Alex & Brown

Wiltshire Aln~~~~~~~~~

and their Founders

Sally M Thomson

Sally Thomson
16 September 2016

HOBNOB PRESS

for the

WILTSHIRE BUILDINGS RECORD

First published in the United Kingdom in 2016
on behalf of the Wiltshire Buildings Record
by The Hobnob Press
      30c Deverill Road Trading Estate, Sutton Veny, Warminster BA12 7BZ.
      www.hobnobpress.co.uk

British Library Cataloguing in Publication Data
A catalogue record for this book is available from the British Library.

ISBN 978-1-906978-35-8

Typeset in 11/13.5 pt Scala. Typesetting and origination by John Chandler
Printed in Great Britain by Lightning Source

The Wiltshire Buildings Record is a voluntary society and educational charity, with members in historic Wiltshire and beyond. The archive of the Record, gathered together since 1979 from fieldwork and from a variety of sources, covers over 17,500 sites representing buildings of all dates and types. The collection is housed at the Wiltshire & Swindon History Centre, Cocklebury Road, Chippenham, Wiltshire SN15 3QN, telephone 01249 705508. www.wiltshirebuildings record.org.uk. It is open to the public on Tuesdays, 9 a.m. to 5 p.m.

Also available from Wiltshire Buildings Record:

Wiltshire Farmhouses and Cottages 1500-1850	£6
Wiltshire Farm Buildings 1500-1900	£5
Medieval Houses of Wiltshire	£6
Wiltshire Town Houses 1500-1900	£6
Architects and Building Craftsmen with Work in Wiltshire (Part 1)	£6
Architects and Craftsmen with Work in Wiltshire (Part 2)	£8
Wiltshire Village Reading Rooms (Ivor Slocombe)	£8

    All plus £1.50 per copy post and packing.

The Dovecotes and Pigeon Lofts of Wiltshire (J & P McCann)	£7

    plus £2.50 per copy post and packing

You can help the Record by allowing us to copy photographs, drawings and any other information, structural or historical you may have about Wiltshire buildings. Please join the Record and help to record buildings in your locality or assist us by drawing our attention to threatened buildings which may be worth recording.

Contents

THE WILTSHIRE BUILDINGS RECORD WOULD LIKE
TO DEDICATE THIS BOOK TO THE MEMORY OF
GRAHAM EXCELL, ARCHITECT

Abbreviations

Cal.Pat.	Calendar of Patent Rolls
Char.Com.	Endowed Charities Commission reports.
IHR	Institute of Historical Research
OUP	Oxford University Press
Val.Ecc.	Valor Ecclesiasticus
WAM	Wiltshire Archaeological & Natural History Society Magazine (now entitled Wiltshire Studies).
WANHS	Wiltshire Archaeological & Natural History Society
WBR	Wiltshire Buildings Record
WSA	Wiltshire & Swindon Archives.
WSHC	Wiltshire & Swindon History Centre
VCH	Victoria County History

Abbreviations for photographs

CC	Crowe Collection (Wiltshire & Swindon History Centre)
ClC	Clive Carter
JS	John Schlamp
JAT	James Thomson
PMS	Pamela Slocombe
PT	Pamela Thomas
PW	Pauline White
SMT	Sally Thomson
WBR	Wiltshire Buildings Record
WLSC	Wiltshire Local Studies Collection

Abbreviations for heraldry

arg.	Argent	silver/white
az.	Azure	blue
gu.	Gules	red
or	Or	gold/yellow
sa.	Sable	black
vert	Vert	green
erm.	Ermine	fur – black spots on white

Acknowledgements

First and foremost, grateful thanks to Pamela Slocombe of the Wiltshire Buildings Record for her enormous help, advice and encouragement.

To the staff of the Wiltshire & Swindon History Centre, Chippenham, for their unfailing help and kindness, particularly Steven Hobbs.

And to Helen Taylor of the WSHC, for her tireless fetching of books and looking up of document references.

To the wardens and staff of many almshouses, who, over the years have helped me answering questions and feeding me information.

To various institutions and their staff:

Brasenose College, Oxford, for their kind permission to use the portrait of Sarah, Duchess of Somerset.

English Heritage for their kind permission to use various photographs and plans of buildings.

Longleat House Archive for their kind permission to use the portrait of Sir James Thynne.

Salisbury Guildhall for their kind permission to use the portraits of Alderman William Hussey and Bishop Seth Ward.

The Dean and Chapter, Salisbury Cathedral for their kind permission to photograph various memorials within the Cathedral.

The Rachel Fowler Centre, Melksham for their kind permission to photograph the portrait of Rachel Fowler and her gravestone (rachelfowlercentre.co.uk)

Trowbridge Museum for their kind permission to photograph the portrait of Samuel Salter (trowbridgemuseum.co.uk)

Westbury Town Council for their kind permission to photograph the bust of Abraham Laverton.

Wiltshire Buildings Record for their kind permission to use various photographs and plans of buildings.

Wiltshire Local Studies Collection for their kind permission to use various photographs and plans of buildings.

Wiltshire & Swindon Archives for the use of numerous photographs from the Crowe Collection.

And lastly to my husband, Alec, for his uncomplaining company, trekking round the County in pursuit of almshouses and their benefactors.

Preface

The essence of this book was begun more than a decade ago, as a dissertation. Later it was recognised as a potentially useful county book and the Wiltshire Buildings Record kindly offered to publish it under their umbrella series on buildings of the county. The original was an academic work, with a different slant on its subject matter, so it was necessary to rework it, concentrating on the buildings, the history and the constitutions of the almshouses. As work progressed, I also became interested in the founders and this led to an extension of the work into 'brief lives' of the men and women whose generosity (and sometimes 'strategy for the afterlife') led to the founding of so many of these interesting and vital institutions.

Some of the old foundations no longer exist, others have been combined with modern charities and renamed. As a general rule of thumb, a cut-off date of 1900 has been made as, after that time, almshouses tended to be run on different principles. Today, almspeople pay a modest rent for their homes, whereas in the past the almshouse was run on entirely charitable lines, with residents being paid a small sum weekly, or monthly, together with the distribution of clothing and fuel.

Introduction

Almshouses have their origins in medieval refuges and hospitals and it is to these that one must look to see how these institutions developed. Numerous good books have been written on the subject, so this introduction will give only a brief overview of their development in Wiltshire.

With the founding of monasteries and abbeys in the Saxon period, the care of the poor, sick, needy and weary became an integral part of religious life. The Rule of St.Benedict, founder of the Benedictine Order, says: 'Guests are to be received as if they were Christ Himself' (Clay, 1909/66:3)

Most monasteries were built with a guest-house, where important visitors or travellers were housed and they would be expected to give a donation towards their hospitality. Others were accommodated elsewhere, but food and shelter were given to all. The poorer wayfarer could offer only his prayers of thanksgiving and this should have been enough for an ecclesiastical body; but doubtless charity was not always administered with an open heart. An extract from the Exeter Pontifical of ca. 1000 AD and used in St.Osmund's Sarum Use asks: 'Wilt thou show mercy and kindness, for the name of the Lord, to the poor, the stranger, and all in want?' (*ibid.*: 2).

In 12th and 13th century Wiltshire there were at least seventeen religious houses, all of which could have provided relief within their walls and alms at their gates. In addition there were houses of Templars at Rockley, near Marlborough (Kirby, 1956: 327-8) and Hospitallers at Ansty, near Tisbury (Kirby, 1956: 328-9; Larking, 1857: 79).

Some shelters were especially built, but were usually small and ephemeral and these were often known as *maisons dieu* or *domus dei*. St Nicholas's Hospital at Harnham, on the southwest edge of the City of Salisbury, also known as a *domus dei*, may have begun life as a simple shelter run by the Augustinian brothers and sisters. It was situated close to the fording point of the River Avon, an isolated spot in those days, since the original City of Sarum was two miles or more away to the north. The valley of the Avon was marshy and subject to flooding and travellers would have been grateful for a night's shelter and food at the refuge dedicated to St.Nicholas. The inmates were known as *transeuntes* – passengers, in the sense of people passing through (Clay 1909/1966, 5).

Domus Hospitalis: St Nicholas' Hospital, Harnham CC

Other refuges were found on pilgrimage routes. Chapel Plaister, near Box, is believed to have been a hospice for travellers and pilgrims on their way to Glastonbury. Little is left of it now, though the remains of its late 14th/early 15th century chapel have been renovated and can still be seen.

Chapel Plaister from the north, a sepia drawing by William Walter Wheatley WBR

It stands alongside the B3109 road between Corsham and Bradford and is still used for services. It underwent a great deal of haphazard alteration until the 16th century, with no definite standard plan and it was probably too small a foundation to survive the Reformation. Pevsner says the chancel had transverse arches across it to support the roof, which was of stone, and he thinks the nave and probably the transept were made two-storeyed quite early on. He wonders if the nave was the original hospice, the transept the priest's room and the chancel reserved for services (Pevsner, 1963: 112).

Chapel Plaister today SMT

At South Wraxall, further along the route, another hospice, now called Manor Farm, remains at the site of St Ouen's chapel. It had an open hall, tree-ring dated 1300-19 and a two-storey crosswing dated 1291-1316. (Dendrochronology Project, WBR & EH, 2011). The chapel itself was demolished, so the present remains were for domestic use by the priest and travellers.

The heavily-restored remains of a hospice and chapel can be found at Tory, high above the town of Bradford on Avon. These were occupied by a hermit in the 15th century. Directly below the foot of the hill is a pre-Reformation stone well house, covering the spring called Lady Well.

Unlike St Nicholas' Hospital, East Harnham, which probably developed from a hospice, most hospitals were originally part of a monastic site. The hospital was not just a place of healing as we know it today, but more of a hostel, where people

Manor Farm, South Wraxall WBR

could find succour. Inevitably they became places where the sick, the traveller and the elderly found shelter, at first temporarily, but later on a more permanent basis. Such hospitals were often endowed by the wealthy as a safeguard for eternity, or, as Simon Roffey says, 'Strategies for the Afterlife' (Roffey, 2009: 16). In an age when Purgatory was in the forefront of people's minds as the place where the souls of sinners went while awaiting entry to Heaven, the prayers of the Faithful who remained on earth were extremely important in reducing the time spent in Purgatory. The soul of the departed, once in Purgatory, could no longer shorten his or her own time there, but relied on the prayers and intercessions of those he or she left behind. Hence the great upsurge in the foundation of chantries, where constant prayer could be offered up, and hospitals, where works of charity could be promulgated, in order to reduce time in Purgatory for the founder and his family.

It is frequently difficult, or even impossible, to give a founding date for early hospitals; foundation charters (if they existed) have been lost and the distance in time since their foundation is great. In most cases, a reference to the hospital in another document is the only evidence we have for its existence. Hence, most foundation dates are approximate.

In Wiltshire, only four early hospitals are known to have been founded by ecclesiastics: St James and St Denis at Southbroom, Devizes, Trinity Hospital at Easton Royal, St John the Baptist, Wilton, and St John the Baptist at Wootton Bassett. As far as is known, all the other hospitals in the county were founded by royalty, aristocracy, gentry or laymen and women.

In addition to the early forms of relief, there were also units, away from the main body of a monastery, known as leper colonies. Originally these were in the form of a number of small huts, or a single building divided up (a Lazar House), but within an enclave, which kept the victims of the disease away from the public. In 1175 it was decreed from Rome that lepers should live apart from the healthy community and by 1179, leper communities were required to have their own priests, churches or chapels, and graveyards (Sweetinburgh, 2004: 31) and they were tended by members of religious orders. Leprosy reached its climax in the middle of the 12th century and by the 14th century had all but disappeared.

Between 1100 and 1250, at the height of the leper contagion, there were many leper colonies throughout the country, and in Wiltshire eight are known by name (Hatcher, 1998). The vast majority of these colonies would have been fairly transient affairs, built of wood and thatch – small, individual huts around a crude chapel, (for the centre of the community was always prayer and worship) and surrounded by a stockade. These have left no trace; but just a few were more substantial and were even endowed foundations. Grants of protection were issued by the king to leper colonies, such grants being found in the Patent Rolls of 1201-1204. Eighty per cent of them mention leper hospitals; by 1300, this was reduced to thirty five per cent (Hatcher, 1998).

Modest and limited excavations in 2002, by Wessex Archaeology, revealed an enclosure and the foundations of a substantial building to the east of Old Sarum, alongside the Roman road between Old Sarum and Ford. Material from the excavations was mostly from the 12th and 13th centuries (Powell, 2006: 219). It is thought that this may have been one of the leper hospitals founded in England during the height of the disease. The cemetery found at Old Sarum in 2002 contained burials within the enclosure and close to the east end of the building (ibid.).

The seven leper hospitals in Wiltshire, known to have existed in the 12th century, were:

St.Margaret's, Bradford on Avon
St.Mary's, Maiden Bradley
St.James and St.Denys, Southbroom, Devizes
St.Mary Magdalen, Burton, Malmesbury
St.Thomas, Marlborough
St.John the Baptist and St.Anthony at Old Sarum
St.Giles, Fugglestone (Wilton)
There was possibly also one at St.Lawrence, Chippenham
When the Black Death of 1348 wiped out most of the remaining lepers,

the hospitals either closed or changed their function. Therefore leper hospitals had a fairly limited life-span; some were converted to almshouses, or hospitals of the hospice type, when no longer required for their original purpose. (Powell, 2006: 219). Two remaining leper foundations in Wiltshire, which survived first as a hospital and then as an almshouse, are St Giles, in Wilton, and St Margaret's Bradford.

Yet another form of relief for the poor was the Bede House. This was usually an addition to a chantry, where the bedesmen, who prayed for the soul of the founder, were housed. Bede houses were, perhaps, the closest forerunners of the almshouses as we know them today, though bedesmen (and women) tended to live communally, a reflection of monastic tradition. Since they were mostly associated with chantries, which were abolished at the Reformation, few have survived in their original form. The Terumber Almshouses, which stood in the churchyard of St.James, Trowbridge, were founded on very similar lines to a bede house, in 1496. An abstract of the Terumber deed says: 'and iij other prestes being ate same and helping every of theim shalle have iiijd. The parish clerke of the said chirch attending to the said dirigees and masses iiijd. And the Bedeman going aboute the toowne praing for the soules abovesaide, as the maner is, iiijd.' (WSA Ref: 206/20). Whether the Bedeman came from the almshouses is not clear; his may have been a separate office; but the deed goes on to recite the duties of the inmates of the almshouse.

Apart from this, the only other hint of a bede house in Wiltshire comes from the survival of the name Bedwyn Street in Salisbury. This was originally Bedden Row. Here, in a survey of 1635, there were some 46 named individuals, mostly elderly, sick or infirm, living on weekly relief. Since most of this number comprised unrelated individuals, one assumes they were almsfolk, living in houses allotted for the purpose, though there is no other evidence of an almshouse here. However, the name may well refer to an earlier bede house, whose function was transferred after the Reformation. Old versions of the name are Beaden, Beden or Bedden, so it would seem likely. The author of the WRS volume on Stuart Poverty in Salisbury refers to it as an almshouse. In fact, the survey itself refers to the 'Beaden Row on both sides', suggesting that all the houses there were given over to almsfolk (Slack, 1975: 6, 65, 78).

Over the centuries, each hospital experienced its own vagaries of development and decay or, in some cases, adaptation and survival (e.g. St.Nicholas's, Harnham; Trinity, Salisbury; St.John's, Heytesbury). Adaptation in adversity was the key to the survival of the medieval hospital. By the beginning of the 14th century, the appeal of pilgrimage was well on the wane, as to some extent, was religious fervour. Increasingly, travellers looked to inns for accommodation on a journey. As a result, benefactors tended to make their bequests to smaller institutions, such as the parish church, the friary and the newly-emergent almshouse. (Prescott, 1992: 23) .

At the Dissolution of the monasteries in the mid 16th century, the driving force behind the care of the sick and the poor was suddenly withdrawn. Although legislation endeavoured to distinguish between hospitals run by religious and those run by the laity, many hospital foundations closed, with the funds thus released becoming dissipated under the subsequent rapidly-changing governments (Caffrey, 2006:10). The plight of the genuine poor was extreme, with responsibility for their welfare falling on the shoulders of the local laymen and women in towns and villages across the country. There was now a need and an opening for the wealthy to found almshouses which could help to remove at least the aged deserving poor from the streets. Legislation in the form of the Poor Law Act of 1601 did little to help, putting the onus entirely on the parish. But many new foundations were set up by the rising mercantile class and run by the corporate bodies of towns and cities.

Institutions which could adapt to the changing conditions of the times and which could prove themselves to be non-religious in the running of their establishments tended to survive. Those which failed to adapt, retaining their religious ethos and, to some extent, architecture, were doomed to failure (Prescott, 1992:73,75). The very small, poorly-endowed foundations were those most at risk, as were those foundations with over-ambitious building programmes, which put enormous strain on already slender resources (*ibid.*). One way to survive was by an old custom called 'feoffment to use'; here the legal title to the lands and property of the foundation was transferred to a sympathetic buyer, who then leased back the property to the original owner. As long as the future use was secular and not religious, the foundation stood a chance of survival. This is probably how St.Nicholas's at Harnham survived (Howson, 1993: 83).

Many of the early hospitals and almshouses were founded by wealthy members of the Church and aristocracy or gentry, such as St.John's, Heytesbury, founded by the Hungerford family; Longbridge Deverill Almshouses, founded by Sir James Thynne; and the College of Matrons in the Close at Salisbury, founded by Bishop Seth Ward.

Those in the hospitals who looked after sick guests, or pilgrims, tended to be employed until they were no longer capable of work. Gradually provision was made for them to enter the hospital to end their days. This led to many hospitals taking on the character of the almshouse (Prescott, 1992: 22).

Medieval hospitals were laid out on similar lines to the dorters of monasteries. The building was usually a single, aisled unit, into which cubicles were fitted for individual residents. At one end was the altar, placed so that the bedridden and infirm could see Mass being celebrated. St.Nicholas's Hospital at Harnham, retains some of its original plan of an early hall-type hospital, while the courtyard style is typified by Trinity Hospital, Salisbury, and St.John's, Heytesbury.

As the communal and spiritual buildings of the monastic foundations began to decline over the years, the lot of the hospital inmate began to improve,

with the innovation of private rooms and small extra comforts. This forced a
change in the layout of buildings. The earlier hospitals had been designed on
the monastic layout, with a large infirmary hall divided into cubicles, a chapel
at one end and communal eating quarters. From the mid-14th century onwards,
smaller versions of the infirmary hall were built, while alongside this was a new
style of hospital altogether (Prescott, 1992: 48). This consisted of a series of
buildings gathered round a central courtyard, the buildings housing individuals,
who could use a communal kitchen or cook for themselves over their own hearth,
as at Trinity Hospital, Salisbury, The Duchess of Somerset's, Froxfield, and St
John's Hospital, Heytesbury. With these new forms of building came the change
in function, with long-term accommodation for the deserving poor, in what we
would now call almshouses. Once almshouses were no longer founded and built
by religious orders, they were designed in the vernacular style and usually built
to last; details reflected current fashions in architecture and the wealth of the
patron (Howson, 2008: 77).

The decline of the cloth industry in Salisbury in the late 16th century
resulted in an increase in the numbers of poor people in the area. There was a
great need for relief and as a result many new charities came into being as wealthy
citizens donated or bequeathed funds (Ransome, M. 1962: 128). Almshouses
now began to be founded in small towns and villages across the county, such as
Topp's Almshouses in the tiny village of Stockton in the Wylye Valley, and Farley
Hospital, a large foundation in a spread-out village in the east of the county. Gifts
of land or property, rather than money, were used to endow the new foundations.
These could be let out, to bring in a constant income (Bailey, 1988: 91). The rise
of both the merchant class and the gentry were important elements leading to
new foundations. The gentry often left bequests for poor relief or endowments
to charities in their wills, while merchants formed city companies, similar to the
old medieval gilds; these companies grew in wealth and much of it was directed
towards charity (Howson, 1993: 87).

If individuals were not sufficiently wealthy to endow a new foundation,
they often left bequests of money, wood, coal or other items to the inmates of
existing institutions. For example, in his will, proved in 1456, John Webb of
Bradford left the poor hospital of St Margaret of Bradford twenty shillings and
five wagons of fuel (TNA PROB 11/4/108). Margery Horton of Westwood in 1562
left to the poor people of the almshouses of Bradford, Trowbridge, Norton and
Frome ten shillings to every house (TNA PROB 11/47/348). Boroughs often took
over the running of some charities, as they did in Devizes.

An Act of 1597 gave power to new benefactors and would-be founders to
bequeath or give land in Fee Simple to erect a hospital or almshouse, without
the need to obtain a royal licence or act of Parliament for incorporation. This
encouraged a flurry of building by men of lesser means. The author of *The
English Medieval Hospital* would have us believe that this resulted in a climax of

new buildings in about 1600, which was almost over by 1640 (Prescott, 1992:73). This may have been true of the country as a whole, but in Wiltshire this was not the case. Many new foundations were made between 1640 and 1740, viz.: Hungerford's, Corsham, 1668; Price's, Tidworth, 1689; Yerbury's, Trowbridge, 1698; Suttons, Salisbury, 1699; Hall's, Bradford, 1700; and Frowde's, Salisbury, 1649.

There was less almshouse building during the Civil War and Common-wealth, (roughly 1641 to 1660) when energies were directed elsewhere; though Robert Jenner, goldsmith of London and MP for Cricklade and Widhill in Wiltshire, founded his almshouses at Malmesbury at this time, and John Topp, clothier, founded the 'gem' of the Wylye Valley at Stockton. After the Stuart period, there was less private charity, with the State taking on more responsibility for the poor. But of the twenty-three almshouses founded in Wiltshire during the 17th century, six have been demolished, five rebuilt and twelve still stand. For Wiltshire, this was the most prolific time for almshouse building.

The problem of poverty continued into the 18th century and beyond. In 1697, the first workhouse was tried and became an essential tool for dealing with poverty over the next two hundred years. In 1782, parishes joined into Unions, which set up larger Houses of Industry, the notorious workhouses. In these, the able-bodied poor were provided with work outside the workhouse; indoor relief within the workhouse was for the impotent poor only (Richardson, 1993: 148); such workhouses were found at Zeals, Warminster and Wilton. But such remedies failed to get to the root of the poverty problem and the need to accommodate the elderly poor continued.

During the years of the Industrial Revolution there was a distinct decline in the building of almshouses, with only four built in Wiltshire during the 18th century. This was as a result of social upheaval, preoccupation with the Napoleonic Wars and riots and machine-breaking, leading the ruling classes to fear the poor, as they did in France at the end of the 18th century (Bailey, 1988:156). However, there was some rather undistinguished rebuilding of old foundations during this time (*ibid*.). This is noticeable in Brickett's Almshouses in Salisbury, and, to a certain degree, in the Trinity Hospital in the same city. Also in Salisbury, the tradition of hospital building was continued in the 18th century, when the General Infirmary was built in Fisherton Street. Though not an almshouse, it nevertheless offered relief to the sick and ailing poor. The building still stands, though it has now been turned into apartments; but the original was built in 1767 through public subscription, as the band on the façade of this five storey building proudly proclaims, and was opened in 1771 (RCHM, 1980: p52b).

In the nineteenth century, almshouses were often built by institutions – companies, societies, town councils. The Charitable Trusts Act of the late 1850s appointed Charity Commissioners to safeguard the administration of charities. Many Victorian almshouses were stereotyped in both their appearance and their running, e.g. Zeals, Warminster, Wilton, though from the 1860s there was a conscious raising of the tone. Union Street Almshouses, Trowbridge, for instance, was designed with an arcade on the ground floor and a timber balcony above (Pevsner, 1963: 479). The 19th century was the great age of philanthropy and eighteen almshouses were founded in Wiltshire during this time, only four of which have been demolished.

With the coming of the Welfare State and old age pensions, almshouses should have become redundant; but yet again, they have adapted and many are used as sheltered accommodation, cottage homes for the elderly or retirement homes. Residents now pay a modest rent, but the property is often maintained by the National Association of Almshouses.

It will be seen from the accompanying graph (fig.1) that there were three surges of charity building in Wiltshire between the 12th and 20th centuries. The 13th century, the great era of hospital building; the 17th century, when the rising class of merchants and gentry became dominant founders; and the 19th century, the great age of Victorian philanthropy.

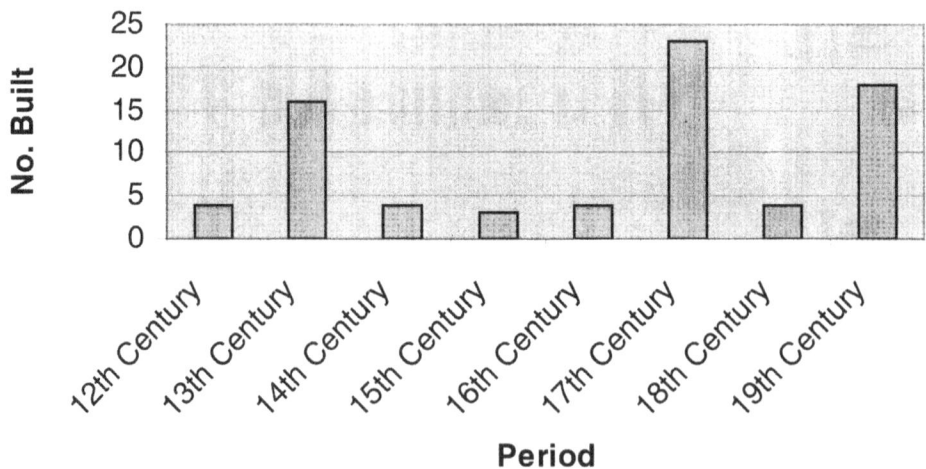

fig.1 Almshouse building in Wiltshire

This pattern is somewhat peculiar to Wiltshire when one considers, for instance, that in the 18th century, many almshouses were built in other parts of the country, inWiltshire only four. This may have been due largely to the fact that all the almshouses that were needed had been built during the 17th century. Of the four built during the 18th century, three were in textile towns, where the population was rising and there was probably an immediate need.

Hospitals

Hospitals have been mentioned in the above Introduction, because they were the forerunners of the later almshouses. But this is a book about almshouses, not hospitals and so they have not been looked at in detail. However, it might be of interest to the reader to have some idea of the location of known medieval hospitals in Wiltshire. What follows is a list with their dates of foundation, where known, and their possible founders. Of the twenty-six known hospitals in Wiltshire, eight are believed to have been leper hospitals and seven survived in the form of almshouses.

PLACE	NAME	DATE	FOUNDER
ANSTY	Preceptory of St John	1211	Walter de Turbeville
BEDWYN, Gt.	St John the Baptist	ca.1279	Walter le Bret
BRADFORD	St Margaret	1235	The King
CALNE	St John the Baptist	1202	Richard the Tanner
CHIPPENHAM	St Laurence	1338	?
CRICKLADE	St John the Baptist	1231	Warin
DEVIZES	St John the Baptist	ca.1314	?
" Southbroom	St James & St Denys	1207	?Bishop of Sarum
EASTON ROYAL	possibly Holy Trinity	1246	Archdeacon Stephen
FUGGLESTONE	St Giles	ca.1135	Queen Adeliza
HARNHAM (Bridge)	St Nicholas	1215	Richard Aucher
HARNHAM (East)	?	1361	?
HEYTESBURY	St John & St Katherine	1472	Walter, Lord Hungerford
MAIDEN BRADLEY	St Mary	ca.1190	Manasser Bisset
MALMESBURY (Burton)	St Mary Magdalene	ca.1222	?
"	St Anthony	1245	?
"	St John the Baptist	1247	?
MARLBOROUGH	St John the Baptist	ca.1215	Levenoth
"	St Thomas the Martyr	ca.1231	?
SALISBURY	Holy Trinity	ca.1379	Agnes Bottenham
SARUM (Old)	St John the Baptist & St Anthony	ca.1195	?
STRATFORD	St John the Baptist	1231	?
WILTON	St John the Baptist	ca.1195	Prior Hubert
"	St Mary Magdalene	mid-13th C	?
WOOTTON BASSETT	St John the Baptist	1266	Sir Philip Bassett & the Rector

Almshouse Gazetteer

The architectural descriptions have made extensive use of the Listed Buildings descriptions, published by the former Department of the Environment. Copies are available at the Wiltshire Buildings Record in Chippenham, or see Images of England online.

Amesbury   Name and location unknown

The almshouses here were mentioned in a lease dated 15 September 1590 in the Antrobus Deeds, as being part of the property and demesne lands of Richard Moody and his wife of Oxford. The lease was granted to Philip Poore of Durrington, gent., for forty-one years: '. . . reserving the house called the Resceavors House late parcel of the premises and the garden thereto belonging and all houses called the Almeshouses near the Resceavors House...'.[1]

The Receiver's house and a lodging for five chaplains of the priory, were ear-marked for demolition in 1539, but were apparently still standing, along with several other priory buildings in about 1574.[2] It is possible that the chaplains' house was used for the continuation of the giving of alms after the dissolution of the priory itself.

The Antrobus Deeds are deposited at the WSA[3] and the Wiltshire Record Society has transcribed those between about 1250 and 1625.[4]

Notes:
1 Pugh, 1947, 64.
2 Crowley, 1995, 21.
3 WSA Ref : 283/79.
4 Pugh, 1947.

Boscombe (Allington parish)   Kent's Almshouses   SU 20238

A little way north-east of the church on the north-west side of the village street, now the A338.

Kent's Almshouses, Boscombe CC

Founded by the will of John Kent, dated 20 December 1707, proved in June 1710[1], in which he devised to his nephew, Robert Kent, a fee-farm rent of 11s 0d per annum in Wiltshire and Gloucestershire; and a fee-farm rent in Northumberland of £57 per annum, subject to payment of £24 for the maintenance of the almspeople. By the turn of the 19th century, the endowment of £24 per annum was being paid by the Earl of Ilchester and was said to be charged on property in the parish of Pitton with Farley.[2]

Constitution: For four poor persons, two widows and two widowers. A weekly allowance of 2s 4d was made to each recipient, who was nominated by the parish. Each almsperson had one room and a piece of garden.[3] The privilege of selection was later extended to Winterbourne Dauntsey.

By 1833, the parish held three of the four tenements in order to house paupers, the fourth being left empty. Towards the end of the century, almspeople were not required to actually live in the almshouse, so that the latter often stood empty or were let out, though weekly doles of 2s 4d or more were made to three or four recipients during the first half of the 20th century.

The almshouses were sold in 1930 to the Bourne Valley Nursing Association and were made into a house for a nurse. The building is now a private house.[4]

The almshouses were erected in John Kent's lifetime. They consisted of a row of four, low, one-storey cottages, each containing one room. The cottages were brick-built with tiled roofs. The small garden in front was divided into four plots, enough for the growing of a few vegetables, and was surrounded by a low wall.

The almshouses today (2010), now converted to a private dwelling   SMT

Today, though converted into private property, the almshouses retain their recognisable outline.

Plaque on the wall of the almshouses   CC

A stone plaque affixed to the wall of the cottages reads:

Dei Donum et Deo
solas quas dederis semper
habebis opes.
1708

This translates roughly as:

The gift of God and the gift to God
The riches that you impart will be the only riches you retain

The plaque, still in place on the porch today SMT

Notes:
1 Will of John Kent, TNA, PROB 11/515/326.
2 Ch.Com. 1837, 468.
3 *ibid..*
4 Stevenson, 1995, 61.
Charity Commission references:
1837: 468

Bradford on Avon　　　　Hall's Almshouses　　　ST826606
On the east side of Frome Road, at the junction with Trowbridge Road.

John Hall of The Hall, Bradford on Avon, purchased Paxcroft Farm (east of Hilperton and then in Steeple Ashton parish) in 1697.[1] This large freehold property brought an annual rent of £80. In 1700, he founded the almshouses

Hall's Almshouses SMT

and gave from the Paxcroft rent the annual sum of £40, paid quarterly 'for the maintenance of four poor old men'. His will of 10 September 1708 perpetuated the arrangement. He died in 1711 and his estate passed to Rachel Bayntun, probably his illegitimate daughter. She died in 1722 and in 1726 her son became the second Duke of Kingston on his grandfather's death. In 1735 the Duke conveyed Paxcroft Farm to six trustees. He died in 1773 after a bigamous marriage to the notorious Countess of Bristol. Despite a court action, she enjoyed the estate till her death in 1788. The almshouses were said to be under her governance in 1783. [2]

The estate reverted to Charles Medows, son of the Duke's sister, Frances. In 1796 he was created Viscount Newark, then became Earl Manvers in 1806. Though he sold The Hall in 1802 he retained the rest of the Bradford estates, Paxcroft Farm and specifically the patronage of the almshouses. At his death in 1816, his son the second Earl Manvers inherited, the latter in due course handing over the nomination of the almsmen to his agent. [3] However, in 1858 the Charity Commissioners said that for a long time past there had been no legal trustees. The Hall was purchased by Stephen Moulton in 1848 and in 1861 the Commissioners denied the right he claimed as owner to nominate almspersons. A new scheme was agreed in 1887. [4] His son Horatio bequeathed £1,000 to the trustees in 1894, the interest from which added £31 10s to the annual income.[5] Paxcroft Farm was purchased by Walter Long of Rood Ashton House in the period 1879-86 and when sold again in 1911, a rent charge was still payable to the Trustees of Hall's Charity.

Constitution: The four poor men were originally each to receive a gown as the Trustees decided and after this had been effected and after any repairs to the building carried out, the residue of the income was to be equally divided between the men and paid monthly.

Vacancies were in the gift of the owner of The Hall and the Vicar of Bradford was to be always one of the Trustees. Later, the men received a weekly allowance, a coat or gown every two years and a pair of shoes yearly. In 1834 the weekly allowance was 3s 6d and married men were admitted with their wives.[7] In 1901 the allowance was 6s and two coats per year were given, one for the summer, one for winter, with the arms of John Hall as a badge on the sleeve.[8]

Badge used by almsmen from Hall's Almshouses PS

In 1908 the allowance was 7s 6d a week, but by 1935 it had been reduced to 5s, plus their old age pension.

The building is Grade II* listed, the exterior largely unaltered. It is rectangular in plan and of local limestone, ashlar at the front, with coursed rubble stone on the other elevations. It is two storeys high with a high-pitched hipped roof with stone tiles and projecting eaves.

Each unit has one window on each floor. These are leaded casements with stone mullions, with small ogee mouldings. The two doorways in the centre of the front and the two further doorways, one at each end, are plain with a square head.

There are two tall chimneys in ashlar, each bearing a carved initial (K or M), surmounted by a coronet (for the Duke of Kingston and Earl Manvers).

The front area is bounded by a stone wall with decorative urns and steps up to a gateway flanked by pillars capped by stone balls. The gates, railings and front paving slabs date from 1889-1893. The small garden was divided into four plots.

Hall's Almshouses from the rear WBR

Internally the building was divided into four tenements, each with a room below and one above. Repairs and reroofing were carried out in 1890 at the expense of Horatio Moulton.[9] In 1961, bathrooms and central heating were installed and in 1989 the steep winder stairs were removed and the interior was made into four flats.

Coat of Arms SMT

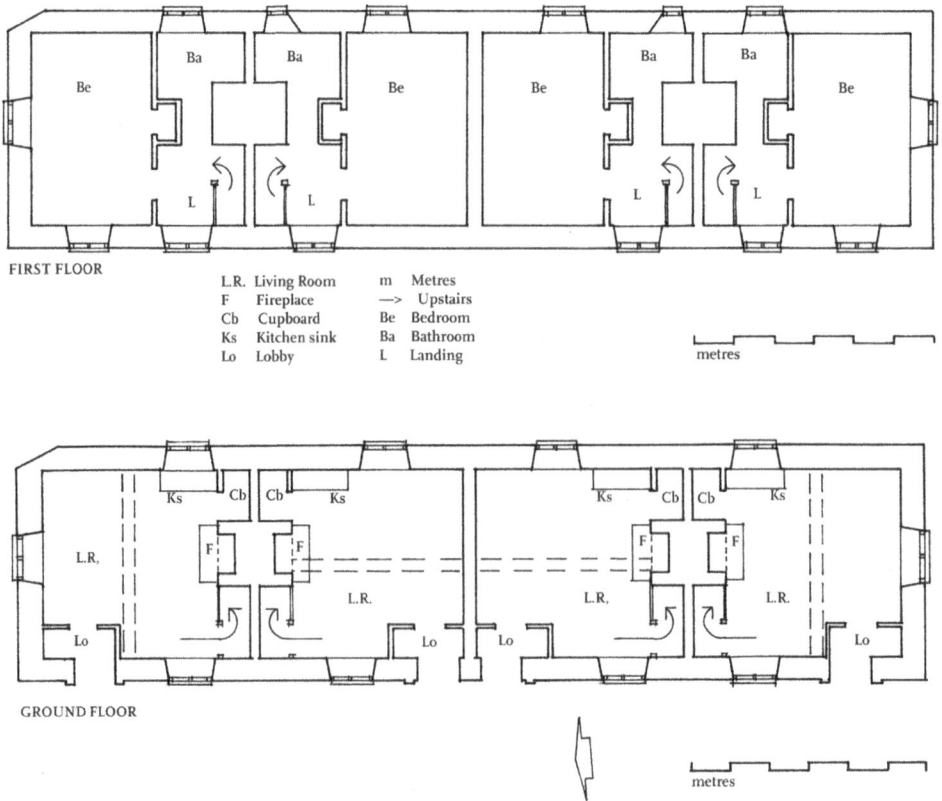

FIRST FLOOR

L.R.	Living Room	m	Metres
F	Fireplace	—>	Upstairs
Cb	Cupboard	Be	Bedroom
Ks	Kitchen sink	Ba	Bathroom
Lo	Lobby	L	Landing

GROUND FLOOR

Ground floor and first floor plans of Hall's Almshouses CIC

Over the twin doorway at the front of the almshouses is a panel bearing the arms of the Halls: Sable three poleaxes argent, and the motto:

> Deo et Pauperibus (for God and the poor)

To this has been added:

> Improved, restored and further endowed 1891-3 by
> Horatio Moulton, of Kingston House (The Hall)

The returns to the Visitation Queries of 1783 read as follows: 'There are two hospitals here, one founded by the lord of the manor for three old women and still under his direction; the other endowed by John Hall Esq., with an annuity of £40 per annum net, paid out of an estate called Packscroft Farm in the parish of Steeple Ashton, for the support of four poor men, now under the government of the Countess of Bristol, and both foundations are properly supported.'[10]

Notes:

1 British Library Eg. 3654
2 Ransome, 1972, 23.

3 Jones, 1859, 347.

4 Notes on Hall's Charity made for the trustees, Wiltshire Buildings Record.

5 Pugh, 1953, 50

6 Ransome, 1972, 23

7 Charity Commission Report

8 Pugh, 1953,50.

9 Fassnidge, 113.

10 Ransome, 1972, 41.

Charity Commission references:

1837:   1214-15

1908:   94-5

Bradford on Avon Almshouse

St Margaret's Hospital, refounded as St. Katherine's
ST 825605

51-53 Frome Road, on the west side, a short distance before the canal.

St Katherine's Almshouse, Bradford on Avon SMT

St Margaret's was a leper hospital and the Shaftesbury Abbey Cartulary, Survey C, of ca.1190-1200, has a reference to a lazar (leper) house in Bradford, *habent tedracam uno anno ad maladariam.*[1] Leper Hospitals were always situated well outside a settlement because of contagion and the site of St Margaret's would have been ideally placed at the end of Frome Road, formerly called St Margaret's

Street. A letter of protection was issued to St Margaret's in 1235, a year when many other letters of protection were distributed to hospitals: Protection with clause *rogamus*, without term, for the brothers and sisters of the lepers' hospital of St Margaret, Bradford.[2]

The foundation is mentioned again in 1456 when John Webb of Bradford left to the poor hospital of St. Margaret of Bradford 20s and five wagons of fuel and in 1490, when Henry Long of South Wraxall manor left ½ mark (6s 8d) to the poor of the house.[3]

Leland, writing in the 16th century, says: 'There is a little streate over Bradford bridge and at the end of that is an hospitale of the Kinges of Englandes foundation. As I turned up at this streat end toward Through-bridg, there was a quarre of fair stone on the right hand in a felde.'[4] He is likely to be describing the Rowden Lane route to Trowbridge over Trowle Common and passing the quarry on Jones's Hill.

In 1535 twelve poor persons received £3 6s 8d yearly out of the Rectory for offering prayers for the soul of the founder of Shaftesbury Abbey.[5] This implies that there was a chapel on the site. Canon Jones suggested that at the Dissolution, when the Abbey lapsed to the Crown, provision was made for a smaller number of poor persons out of Bradford manor; at one time there were ten.[6] Manorial accounts record annual pensions totalling 32s. to six poor people in 1577-79 and in 1585 and repairs to 'the almshouse of Bradford called "St Margaret's" in 1578 costing £19 6s. 8d.[7] In the 16th and 17th centuries, the only recorded burials of inhabitants of the almshouse were for four men and one woman. The entries recorded the deceased as 'of the Allemshows'. It may be that, after the foundation, in 1700, of Hall's Almshouse as a men's establishment in the parish, St Margaret's was restricted to women of the parish who were not in receipt of parish relief.

The name 'St. Margaret's' gradually lapsed. In her will of 1562 Margery Horton of Westwood left ten shillings to each of the poor people of the almshouses of Bradford, Trowbridge, Norton and Frome.[8]

John Aubrey, writing in the 1660s, said: 'A little beyond the bridge is a chapel and almshouse of ancient date.'[9] He wondered who the founder might have been.

The number of almspeople further decreased. The Returns to Visitation Queries of 1783 state that there were two almshouses, one endowed by John Hall Esq, the other founded by the lord of the manor for three old women and still under his direction.[10] In the mid 19th century there was still a tradition that the site had included a chapel, with a bell and outbuildings, and a chaplain was said to have been paid £10 a year to serve the spiritual needs of the community there. The bell was believed to have gone to Winsley Church, but when enquiry about the chaplain was made by the Charity Commission of 1834, no evidence was found.[11] The chapel is marked on Andrews and Dury's map of 1773. Much of the stone was taken from the site in about 1794 for road mending and this may be when the chapel and outbuildings were demolished.[12] In 1799, several pieces of ground belonging to the almshouse site were conveyed to the Canal Company, when they constructed the Kennet and Avon Canal. When the road over the canal was built, it reached above the level of the original window sills and the space occupied by the almshouses was much reduced.[13]

Extract from Andrews' and Dury's map, 1773. (Crittall, 1952)
The site of the Chapel is above the word 'The' and Clay Farm, now the Barge Inn, is to the right of the road.

1864 Town map of Bradford, showing position of the almshouses WSA

Two large town maps of Bradford, dated 1837[14] and 1864,[15] show the old buildings of St Margaret's occupying a triangle of land between two roads and the canal. Before the construction of the canal, the lane to the west continued up Jones's Hill, then called Almshouse Hill. The almshouses, known as 'The Old Women's Almshouse', were still there in 1859 in a very ruinous state. They were low in the walls and, according to Canon Jackson, very damp. The access road to the canal bridge had been built at a higher level than the earlier lane, leaving the buildings in a sunken position. The valuation book accompanying the 1864 map of the town describes the site as 'Yard, sheds and old Almshouse'.[16]

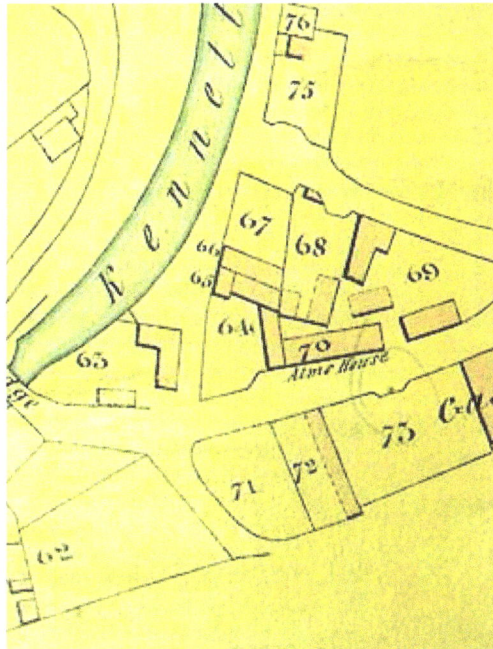

From at least 1702 the almshouse was endowed with 12 ½ acres of lands in various parts of the parish which had been Shaftesbury Abbey's.[17] A newspaper report of 21 February 1861 announced that the almshouse, the oldest charitable institution in the parish, had now been placed on a satisfactory footing, a matter which had been before the Charity Commissioners for some years.[18] An act had been passed at the close of the session of 1860 to appoint legal trustees. These were the Vicar, the Lord of the Manor, the Churchwardens for the time being and three gentlemen nominated by the Vestry. They were Ezekiel Edmonds (a clothier), George Spencer and Samuel Taylor. A scheme for the management of the charity was also set out. In 1906, the endowment included £10 from the Bradford Gas Company and £11 from the Canal Company, both of which leased adjoining land, formerly part of the almshouse site.

The almshouses were rebuilt in 1868 to the design of C.S.Adye of Westbury House, Bradford on Avon, later the first County Surveyor of Wiltshire. John Bubb, a bookseller, stationer and silversmith in the town, who never forgot his boyhood in the workhouse, paid for the rebuilding.[19] He also left £1000 in his will of 1860 to provide income to buy coal for the deserving poor who would pay half the cost. The name 'St Katherine's' may have been given by Canon W.H.Jones, as there is no earlier reference to the almshouses using that name, though there had been a cult of St. Catharine, the patron saint of spinners, in the town.

The building today consists of three units in a restrained Gothic style. They are two storeys high and built of ashlar limestone in small blocks. In 1878, a further unit was added by the Trustees in the same style at the north end, running forwards towards the road, to accommodate a fourth almswoman. There are three front doors and a fourth has been blocked up. The gable end of the 1878 extension bears the name of the almshouse, the Hobhouse coat of arms and the apt motto 'Spes vitae melioris' (Hope for a better life), all carved in stone. On the north chimney is the date 1878.

St Katherine's Almshouse, East face of north gable. PMS

St Katherine's Almshouse, Building date on north chimney PMS

The almswomen were still receiving 4 shillings weekly, as set out in 1861, when the Old Age Pension Act of 1908 was passed. The allowance was reduced to 2 shillings as a result and was still the same 27 years later. The late B.S.Niblett, whose grandmother was an almswoman, described her thus: 'I can see her now, dressed, as were all the other old ladies there, in a black blouse which fastened up the front with black buttons. She always wore a brooch at her throat. Her black skirt reached down to the ground, and she wore a black poke bonnet, which tied under her chin with long black ribbons. On her feet she had black stockings and button-up boots. She almost always wore a white apron and had a black cape to wear for walking out.'[20]

Notes:

1 Stacey, 200.

2 Cal. Pat. 19 Henry III, 115.

3 Wills of : John Webb 1456, TNA, PROB 11/4/108; Henry Long, 1490, PROB 11/8/472.

4 Toulmin Smith, vol 1, 136.

5 Val. Ecc., vi, 276.

6 Jones, 1907, 165.

7 WSA Ref. 947/1350.

8 Will of Mary Horton, 1564, TNA, PROB 11/47/348.

9 Aubrey, J., 21.

10 Ransome, 1972, 41.

11 Ch. Com. 1908, 92

12 *ibid.*, 93

13 WSA Ref: 1118/2.

14 Ashmead ref: WSA G13/990/13L

15 WSA Ref: G13/990/13L

16 WSA Ref: G13/990/17

17 Ch. Com. 1908, 91-2

18 WSA Ref: 1118/2.

19 *ibid*. 105 & Society of Antiquaries, Ref: SAL/MS/817/2

20 Niblett, 14.

Charity Commission references:

1837: 1210-4

1908: 91-4

Brinkworth   Name and location unknown

Nothing is known of the whereabouts or constitution of the almshouses at Brinkworth, but evidence of their existence is found in the Court Records of Brinkworth and Charlton.[1]

In the autumn of 1630, the details emerge in a View of Frankpledge that John Berry, perhaps the Bailiff of Grittenham, at the command of John Ayliffe, gent.,(the lord of Grittenham), 'cast down, destroyed, and threw to the ground a cottage built by the churchwardens, and overseers of the poor, of Brinkworth parish on the waste of the lord of this manor for an almshouse. John Ayliffe is amerced 40s'.[2]

It may have been a genuine misunderstanding on the part of the churchwardens, but it may also have been that the lord of Grittenham did not wish to fund provision for paupers of Brinkworth by means of his own rates.[3] He was fined in the Brinkworth Court.

In 1632, the bailiff for Brinkworth manor had to decide on a location for the site of an almshouse.[4] Nothing further is heard of it.

Notes:

1 Crowley, 2009.

2 *ibid*. 180

3 *ibid*. 81

4 *ibid*. 67

Bromham   College of the Poor   ST 962652
Originally on the left hand side of Church Hill heading west towards Melksham, where Baynton Close is now sited.

Foundation Charter of James I WSA Ref: 518/11

The College of the Poor was founded by Royal Charter in 1614 by Sir Henry Baynton of Bromham House. In 1783, the almshouse was supported by Sir Edward Baynton 'at his own pleasure'.[1]

Constitution: Provision was to be made for six or more poor people, from the parish of Bromham; but ideally four old men and two old women, the latter to attend the men when they were ill. They were all to attend church on Sundays, Wednesdays and Fridays, in the dress provided by the founder. £20 a year was to be divided among them.

College of the Poor, with occupant CC

A list of forty-one Statutes and Rules is included with the Charter, signed
and sealed with a very clear coat of arms. An indenture between Sir Henry
Baynton and Robert Richards, the parson of Bromham parish church, on the
one part, and Richard Lynnte and William Webb, churchwardens, on the other,
constitutes these persons as Governors. This corporate body was to be known as
the 'Governors of the College or Hospital of the Poor', and the President was to
be Sir Henry during his lifetime, and afterwards his heirs and successors. The
owners of Spye Park subsequently always took an interest in the College until the
20th century.[2]

The almshouses comprised a single-storeyed, six-gabled, stone and timber-
framed building, divided into six tenements. Pevsner says the ground floor was
of stone, but it appears from all existing photographs that the whole building
was stone-built, with timber-framing in the attic gables. The building was in a
'decayed' state when Pevsner visited, in 1962 or 63.[3] After efforts to secure the
future of the almshouses failed, they were demolished in 1964 and a number of
bungalows, with no almshouse connection, was built on the site.

College of the Poor, prior to demolition (Reproduced by permission of English Heritage)

When the almshouse still stood, there could be seen in the centre of the
front wall a stone with an inscription. When the building was demolished, it was
removed to the parish church.

College of the Poor, from the back, prior to demolition
(Reproduced by permission of English Heritage)

I WAS HUNGRIE AND YEE GAVE MEE
MEATE I WAS THIRSTY AND YEE GAVE
MEE DRINK I WAS NAKED AND YEE
CLOTHED ME I WAS HARBERLES &
YEE GAVE MEE LODGINGE CVM YEE BLES
ED OF MY FATHER INHERIT THE KINGE
DVM PREPARED FOR YOV MAT.15
ANNO CHR 1612 ET ANNO
REG IAC REGIS MAGN BRITTAN 10

(In the year of Christ 1612 and in the tenth
year of the reign of king James of Great
Britain)

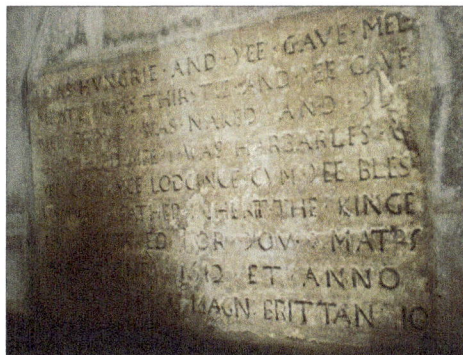

Plaque removed from College of the Poor PT

This plaque has been inserted into the floor of the south chancel in St. Nicholas's church in Bromham, the only reminder of Henry Baynton's legacy to the poor.

The Royal charter bears the seal of James I, depicting the King seated on his throne. The constitution carries Henry Baynton's seal with his arms:

Quarterly of six:

sa a bend lozengy ar (Baynton)

ar 2 bars gu each charged with 3 crosses crosslet of the field (Beauchamp)

gu a fesse between 6 martlets or (Beauchamp St.Armand)

az 3 roches naiant ar (Roche)

gu 2 lions passant guardant in pale ar (de la Mere)

ar on a chevron sa 3 eagles displayed of the field (Wanton)

These arms are reasonably clear on the seal, but were verified in Rev.J.Battersby's Heraldry of Wiltshire.[4]

Notes:

1 Ransome, 1972, 29.

2 Wiltshire Gazette, 3 Feb 1936.

3 Pevsner, 135

4 Battersby, 10.

Charity Commission references:

1837:   370-1

1908:   146-9

Calne   Dr Tounson's Almshouses   ST990708

On the south west side of Kingsbury Street, nos. 10-13

Grade 2* (formerly listed as Nos. 10-17)

Dr Tounson's Almshouses WBR

In his will, dated 1685, Dr John Tounson, DD, mentions that he has already built an almshouse 'for eight poor antient people' and that he has purchased several lands in Calne for the perpetual endowment of the same.[1] He gives the

Almshouse to his nephew, Robert Hyde, of Dinton, and to his heirs for ever, trusting that he will maintain the inhabitants out of the rents, profits, etc.

Constitution: For eight poor men or women, over fifty. To have two rooms each and a garden.

According to Tounson's will, the nominations to the vacancies were to be made by the Bishop of Salisbury and the Vicar of Bremhill, his own nominations being first made by will/codicil. The vacancies were to be allotted as follows: The first, second and third vacancies from Highworth; the fourth and fifth from Bremhill; the sixth from the chapelry of Highway, Bremhill; and the seventh and eighth from Calne.

Almswomen from Dr Tounson's Almshouses CC

A two-storey terrace of originally eight paired almshouses, built round a curve of the road, the building is constructed of limewashed limestone rubble, the ridge stacks being of ashlar. The roof is of stone slates.

The plan was of single depth, there originally being only one room for each person. This arrangement was altered in 1973 to accommodate four residents, with more space each. There are now (2008) through passages and side entrances and the rear elevation has a full-width timber veranda, small single-light windows and three half-dormers with leaded lights, all features inserted in the late 20th century.

The heavy three-plank doors are paired and bear their original wrought-iron strap hinges, each terminating in a fleur de lys. Each door has its original peep-hole, covered by a wrought iron grille.

The windows are stone mullioned with ovolo surrounds. The ground-floor windows have label mouldings and the lead casements have metal stays. The interiors have chamfered oak beams with roll stops.

A plaque over the centre of the row bears the following inscription:

TO THE GLORY OF GOD AND
THE GOOD OF THE POORE
WAS THIS HOVS ERECTED
BY IOHN TOUNSON DR.D
SON OF ROBERT LATE
BISHOP OF SALISBURY. 1682
LET YOUR LIGHT SO SHINE
BEFORE MEN THAT THAY
MAY SEE YOVR GOOD
WOORKS AND GLORIFIE
NOT YOV BVT YOVR FATHER
WHICH IS IN HEAVEN MATH: 16

Notes
1 TNA, PROB 11/389
Charity Commission references:
1837: 1226-7
1908: 154, 167-8

Chippenham, Lowden   Mrs Utterson's Almshouses   ST913730
To the right of St.Peter's Church, Lowden Lane.

Utterson's Almshouses, Lowden, Chippenham SMT

In the parish records for Chippenham are two entries for burials from the almshouses, dated 1653 and 1656.[1] No other records exist of these almshouses, though it is believed there was once a leper hospital in the town; it is possible that the 17th century almshouse was a descendant of such a hospital.

By an Indenture of 28 March 1884,[2] the Rev.J.Rich sold land to Mrs Elizabeth Utterson, widow, and she had five cottage almshouses built on the site.

Constitution: The almshouses were gifted to St.Andrew's Parish Church, Chippenham, and were to be run by the Vicar and four bona fide members of the Church of England, constituting the Trustees. The inhabitants were to be five maiden ladies of Chippenham, all bona fide churchgoers.

The almshouses now operate under the Charity Commission, run by a Committee of five persons, chaired by the Vicar. The five ladies now pay a nominal rent and the maintenance of the buildings is undertaken by the Committee.

A row of five stone-built houses with red brick quoins and window surrounds. There is a small strip of garden ground at the front. Four gables, two either side of a central large one. There are Gothic-style vertical slits in the wall above each window.

There is a small, circular, modern plaque in the central gable, which reads:

Elizabeth Utterson's Almshouses
November
1884

Notes:
1 WSA: Chippenham St Andrew parish registers: burials.
2 WSA Ref: 2568/13
Charity Commission references:
1908: 274-6

Modern plaque on Utterson's Almshouses SMT

Corsham   The Hungerford Almshouses   ST874701
At the junction of South Place, Lacock Road and Pound Pill, east side of Pound Pill. Almshouses and school listed Grade I, front wall, Parish Room and summerhouse listed Grade II.

Margaret, Lady Hungerford, who died in 1673, gave £60 a year from her manor of Stanton St Quintin to a school and almshouse at Corsham. From 1920, the £60 was a charge on Lower Stanton Farm.[1]

The Hungerfords endowed Corsham Court at this time. Lady Margaret was the daughter and co-heiress of William Halliday, a London merchant and built the almshouses in memory of her father.[2]

Four acres of land were specially purchased at the town's end, on the

The entrance to the School and Almshouses WBR

London-Bath Road. Building appears to have taken place between 1668 and 1672. Various original working drawings survive but were not followed in some of their details.

This is an excellent example of a well-organised, largely self-sufficient complex, providing a range of social functions. The building is in the form of a letter L, of which the long side on the north contains the six almshouses; the short side to the west contains the master's house and school. Both aspects have fine entrance doors with heraldic enhancements and plaques. The chapel/ schoolroom has a panelled ceiling, fixed benches, a settle by the fireplace and a three-tier pulpit or master's desk with carved hands to hold candles. There is a gallery over the entrance passage. The attic above has a clothes press and may have been the boys' dormitory. A bell-tower rises above the west porch and contains a single bell.[3] John Buckler's painting of the buildings in 1809 shows a tall, open tower with a flagpole.[4]

The almshouse range is of rubble stone with a stone-tiled roof, two and a half storeys high, with paired, oak-plank doors. Facing Lacock Road is a regular range of six three-light windows on the first floor, with a baroque pediment bearing the armorial achievement in the middle. The ground floor doors and windows are arranged as three-light window, paired door, two-light window, paired door, three-light window. The paired doors are under a stepped dripcourse. Over the arms, between the gables, is a stepped ashlar parapet. To the rear of the block are six chimney gables and a similar arrangement of doors and windows as at the front.

A covered walkway gave access to the water pump and individual storage areas for wood, coal and ashes. The almshouses each have a ground floor room with a fireplace, and the entrance area leads to a small service area fitted with a dresser. A winder stair with handrail leads to an upper bedroom. The long attic above the almshouses could be used as a hospital and women in the two end houses had access to it to attend the sick of Corsham.[5]

The Almshouses, Corsham, late 19th century CC

The schoolmaster's house has more spacious accommodation. It underwent some modernisation in the 18th century, but retains a dog-leg stair, a more ornamental dresser and an original table. Amongst the residents a married couple were designated to clean and repair the schoolhouse and a woman was the schoolmaster's house servant.[6]

The outbuildings: These include a washhouse/privy for the schoolmaster, a combined kitchen/brewhouse/coachhouse/stable/pigsty and poultryhouse (later used as the Parish Room), a washhouse/privy for the residents and, in the close to the south, which provided grazing for the master's horse, an unusual double-sided summerhouse. The close has been built over for housing. There were vegetable plots for the residents, a garden for the schoolmaster and a hedge on which to dry clothes.[7]

Both the north and west fronts bear tablets with the following inscription:

This free School and Almshouse was founded and endowed by Margaret Lady Hungerford, relict of Sir Edward Hungerford, Kt., of the Honourable Order of the Bath,

daughter and co-heir of William Halliday, Alderman of London, and Susan his wife,
daughter of Sir Henry Row, Knight, and Alderman and Lord Mayor of London.
On identical hatchments over the north and west doors appear the arms of
Halliday: Sable three helmets argent, garnished or, a border engrailed of the
second. The Hungerford arms are on a shield surmounting the hatchments:
Sable two bars argent in chief three plates. There are various heraldic devices in
stone about the two entrances, depicting badges of the Hungerfords and their
family connections.

*Constitution: Originally for a master and six poor, childless men or women.[8]
Women in the two end houses had to attend the sick of Corsham here, when it was used
as a hospital.[9] The original funds provided £20 a year for the master, though in the
early 19th century the master was not teaching, and £30 yearly for the six residents, but
the endowment was increased at the end of the 19th century by a Mrs Mary Alexander[10]
and the Charity known as the Alexander Charity provided, among other things, for a
wheelchair for the community.[11] The Governor of the Almshouses is now the Earl of
Radnor, to whom all the Hungerford estates passed. Until the 20th century, qualified
paupers of Stanton St Quintin were preferred when vacancies arose in the almshouses.[12]*

A list of forty-five rules and regulations was drawn up for the inhabitants.
A black gown with a silver badge with Lady Hungerford's crest was worn.[13] The
school had ten free pupils and probably fee-paying pupils in addition.

*Silver-plated badge worn by the almspeople of the Hungerford Almshouses,
WSA ref: 490/22 PMS*

The RCHME report of 1991[14] concludes that 'The survival of the almshouses
and schoolroom in their present state, with so few alterations or additions, make
them both rare and extremely important.' After extensive repairs in 1998-2000
the schoolroom and schoolmaster's house are now regularly open to the public.

HOSPITAL & FREE SCHOOL of CORSHAM, founded by
Margaret (Halliday) widow of Sir Edw. Hungerford. KB 1660
copied from a small drawing taken in 1684 by Mr Thomas
Dingley (See Camden Society's Publication); showing
the there was originally a small Turret.)
1982.3722

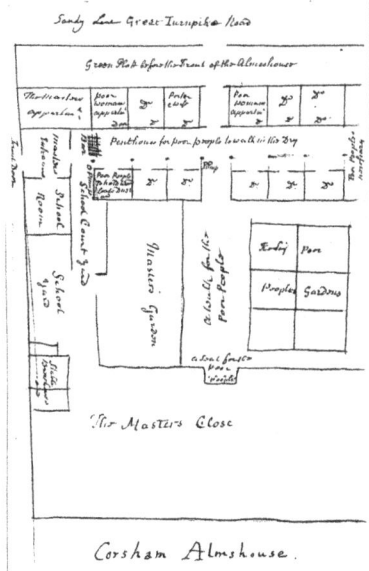

Corsham Almshouse.

*Above: 1684 drawing of the main front, by Sir Thomas
Dingley (Wilts. Museum Devizes: 1982:3722)
Right: Early plan of Corsham Almshouses
(WSA Ref: 490/11)*

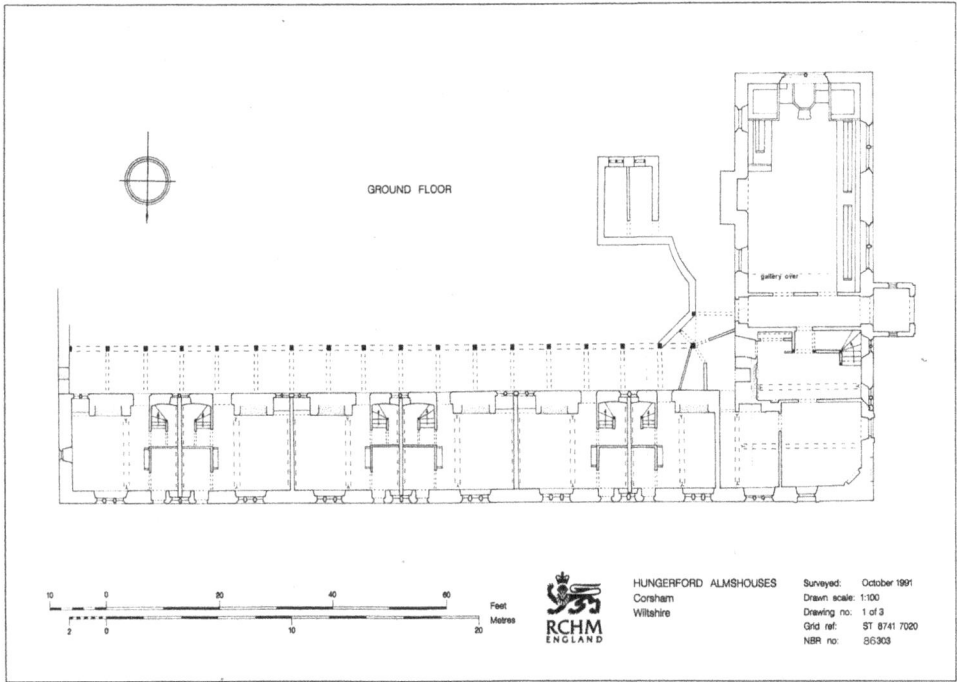

*Ground plan of the Almshouses, Corsham (© Crown Copyright, EH, with thanks to the
Wiltshire Buildings Record).*

Notes:
1 Crowley, 1991, 217.
2 Char.Com. 1837, 624.

3 Pevsner, 175-6.

4 Watercolour by John Buckler, 1809. (Wiltshire Museum, Devizes).

5 Fuller details in reports by RCHME (1991), Keystone Historic Building Consultants (1999) and Quercus Consultants (1999). All in WBR, Chippenham, ref: B214.

6 Hird, 206.

7 *ibid.* 209.

8 *ibid.*45.

9 *ibid.* 46.

10 Ch.Com. 1908, 330.

11 *ibid.* 331.

12 Hird, 45-51.

13 WSA Ref: 490/23.

14 RCHME Report (1991).

Charity Commission references:

1837:   1254-56

1908:   308-10, 330-32

Dauntsey   Earl Danby's Almshouses   ST980825

By Dauntsey village green.
Grade 2.

The original Earl Danby's Almshouses and school CC

In 1420 there was an almshouse here with at least five residents.[1] Nothing further is known of it.

The will of Henry, Earl Danby, proved in 1645, gave a site in Dauntsey and an annual income of £50 from 1667 for a school and almshouse.[2] They were both open in 1673 and possibly by as early as 1667.[3]

Constitution: There were to be six inhabitants, aged fifty years or more, unable to support themselves. Preference was given to natives or residents of Dauntsey, though from 1967, others who were entitled to enter included poor from Brinkworth, Great Somerford and Little Somerford.[4]

Under the terms of the will, £47 4s was to be made available each year: each resident was to receive £5 4s a year and clothing, provided the finances of the almshouse could afford it. £16 was to go to the schoolmaster in quarterly payments and the remainder was to reside with the churchwardens, to be used for maintenance, repairs and, every second year, towards the almspeople's clothing. This was to consist of 43 yards of Bristol Breize or other broad cloth and would go to making the men's coats and the women's gowns, in plain fashion, at Eastertide. For firing there was to be a wainload of wood or 10 bushels of coals at Michaelmas, to each of the six almspeople.

Almshouse occupants. the women holding little nosegays of marigolds and pansies. The almspeople are named as Mrs Still, Martha Dark, unknown, Mr Baker in red waistcoat, and Mrs Smith, c. 1900 CC

In 1905 there were eight residents, including two married couples; in 1986, six residents. From 1865-1905 almost all the income from the endowment was paid into the almshouse.[5] By 1905 the income was £62. After this date, part of the income was again paid into the school.

The original building, erected by 1673, was known as The Stripes, for the obvious reason that it was a closely-studded timber-framed building. The almshouse was on the ground floor, while the School and Schoolmaster's accommodation were on the first floor. After the School and almshouse moved to their new site, The Stripes lost its bell cote and was sold.

'The Stripes' CC

In 1864-6 a new building was erected and the almshouse occupied the east wing, abutting onto the school. It is a long, single-storey building of reddish brick and ashlar dressings, with two non-matching gable ends, each of these giving an upper floor. The chimneys are tall, slender and of decorated brick, looking much older than Victorian. The roof is banded with plain roof tiles. The shallow, ten-bay verandah along the front of the tenements is an echo of the original building, with the centre roof swept low over it.

Notes:
1 Reg.Hallum (Cant.& York Socy.) 224
2 TNA. PROB 11/194/124.
3 Freeman, 1991c, 73.
4 ibid., 25, 204, 211.
5 WSA Ref: 1033 (account book 1804-1905).
Charity Commission References:
1837: 1316-132
1908: 377-9, 381-4

Deptford (Wylye parish)   Name not known   Location not known

Shortly before her death in 1583, Susan Mompesson built an almshouse in Deptford. This much is known from her will, dated that year: 'Item my will and mynde is and I doe by theise presents chardge as well the saide Thomas Mompesson and his heyres males, as also all other suche person and persons as Shall have and enjoye eyther my Landes or Tenementes goods and cattells that theye doe from tyme to tyme as anye neede and occasion shalbe, sufficientlie repaire for ever, thee Almeshowse whiche I have erected and made at Deopford. . .'[1]

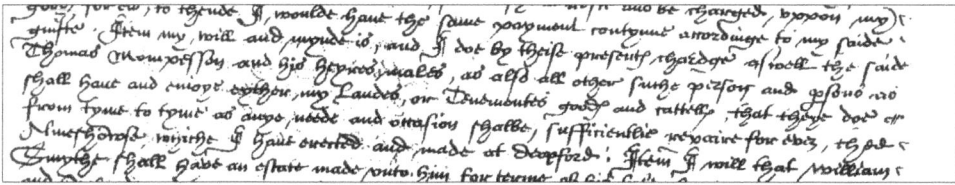

Extract from will of Susan Mompesson, 1583 SMT

Burial registers for Wylye, in which parish Deptford was a tithing, also give a few clues. Two entries in 1620 refer to almsmen and a third in 1621. But beyond this, nothing further is known.

Notes:
1 TNA, PROB 11/66/67.
2 Crittall, 1952.

Extract from Andrews & Dury's map of Wiltshire 1773.[2] WRS

Devizes

In the medieval period there were two hospitals, one outside the town at Southbroom and one in St. Mary's parish. By the 18th century there were at least three almshouses which were at different times rebuilt and relocated. The VCH vol. x gives a fairly good summary of the various charities for the town and how they were applied to the almshouses. Since the 18th century, there have been some amalgamations of the almshouses and also many new foundations within the town, some of them using old charity funding.

The Hospital of St. James and St. Denis, Southbroom   SU 012616

This leper hospital is thought to have been founded by the Bishop of Salisbury. Southbroom was formerly part of Bishop's Cannings. In March 1208 King John granted a two-day fair at the house on the vigil and feast of St. Denis. In 1227 the Southbroom fair was extended to four days. Henry III in 1232 granted wood from Melksham Forest for building the lepers' chapel thought to be the origin of the present St. James' Church. The hospital was granted protection for collecting alms in 1336-8 which was carried out by Richard de Breton, 'hermit'. The site was later represented by a house called Spitalcroft which is marked on a map of about 1835 and in 1900.[1]

c. 1835 map, from Book of Devizes, Edward Bradby.
Spitalcroft shown to NE of St James's Church

The Hospital or Priory of St. John the Baptist   SU 007614

At the corner of Monday Market Street and Sidmouth Street

The earliest reference to the hospital is in 1314 when the Mayor and Burgesses of Devizes presented the priest John Wyt of Potterne to the hospital. When a hospital was run by members of a religious order it became a cell of that order and was called a 'priory'. By 1326 it had a free chapel. In 1399 the king granted the custody of the hospital to Nicholas Coventry. [2]

In the 15th century William Coventry, a relative, founded a chantry in St Mary's Parish and his will charged his lands with payment of £1 12s 8d to four almswomen, in alms, wood, coals and four beds.[3] This was still being paid in 1549.[4] Also, John Coventry the younger, who died before 1475, in his will charged the endowment of his chantry in St Mary's church with £4 to the almshouse poor.[5] Chantries and hospitals were dissolved in 1547 and in 1550 the chapel was sold by the Crown to Richard Roberts of London. The hospital by then may have been named the Old Almshouses, mentioned in 1552. The name Chapel Corner persisted for the site, until at least 1851.[6]

The Old Almshouses   SU007615

In the northwest corner of St John's churchyard
Grade 2.

The Old Almshouse CC

Cunnington's Annals state that the Old Almshouse was built formerly of timber and was rebuilt on a new site 'in the orchard', presumably in 1615 (see below). '1615 – This year and the next the old Almshouses being ruinous were new built with freestone and removed from whence it formerly stood to a more convenient place where it now is, and the poor people placed therein by the Maior and Burgeses on 1st Janry and divers good orders sett up in a table in the said house from thenceforth to be duly observed. Mr Wm. Barrett Citizen and Grocer of London and Mr Cleophes Smythe citizen and draper of London both born in the Borough contributed £5 each towards the expense of the building.'[7]

The building retained the name St. John's Hospital on Edward Dore's plan of Devizes in 1759. When the Old Almshouse was investigated in 1834 for the Charity Commission, it was described as a building of 1615, in St. John's Churchyard at the top of Estcourt Hill. There were four rooms occupied by two widows from St John's parish and two from St Mary's. Two underground rooms were let by the overseers of St John's to parish paupers. Since 1726 there was a small garden for the use of the almswomen. Endowment came from fifteen plots within the Borough.[8]

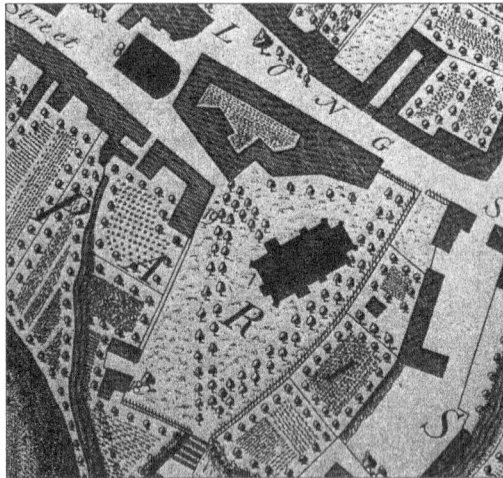

Extract from map of Devizes by Edward Dore, 1749.
Wiltshire Museum Library, Devizes
From the top: No.19 New Almshouses, No.1 St John's Church, No.18 Old Almshouses

The two-storeyed cottage is of coursed dressed stone, with a stone-tiled roof and brick chimneys on either gable. There are two gabled half-dormers on the first floor with 3-light casements and moulded stone mullions. There are two similar windows on the ground floor. There is a central gabled porch with a stone-tiled roof and a flat-arch entry. Interior partitions are timber-framed. The

The Sexton's House, formerly The Old Almshouses SMT

end gables and the dormers have bargeboards. After 1896, it was known as the Sexton's House, the name by which it is known today.

The New Almshouse   SU 008615
At the corner of St.John's churchyard and St.John's Court

The New Almshouse   SMT

Marked as 'An Almshouse' on Edward Dore's map of 1759.

By the time his will was proved in 1451, Thomas Coventry, probably William Coventry's brother, had founded an almshouse and his will exhorted his widow to use his lands to support ten beds there. On her death, the lands were to pass to the Borough Corporation to continue the maintenance. Any surplus from the income of the lands was to be used for the support of the almspeople themselves.[9] Coventry's foundation is thought to have been the New Almshouse, so-called in 1552, situated within the plot of his stone house, 4 St. John's Court.[10]

4 St. John's Court   PMS (WBR)

In 1576 there is a reference to two stewards of the Old and New Almshouses and in 1573-6 a warden, Stephen Flower.[11] In 1576, two wardens of the New Almshouse are mentioned.[12]

The Corporation continued to receive and pay the endowment of both Old and New Almshouses for many years, as was recorded in the Returns to Visitation Queries in 1783.[13]

As there were ten beds in 1451 the buildings then may have stretched further along the plot. The one and a half storey timber-framed building of about 1600 called Tower Lee next to the present building may perhaps have been part of the group. In 1834, the New Almshouse was described as standing where St John's Court meets St John's churchyard. There was a large communal kitchen, with sleeping places on two sides of it, with a lumber room over the top. There were three plots of land in the Borough which formed the endowment of the foundation.[14] During rebuilding in about 1855 the old building was found to contain Romanesque stones thought to be from the Norman nave of St John's church, though they could equally have been from Devizes castle.[15] In 1901, three women were chosen alternately from either parish to fill the vacancies; there was no defined age and they received a weekly dole and coals.[16] In 1895, the building was altered and by 1971 formed two separate dwellings.

The present building is a pair of one-storey cottages in Tudor style, of coursed rubble stone with stone dressings. Below the parapet is a moulded string. The roof is of stone tiles and the gable ends each have a chimney. There are three pairs of iron-framed leaded casements with stone surrounds under hooded dripstones. The two doors, with 3-centred arches, are set between the three windows.

Eyles' Almshouse

By 1668, Sir John Eyles had founded an almshouse in Devizes. This was situated in Short Street in St Mary's parish and was said to be in or near the gatehouse there.[17] It is marked on a plan of 1801. The Market Place end of Short Street was made into the Shambles covered market in 1803.

Sir John's will, proved in 1703, [18] settled the house of eight rooms, in trust, on the poor of St John's parish, and the building was used until 1829. He also left two houses in Short Street for the poor of St Mary's; these were rebuilt in 1812, but demolished in 1828.

By a deed of 1704, Mary Eyles settled, in trust, a rent of £8 on the Salutation Inn (now the Elm Tree Inn, which still stands). £1 4s 0d was to be used for fuel for six women in Sir John Eyles' almshouse, with the residue being used for teaching and clothing.[19] The Inn was sold in 1886, the rent-charge was redeemed and the proceeds invested. Some of the resultant income was used to repair the almshouses in St John's parish.

Later developments

In 1828-9 both parishes built a combined almshouse/poorhouse near Devizes Green, with the stipulation that six of the twenty-four rooms were to house the Eyles Almspeople. The building was known as St John's Buildings.[20] After the Union Workhouse was built, the building was shared with members of the Old Almshouse.

In 1828 St Mary's also had a site on Commercial Road, with a two-storey brick building of two blocks, facing across a garden. Each block had sixteen rooms, two for each resident.

In 1896, seven cottages were bought in Sutton Place, near Southbroom, and converted to two-room almshouses. The residents of the Old Almshouse

St Mary's Almshouses, Devizes, opened 1911 CC

were transferred thence. In 1904, there were four widows receiving a weekly dole and quarterly fuel.

In 1914-15, new regulations were drawn up for both the Old and New Almshouses by the Corporation, under whose aegis both foundations had come. It would appear that while the New Almshouse was open to people of both sexes, the residents of the Old Almshouse continued to be women only.

Notes:

1 Chettle & Crittall, 1956, 362; WSA OS map 1900; www.St-James-Devizes.org.uk
2 Chettle & Crittall, 1956, 337.
3 Kite, 251.
4 Pugh, 1975, 307.
5 Will of John Coventry, Pugh, 1975, quoting Cal.Pat. 1555-7, 152.
6 Pugh, 1975, 235n.
7 Cunnington, vol.i, 64.
8 Charity Commission, 1837, 733; 1908, 440.
9 Will of Thomas Coventry TNA, PROB 11/1/228.
10 Kite, 254.
11 Cunnington, vol.i, 66.
12 *ibid.*
13 Ransome, 1972, 66.
14 Charity Commission, vol. i, 339-40.
15 Kite, 254n.
16 Charity Commission, vol.i, 440.
17 *ibid.* 392.
18 Will of Christopher Eyles TNA, PROB 11/470/314.
19 Charity Commission, vol.i, 392.
20 Pugh, 1975, 309.

Charity Commission references
1837

New: 1367-69
Old: 1362-66
Eyles: 1347, 1360
1908
New: 411, 439-41
Old: 406-10, 435-39
Eyles: 392, 445, 455-6, 457

Farley (Pitton & Farley parish) Sir Stephen Fox's Hospital   SU225296
Opposite the parish church.

Sir Stephen Fox's Hospital   SMT

Hospital building Grade 1, North and West walls Grade 2.

Sir Stephen Fox, the son of a yeoman, was born in this village and, as part of a charitable scheme, which extended to other parts of the country, he founded and built these almshouses in 1688 and rebuilt the parish church, which stands opposite.

Constitution: The original document remains with the almshouses. It made provision for twelve poor, aged persons, six men and six women, over fifty years of age,

*to be widowed or unmarried. They were provided with two rooms each plus a garden.
The privilege was extended to the parish of Maddington, near Shrewton.*

The almshouses are an architectural statement. The long, low, two-storeyed brick building, of Flemish Bond, was designed by Alexander Fort, a master mason employed by Christopher Wren. Despite speculation it is unlikely that Wren had a hand in it. Fort died in 1706.[1] The central warden's house is of four bays, with four leaded casements with stained oak bars and surrounds on the first floor. Two windows and two central, half-glazed doors are on the ground floor. In the centre of the steeply-pitched hipped roof are two hipped dormers with leaded casements. There are four brick chimneys at each corner of the roof. The centre of the building is in line with the churchyard gates opposite. Inside is a portrait of Sir Stephen Fox, thought to be by Lely.

The almshouses themselves were originally two-roomed apartments, with a store at the rear. They were later altered to give two bedrooms under the roof, which is hipped. Inside, there is a single fireplace and a newel stair for each apartment. In the late 19th century a village reading room was opened in a cottage which was part of the almshouses, but when the residents were disturbed, it was closed and it transferred in 1902 to a new building opposite.[2] The front garden is enclosed by a brick wall.

Above the main entrance is a stone plaque with Latin inscription, surmounted by a cherub's head:

Plaque on front wall SMT

DEO OPT.MAX Bonorum Omnium Largitori
Isthoc Quantulumcunque Grati Animi
Monumentum acceptum Refert
SCHOLAE hujus et PTOCHOTROPHII
Fundator humilis gratabundus
MDCLXXXI
Quid tibi Divitiae prosunt quas Congeris Hospes
Solas quas Dederis SEMPER habebis Opes

A rough translation is:

To God the best and greatest benefactor
The humble and grateful founder
Of this school and poorhouse
Bears this your welcome monument, however small
1681
'What riches profit you, what can you collect as host?
You shall give up those riches. You will always have wealth'.[3]

On the outside wall, bounding the property, is a small modern tablet, which reads: FARLEY HOSPITAL. It is surmounted by a fox.

Farley Hospital, viewed from the Church SMT

Notes:
1 Pevsner, 216.
2 Slocombe, I., 67.
3 I am indebted to Mr Steven Hobbs of the WSHC for his assistance with this translation.
Charity Commission references
1837: 451-56

Figheldean   ?Poore's Almshouses   Location: ca. SU155474
Supposed to have been just south-west of the church

According to the VCH[1], five almshouses were built here, a little south-west of the church, in 1826, at the behest of Edward Dyke, (d.1859). He inherited the manor of North Tidworth from Edward Poore (died without issue 1803), having assumed the name Poore; he was henceforth known as Edward Dyke Poore.

However, the Charities Commission Report of 1908 gives a different version. Parliamentary returns of 1786 are supposed to have mentioned a sum of £30 given to the poor by Edward Poore, but the Report says there is no trace of such a donation in the parish books. Edward Dyke Poore, lord of the manor of Figheldean, died in 1874 and when his nephew and heir, also Edward Dyke Poore, was approached by the Commissioners, he knew nothing about the benefaction, had never heard of it, and declined to re-establish it. The Report says there was no reference to the Charity in the General Digest of 1867-9, nor in the Charity Commission's Register of Unreported Charities. The Vicar at the time of the 1908 Report had never heard of the Charity, either.[2]

This somewhat muddled account of events concerning the almshouses and Poore Charity prompted a search for Edward Poore's will. The most likely candidate was Edward Poore of Tidworth, (d. 1803), who held estates in Tidworth and Figheldean, the will having been made in 1802 and proved in 1804. In this, Edward Poore says: 'To the residents in my Alms houses at the time of my decease and to the persons not residing who shall be on that Establishment the Sum of Five pounds each.'[3]

Extract from will of Edward Poore, 1802   SMT

This at least establishes that an Edward Poore had indeed founded some almshouses on one of his estates, and since the almshouses at Tidworth were founded earlier by Dr Pierce, one can only assume that Poore refers to almshouses at Figheldean. Although the VCH states that the almshouses were built in 1826, it would appear that perhaps this was a refounding of them and possibly a rebuild, by Edward Dyke Poore. It is not clear from Edward Poore's will when his almshouses were established, but they were certainly in existence by the time he wrote his will in 1802.

Constitution: Not known

The buildings were demolished in the 1960s; they appeared on a provisional list of historic buildings of interest, issued by the Ministry of Housing and Local Government of the time.[4]

Notes:
1 Stevenson, 1995a, 107.
2 Ch.Comm. vol. ii, 171.
3 TNA, PROB 11/1405/42.
4 Information given to the VCH by the Vicar at the time (Stevenson, J., 1995a, 94n).
Charity Commission references:
1837: 472

Froxfield   The Duchess of Somerset's Hospital   SU 300681
North side of the Bath Road, on the east side of Froxfield

Duchess of Somerset's Hospital, the street frontage   WBR

Hospital Grade 2*, Chapel Grade 2*.

Sarah, Duchess of Somerset, (1631-1692), the wife of Lord John Seymour, 4th Duke of Somerset, was believed to have been worth about £50,000,[1] somewhere in the region of £4-5 million in today's currency. Her father gave her £10,000 when she married Lord Seymour and as her father's only heir, she inherited much of his wealth when he died.[2] Before her own death, she made provision for all her family, friends and servants; this was followed by a large number of benefactions to charity, including the Broad Town Charity for training apprentices and the founding of almshouses at Froxfield, both in Wiltshire.

By her will, dated 17 May 1686, the Dowager Duchess bequeathed £1,700 to build an almshouse on two acres of land at Froxfield. The will details the provisions, which are recorded below.

Constitution: The Duchess's will originally specified provision for thirty poor widows; but when the income from her estates permitted, this was to rise to fifty. There are now forty-nine. A copy of the original will is held at the Hospital. Later it was stated that the Hospital provided for 'fifty poor widows, twenty clergy and thirty lay'.[3]

No widow possessing lands or tenements worth £20 or more per annum would be eligible. Each was to be 'poor but honest and such as lead a good life'. The maintenance fund was to provide each widow with a stipend. Remarriage meant their place was forfeit.[4] Provision was also made for a chaplain, a post filled by the Vicars of Froxfield.

The Duchess's will specified the places from which the widows were to be drawn; there were to be 20 clergy widows and 30 lay; of the latter, ten were to be drawn from her manors of Wiltshire (i.e. Froxfield, Huish, Shaw, Fyfield, Milton and Broadtown), five from the counties of Wiltshire, Somerset and Berkshire, five from London and Westminster, and ten from other counties within 150 miles of London. These widows were allocated specific houses within the Hospital and each house carried a number. Of the 20 clergy widows, ten were drawn from the counties of Wiltshire, Somerset and Berkshire, five from London and Westminster, and five from other counties.[5]

The building is in the form of a large quadrangle, with a chapel in the middle of the courtyard; the almshouses are of brick and the chapel and gatehouse of ashlar; these were added in 1813.[6]

The chapel in the quadrangle WBR

Each house consisted of a ground floor room with a chamber above, with a hearth in each room. In recent years the building has been modernised internally, but still presents an impressive range running parallel to the main road, with thirty-seven bays. The building was enlarged in 1775 and the difference between the two building phases is clear.[7]

The eastern half of the Hospital, brick-built in 1694, has doors and windows in stone surrounds with ogee arches. The doors are boarded and have small wooden canopies and lattice sides. The windows are two lights, with brick relieving arches. The eaves are dentilled brick.

Individual house   WBR

The western half, of 1775, lacks the stone detail of the earlier build; there is a brick plat band and the leaded windows are in timber frames.

The gatehouse of 1813 is of stone with tall buttresses and moulded carriage openings under a Tudor arch.

Over the central archway, facing the main road, is a stone plaque, inscribed as follows:

The
SOMERSET HOSPITAL
For Twenty Clergy
And Thirty Lay Widows

FOUNDED and ENDOWED
By the late Most Noble
SARAH
Duchess Dowager of SOMERSET
A.D.MDCXCIV

On the South external wall of the chapel is the following:
The Following inscription was engraved by Order
Of the Trustees of this Hospital
The Original Chapel being in decay
The Right Honourable Thomas Bruce Earl of Ailesbury K.T.
One of the Trustees
Erected the present at his sole Expense A.D.MDCCCXIII
Not only for the Accommodation of the Widows
But out of Respect to the Memory of his late Noble Relative
SARAH DUCHESS DOWAGER OF SOMERSET
The Pious Foundress of this munificent Charity

In the East window of the chapel are two pieces of heraldic glass in the form of lozenges:

Quarterly 1 and 4:
or on a pile gu between six fleurs de lys az three lions of England (for the Duke of Somerset)
2 and 3:
gu a pair of wings conjoined in lure or (for Seymour)
impaling:
az 9 molets pierced, arranged 1,2,3,2,1, or
surmounted by a ducal coronet.

Quarterly 1 and 4:
ar a saltire gu on a chief per pale ar and gu a lion rampant on the first sa
2 and 3:
ar a chevron gu between three ?snails sa
surmounted by an Earl's coronet.

Notes:

1 *ODNB* (Howard Tomlinson quoting N. Luttrell, 1857).

2 Crowley, 2013, 1-2.

3 Ransome, 1972, 90

4 Rix, 2.

5 *ibid.* 3 & 4.

6 Pevsner, 224.

7 *ibid.*

Charity Commission references:

1837: 415-423

Garsdon (Lea & Cleverton parish) Name and location unknown

In the early years of the 17th century, provision was made for the poor of Garsdon in the form of a cottage, built by the wealthy inhabitants. It was confirmed as an almshouse in 1659,[1] but there is no mention of it in the reports of the Charities Commission. Apparently there were four cottages standing just to the east of Garsdon Manor, which, according to a Survey of 1821, were in the hands of the Overseers of the Poor.[2] One of these may have been the original almshouse; certainly the accompanying Survey map shows a small block of what could be three cottages, with another set at right-angles to it.[3] By the time of the Tithe Award of 1840, there were only three cottages listed for the site. They were owned by Lord Methuen and occupied by John Vincent, Hester Whale and Thomas Hinton. The cottages and their gardens occupied 2 roods and 33 perches and the rent was recorded at 2s 6d. There is no mention of almshouses or charity.[4]

Notes:
1 Freeman, 1991a: 92.
2 WSA Ref: 88/7/4/5.
3 WSA Ref: 135/16.
4 WSA: Garsdon Tithe Award 1840.

Great Wishford   Grobham Cottages   SU 340355
North side of West Street, opposite the Church

Grobham Cottages SMT

Grade 2.

Founded by the will of Sir Richard Grobham, dated 16 December 1628, proved 25 July 1629. Lands in South Newton formed the endowment of the almshouses, amounting yearly to about £37 by the late 18th century.[1]

Constitution: For four poor parishioners, men or women, plus the services of a nurse or housekeeper. Men and women were appointed until about 1790; after this the residents were usually men with their wives living with them. By 1904, two couples and a single man occupied three cottages; the fourth was leased and the rent was used to relieve another parishioner. In the mid-19th century, each almsman received 30s a month. A housekeeper was appointed from 1870-1885.

In 1969-70 the cottages were converted into two and there are now only two residents. Originally built as four cottages in a terrace, in banded flint and stone, with a tiled roof, gable end rendered stacks. The plan was baffle-entry and they were single storey with attics. They have four 2-light recessed hollow-chamfered mullioned casements with C20 steel casements, and four hipped dormers with C20 casements.

There are two chamfered stone doorcases to the centre and two to the ends, all with C20 doors, The rear has C20 lean-to extensions and doors, and single-light recessed hollow-chamfered casements. The interiors were altered and modernised 1960s, and have chamfered beams.

Grobham Cottages   JAT

A small tablet on the front of the building says simply: Grobham Cottages

Notes:
1 Ransome, 225
Charity Commission references:
1837: 505-7

Hankerton

One tiny shred of evidence exists to demonstrate that there may once have been an almshouse in Hankerton. The Hearth Tax for Wiltshire lists, under the heading of Hankerton and Cloatley Hundred, the following entries under Hankerton Tything:

Oliver Webb for Richard Hills ten[emen]t 2 yearlye } 2
Webb an Almesma[n] noe distresse to be taken }
Arabella Beale for p[ar]te of Alice Gaggs tenem[en]t
Arabella a poore Almesbody & Excluised by certe 2 hearths

It may, of course, simply mean that these two people were in receipt of alms, perhaps paid by the parish; but such recipients were not usually termed almspeople and it would appear that Olive and Arabella were both inmates of an almshouse (however small) within the parish of Hankerton.

Notes:
1 Hearth Tax Returns for Wiltshire – MSS only. Publication at a future date by the British Record Society.

Heytesbury (St.John's Hospital)

The Hospital of St.John the Baptist & St.Katherine ST929428

North side of the east end of High Street, at junction with slip road to A36 bypass. Grade 2.

The almshouses were founded in 1472 by Walter, first Lord Hungerford, but it was not until the death of his daughter-in-law, Margaret (neé Botreaux) in 1479 that the foundation received sufficient endowment to ensure its perpetuity. This consisted of the manors of Cheverell Burnell and Great Cheverell, with further estates added in later years, and 20 cartloads of wood per annum from Southleigh. By 1633, there was also property in Upton Scudamore, Calne, Stockley and Warminster.

The Hospital escaped closure at the Reformation, being a lay foundation, but its annual revenue of £42 was confiscated by the Crown and given to Sir

Heytesbury, the front of the old building SMT

William Sharington, the new owner of Lacock Abbey. However, the Hospital was restored, with its revenue, by Cardinal Pole and this was confirmed by Elizabeth I. At this time there was also a school.

When the great Heytesbury fire of 1765 occurred, many of the Hospital inhabitants had to lodge in the church until provision could be made for them. The new building took place between 1766-7 and is, in essence, the building we see today.

From the St.John's Hospital guide (By kind permission of St John's Hospital)

New building programmes in the 20th and 21st centuries have been financed by the sale of almshouse estates and the coach house is now a chapel. The new flats behind the main building were designed by the Wyvern Group of Designers, Devizes, who have been responsible for the renovation and redevelopment of many of the Wiltshire almshouses in the 20C.

Constitution: The Foundation Deed of 4 April 1472, reciting Letters Patent Edward IV, names trustees to found, create, erect and establish an almshouse, consisting of a Chaplain, who was also to be the Custos (Warden) and the Schoolmaster, and twelve poor men, with one woman to wash and clean for them and to care for them when they were sick. The almsmen were preferably to be unmarried. They were to lead a communal life, praying for the souls of their founders and benefactors, and were not to leave the Hospital without permission.

The Almsmen of Heytesbury, 1892, with their 'carers' (By kind permission of St.John's Hospital)

St John's Hospital, 1916 CC

A weekly allowance was made to each almsman and every year he was to be issued with two pairs of hose, two pairs of shoes and two shirts. Every second or third year the almsmen were to have a gown and hood of white wool, emblazoned with JhuXrt (Jesus Christ) in black on the breast and shoulder.

In the 18th century this was changed to a scarlet gown with a badge in blue, bearing the initial letters HIS, together with a silk hat. This uniform endured until 1958, when it was abolished.

The constitution was elaborated with forty-eight statutes, giving details of the running of the Hospital and the behaviour of its inhabitants.[1]

Revisions of the Constitution over 500 years mean that women and married couples were later admitted, with a Matron in charge, and with gardeners and maintenance workers on the site. For this the residents paid a weekly service charge.

'Getting Ready for Church' 1926   CC (from The Guardian)

In the 21st century, first consideration is now given to residents of Heytesbury, Knook and Tytherington; but inhabitants of other places are also considered, including those outside the county.

The original Hospital was burnt down in the Great Fire of 1765, which destroyed much of Heytesbury.[2] It was rebuilt 1766-7, in brick, on three sides of a turfed square, under a hipped, slate roof; the architect was Esau Reynolds of Trowbridge. The style is of older, 17th century almshouses. The main, two-storeyed building is of Flemish Bond with stone dressings, under a tiled, hipped roof with a brick stack. The front is 5-sash windowed. There is a former coach house (now a chapel) at the north corner and a clock and bell tower over the main entrance to the almshouse.[3]

A coat of arms over the main entrance incorporates the Hungerford arms. At the main gates is a metal plaque, with the Hungerford coronet, sickles and wheatsheaf at the top. Beneath, it reads:

THE

HOSPITAL OF ST.JOHN HEYTESBURY

THIS ALMSHOUSE WAS FOUNDED IN THE YEAR 1449

BY WALTER LORD HUNGERFORD TREASURER OF ENGLAND

THE PRESENT BUILDING DATES FROM 1769

(St John's)   Heytesbury: the chapel, exterior and interior   (CC)

IN 1952 THE INTERIOR WAS ALTERED TO PROVIDE
NEW DWELLINGS

Several seals in good condition survive attached to the original charters of foundation of the Hospital, including one of unknown date, one of Lady Margaret Hungerford and a Hospital seal of 1633.

Notes:
1 WSA Ref: 251/35
2 Ginever, 27.
3 Grubb, 25.
Charity Commission references:
1837: 739-46

Hilmarton   The Poynder Almshouses   SU 021754
South east of the parish church
Grade 2.

The Poynder family were the 19th century owners of the Hilmarton estate and William Henry Poynder settled in trust (by indenture, dated 28 March 1878) a piece of ground on which he built five almshouses in 1878. The Trustees were to be the Rev. Francis Goddard and two named Churchwardens.

William Poynder also invested £3000 to provide maintenance for the property and its inmates. The almspeople were to be former employees of the Hilmarton estate, preferably members of the parish congregation and not to be already in receipt of parish relief.

In 1952, the payments to residents ceased, having been reduced over the years. In 1961, residents had to make their own contributions towards maintenance of the buildings and themselves. But since 1938 there has been an 'extraordinary repair fund', which helps to maintain the buildings.[1]

Poynder Almshouses, the central porch SMT

The Poynder Almshouses, early 20th century CC

Constitution: Originally intended for five poor married men of 65+ years with their wives, or three poor single men and two poor single women, of 65+ years. Workers or tenants on the Hilmarton estate were to be given preference.

At the time of the foundation, a doctor was to attend the residents and to be paid from the Charity. At that time he was Dr Campbell of Calne.

Built of stone, in a rather ornate style, similar to the other Poynder buildings in the village, each almshouse consists of one storey, comprising a living room, bedroom, kitchen and offices.

The buildings are of rock-faced rubble stone with ashlar dressings. The roofs are of banded fishscale tiles with coped gables and end stacks on each house. The plan is three in a row, with one across each end. Each house has a gabled porch with a 2-light mullioned window under a hoodmould on each side. The houses on each side and at the end have coped gables, with a lancet in the centre. Gables facing the road have ashlar canted bays with 1, 2 and 1 lights. Together with many other buildings in the village, the almshouses were designed by the architect Henry Weaver, who for a time was the agent for the Hilmarton estate.[2]

The two outer plaques, set in the gables, are of red clay and bear the initials of the founder and the date, set as follows:

1

8 WP 7

7

There is a stone plaque with the Poynder coat of arms over the central porch and another bearing the foundation inscription above the inner doorway.

Poynder: Pily counterpily of four traits or and sa, the points ending in crosses formée, two in chief an one in base, in the centre chief point a castle of the second, and in base

The Poynder coat of arms   SMT

two martlets of the first, on a chief az a key erect, wards upwards and to the sinister or, between a rose on the dexter side and a fleur-de-lys on the sinister ar.

Motto: In Christo spes et Gloria – in Christ is hope and glory

Notes:
1 Crittall, 1970, 65.
2 *ibid.*, 52.
Charity Commission references:
1908: vol.i 548-550

Keevil   Possibly called the Poor's Houses   Location not known

In about 1615, the inhabitants of Keevil are known to have petitioned for a licence to build an almshouse, because many of the poor people of the place were forced to live in barns and outhouses for want of better accommodation.[1]

According to the Charity Commissioners' Report, the Poor's Houses were built in the tithing of Bulkington. They were originally two cottages, which fell into disrepair many years before the enquiry. They were bounded by the public road on one side and Thomas Gaisford's land on the others. The site was eventually sold, after a vestry meeting was called in 1885 and it was suggested at the time that the money raised should be put towards a new village pump. In the event, the money went towards the relief of the Poor Rates.[2]

It is not certain if these two cottages constituted the original almshouses, but it seems likely.

Church Rates of 1707[3] and Church Accounts of 1797-1879[4] have no mention of any almshouse and nothing further is known of them.

Notes:
1 Hist.MSS.Com.Var.Coll. 95
2 Ch.Comm. vol.ii, 252
3 WSA Ref : 1497/1
4 WSA Ref : 653/24

Kington St. Michael   Lyte's Almshouses   ST 904774
South end of village, west side of main street
Grade 2.

Isaac Lyte was baptised in Kington and later became an Alderman in London; as a gesture of charity towards his fellow villagers, he founded this block of almshouses by his will, proved 1673. £600 was to be laid out on the building, which took place in 1675.

Lyte's Almshouses SMT

By an indenture of 1707, whose whereabouts is unknown, a piece of adjoining ground was settled upon trust. There was no endowment, but Isaac Lyte gave a £20 per annum rent charge from property in Corston towards maintenance of the almshouses.

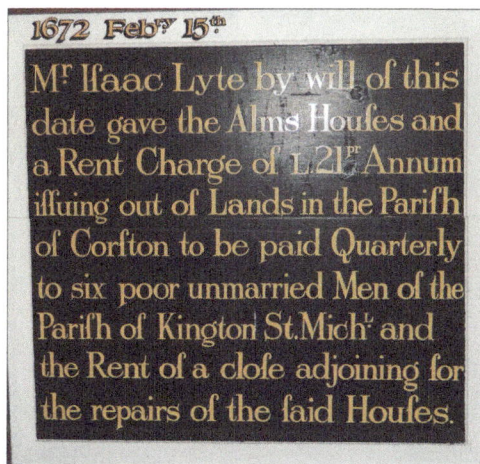

1672 Feb.ry 15.th

Mr Isaac Lyte by will of this date gave the Alms Houfes and a Rent Charge of L.21.r Annum iffuing out of Lands in the Parifh of Corfton to be paid Quarterly to six poor unmarried Men of the Parifh of Kington St.Mich.l and the Rent of a clofe adjoining for the repairs of the faid Houfes.

Benefaction board in Kington St Michael Church SMT

Lyte's Almshouses, early 20th century CC

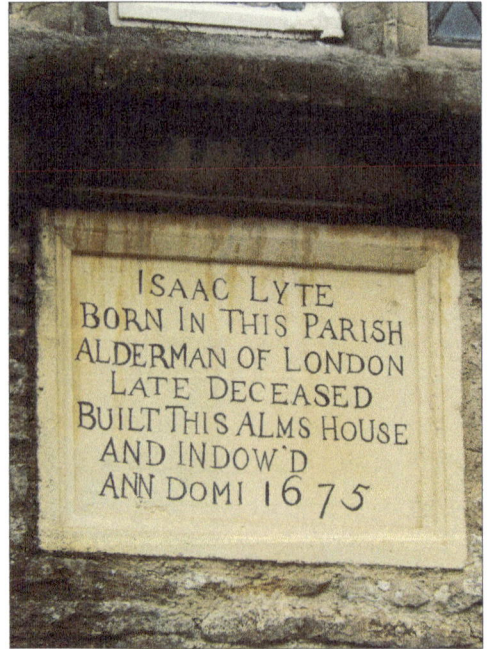

ISAAC LYTE
BORN IN THIS PARISH
ALDERMAN OF LONDON
LATE DECEASED
BUILT THIS ALMS HOUSE
AND INDOW'D
ANN DOMI 1675

Central gable with Lyte coat of arms and foundation plaque SMT

Over the years, various benefactors gave towards the maintenance and upkeep of the almshouses and the poor of the parish, with one Thomas White leaving a bequest of £200 for 'the better maintenance of the poor inhabitants of the almshouses'. This was in 1821.

Eventually, all the various charities of the parish were amalgamated and came under a board of trustees, which administered the almshouses.

Constitution: For six poor men, originally to be unmarried, to be appointed by the Vicar and Churchwardens of the parish.

The almshouses consist of six stone houses, built in a terraced row of rubble stone with ashlar dressings and a stone slate roof. Each of the houses has a coped gable and there are three large chimneys to the rear.

The windows are 3-light stone mullioned, with ovolo mouldings and hoodmoulds on the upper windows, dripcourses over those on the ground floor. Each door has a semi-circular hood and there are steps up from the street.

A plot of garden is attached to each tenement at the rear.

In the third gable from the left is a cartouche with the Lyte coat of arms and below it is a stone tablet detailing the foundation.

Arms: gules, a chevron between three swans, ar.

Further almshouses acquired by the Lytes Almshouse Charity, 2013 SMT

A further three almshouses have been acquired (as of 2013) in the village; these are sited in old buildings along the High Street.

Charity Commission references
1837:   330-33
1908:   587-9; 593

Leigh Delamere (Grittleton parish)   Neeld's Almshouses   ST 885793
Between the church and the rectory.

Neeld's Almshouses , showing the original path to the entrance CC

Grade 2.

By virtue of his will and two codicils, proved in 1856, Joseph Neeld of Grittleton House founded an almshouse for six poor people, though it was evidently some time before there were any almspeople appointed. He left £5000 to named trustees.

No conveyance of the site was ever made and when approached about the matter by the Charities Commission in 1908, Sir Audley Neeld, Bt., then heir to the Grittleton Estate, regarded the Neeld Charity and the Almshouses as connected with the estate and said he would object to any interference in the management of the same.

The church is very large and the almshouses very grand and set well back from the road. Leigh Delamere village is almost non-existent. The churchyard is full of professional deceased – soldiers, sailors, a general, etc. A villager I spoke to had found a number of symbols about the church, which related to Templars and

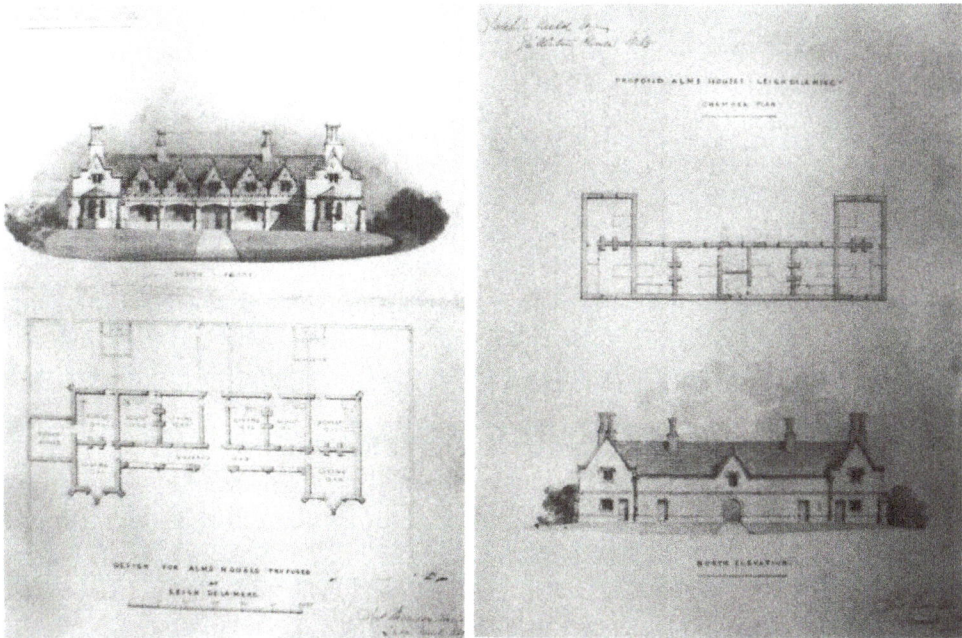

Plans for the Neeld Almshouses, front and rear elevations respectively CC

Neeld's Almshouses   CC

Masons. He discovered that Joseph Neeld was indeed a Mason and the church and almshouses were built for his Masonic colleagues; hence the reason why these two buildings seem out of context in such a tiny place.

Constitution: Originally founded for six poor men, sometime old servants of the Neeld estate were also appointed to the almshouses.

Designed by James Thompson, architect of Grittleton House, there are six tenements, with strips of kitchen garden to the rear. The front is laid to grass, which now covers the original path. The drive to the almshouses is to one side.

The buildings are low, two-storeyed, built of squared stone rubble, with five gables and projecting wings. The roofs are of stone slate and the clustered chimney stacks of ashlar, a group of four on each wing and two on the central ridge.

The style is Tudor with a raised plinth and a dripcourse.

The windows are two-light stone-mullioned, with hoodmoulds. The wings have triangular bay windows on the ground floor south end walls, with central buttresses and two Tudor-arched lights each side.

There is a blind shield on each of the two end gables facing the front and a third over the doorway. This latter is surmounted by a bas relief of a wolf's head erased (for Neeld).

Charity Commission references
1908: 495-6

Longbridge Deverill   Thynne's Almshouses   ST 867413
The east side of the A350, entering Longbridge Deverill village
Grade 2.

Thynne's Almshouse, Longbridge Deverill SMT

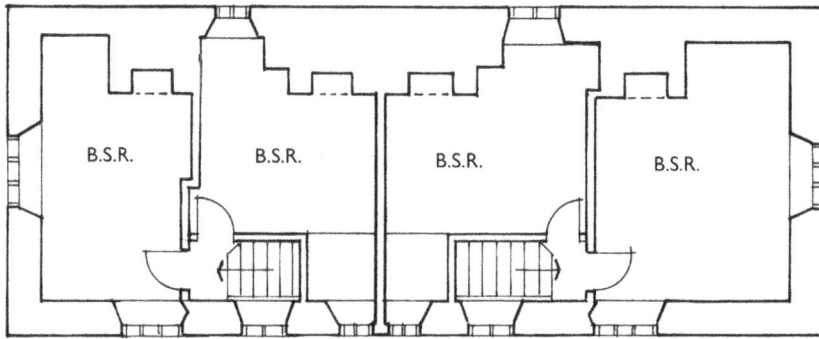

FIRST FLOOR

0 1 2 3 4 5 6 metres

B.R. bedroom
B.S.R. bed-sitting room
C cloakroom
Can canopy
W.C. water closet

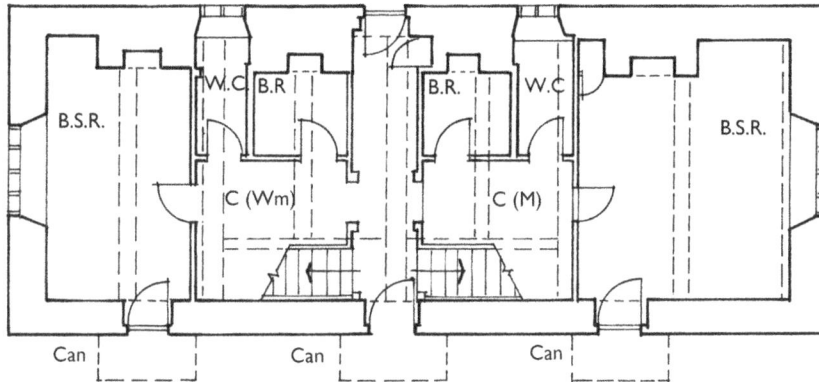

GROUND FLOOR

Plan of ground and first floor of Thynne's Almshouses ClC

The almshouses were founded by Sir James Thynne of Longleat. A deed of Feoffment, dated 27 November 1665, between Sir James of the one part and Sir Henry Cocker of Hill Deverill, and nine others of the second part, conveyed to Henry Cocker 'all that messuage or tenement and house called Sir James Thynne's Almshouse, together with the garden and appurtenances'. So presumably the almshouse was already in existence at this point, but probably fairly new.

By indenture, dated 28 November 1665, a rent charge of £80 per annum was granted to the trustees on a farm at Fifield.

It has been suggested that the building was originally a mill, but from the details of the deed above (recited in the Charity Commissioners' Report of 1908) it would seem to have been purpose-built.

There are a number of 18th century receipts of various tradesmen, issued to the Almshouses[1] and a few records of entries to the Almshouse.[2] Almspeople appear regularly in the burial registers of the parish from 1678 to 1781, with just one entry for Monkton Deverill in 1773.

Constitution: For six poor men and two poor women, single or widowed, but over fifty years of age. The privilege was extended to Monkton Deverill and 'Hussey' Deverill. They were to be members of the Church of England and upwards of 60 years of age.[3]

The feoffees, their heirs and assigns, were to be trustees after Sir James Thynne's death and a Steward was appointed to ensure that the number of trustees was maintained. For this he was paid 40s. He was also paid £4 per annum as a stipend.

The trustees were to provide eight cloth gowns at 30s and £5 6s 8d a year for coal.

There was also to be a chest with three locks, to contain the documents which would accrue, pertaining to the almshouse and its running.

Some of the later trustees are named in the Charity Commissioners' Report, page 285.

The building is set end-on to the main road. It is built of rubble stone, four rooms up, four down, with three gables, under each a three-light transomed window. Small two-light windows under the valleys. The doorways are hooded.[4] The roof is of stone slates and the north front had three tall chimney stacks with two 2-light mullioned casements on each floor between the chimneys. The chimneys were demolished in 1982.

The double-faced wooden clock projects from the gable end over the road on a carved bracket, with a hipped, tiled roof; and behind it is a louvered bellcote with tiled pyramidal roof and a ball finial. This clock was donated in 1863 by Mary Morrice, the mother of William D.Morrice, Vicar of Longbridge Deverill. She had the clock erected at her own expense and gave £125 into the hands of three trustees for the almshouse. Part of this was invested and became the Clock Fund.

The rear, showing chimneys, since removed   *Before restoration of the fabric*

Both CC

The small garden was originally divided into eight plots and there were eight sets of outhouses at the back.

Notes:
1 WSA Ref: 1020/39-49.
2 WSA Ref: 1020/50, 51.
3 Ransome, 1972, 65
4 Pevsner, 271.
Charity Commission references
1837: 720-24

Malmesbury　　　　　**Hospital of St.John**　　　　**ST 935869**
East side of south end of High Street

The main block of St John's Hospital SMT

Grade 2*.

The leper hospital of St John was founded on this site, probably in the late 12th century.[1] It seems probable that some of the revenue accruing after the dissolution of the monasteries and religious institutions was used when a school and an almshouse were newly founded on the same site.

　　The property had eventually come into the hands of three prominent citizens of the town and in 1580 the Hospital was conveyed by John Stumpe to the Burgesses, with the onus on them to maintain both the almshouse and the school. From 1609, the burgesses gave £10 of the £20 paid to them for their enclosure of King's Heath for the maintenance of five almspeople. From 1616 onwards the Court of the Burgesses was held in the courtroom, part of the old Hospital buildings.

In 1629, an allotment of land was made for the upkeep of the almshouse and in 1694, Michael Weeks, a former resident of Malmesbury but later of London, endowed a charity for the support of the school and almshouse. The foundation of the almshouse is sometimes taken as being from this date, though it was obviously functioning well before this time.

Constitution: Originally, the almshouse was for five poor people. In 1904, there were three cottages for six widows of Freemen, converted to house only three in 1967.

The habit was to be a black gown with a white cross.

West gable end SMT

The almshouses are now a terrace of three single-storey houses, built of limestone rubble with ashlar dressings, under a stone slate roof. The terrace is two rooms deep, set at right angles to the main road. Each house has an attic and the front has three full-width dormer gables. The windows are 3-light, leaded casements with mullions.

Incorporated into the south end wall is a late 12th century pointed arch doorway, probably the entrance to the chapel of the medieval hospital. Above it is a contemporary blocked window arch with hood moulding.[2]

A stone plaque is inserted in the upper blind arch of the west end of the row. Its inscription reads:

Plaque in gable end   SMT

Memorand that whereas King Athelstan
Did give unto the Free School within this
Burrough of Malmesbury Ten Pounds and to
The poor people my Almshouse at St.John's
And Burgesses of ye same Borough for Ever
That now Michael Wickes Esq late of
This sd Burr and now Citizen of London
Hath augmented and added to ye aforsd gift
Vnto ye sd Free School Ten pounds only to be paid
Yearly to St.John's aforsd within this sd
Burrough by his Trustees for Ever and hath
Also given to the Minister of this Toune
For ye time being 20s only by Year for Life
To preach a sermon yearly on the 19th day
Of July and to his sd Trustees 20s by the
Year beginning on ye 25th day of March
Anno Dom 1694

Notes:
1 Chettle & Crittall, 340.
2 Luce, 120.
Charity Commission references:
1837: 1327-28
1908: 672, 683-4

*Early photo of the St John's Almshouses, left, with the old Hospital arch incorporated
into the gable end CC*

Old painting, showing the bridge, with the gable end of the almshouses to the left CC

Malmesbury   Jenner's Almshouses ST 938875
Northern extremity of Oxford Street, near junction with Holloway
Grade 2.

These almshouses were founded between 1643 and 1651 by Robert Jenner MP, goldsmith, of London, Cricklade and Widhill.

In 1643, Jenner gave a rent charge of £40 from his manor of Widhill, near Cricklade, for the upkeep of the almshouse residents. His will of 1651 provided for this payment to continue indefinitely.[1] However, in the 17th century, actions were brought against his heirs for failure to pay; and payment ceased altogether in about 1740.

In 1805, the churchwardens held a 21-year lease on what may have been part of Jenner's Almshouses at the corner of Holloway and Oxford Street. Four of the original eight buildings were demolished in 1825 and a new poor house was opened on part of the site. In 1834, the rest of the almshouses were used to accommodate poor families on parish relief. This is presumed to have ceased when the Union Workhouse opened in 1838.[2]

According to the VCH (vol.14), four of the houses were demolished in 1825 and the rest in the late 19th century. However, the DoE Listed Buildings suggest that only the northern range was demolished.[4]

Site incorporating Jenner's Almshouses SMT

Constitution: For eight poor people.

Single-depth terrace of five houses, built of limestone rubble and dressings under a stone slate roof, with rear brick stacks. The buildings consist of two storeys and an attic.

The burial registers date from 1591, but it is not until 1651 that the first mention is made of the almshouses, when an entry says 'of the new almshouses', this evidently referring to Jenner's new foundation. Further entries make reference to 'Mr Jenner's almshouses' or 'Mr Ginner's almshouses'. Sometimes the simple label of 'almsman' or almswoman' is attached, but usually it is the foundation itself which is recorded.

The last entry mentioning the almshouses is in 1729/30.

Notes:
1 TNA, PROB/11/219/736.

2 Freeman, 1991, 160-1.

3 Moffat, 1805.

4 Freeman, 1991, 160.

Charity Commission references:

1837: 1333-4

1908: 677, 698

Marlborough   Name not known   SU 190685
Between The Parade and London Road

Before 1215, a member of an ancient Marlborough family, Levenoth, gave a site in the Marsh, near the ford over the river Kennet, for the foundation of the Hospital of St John. Other lands in both Marlborough and Preshute were given for its endowment and maintenance; all of which were confirmed by King John in 1215.[1] The site was in the area between the present day Parade and the London Road and the Hospital would have served pilgrims en route to Canterbury, Winchester or Gloucester.[2] The present St Peter's School stands on the site.

In 1550, after the Dissolution, the mayor and burgesses of the town were granted permission to use the hospital site and buildings, together with its endowments, as a free Grammar school, which continued in existence till 1962, the original buildings having being replaced in about 1578.

By 1575, an almshouse was being maintained next door to the school.[3] This is the almshouse referred to by the Charity Commissions Report of 1908.[4] According to the Chamberlain's Accounts, repairs were carried out to the School House, the Almshouse and the Blindhouse in 1617.[5] By an agreement of 18 March 1725, the Borough Corporation conveyed the almshouse to St Mary's churchwardens and overseers for lodging and employing any poor who wished to receive parish assistance. The parish may have had a workhouse near St Mary's church in 1698,[6] where 'Mr Williams' workhouse' is mentioned on the south side of the churchyard. It is not clear whether this was a private workshop, for an artisan, or a workhouse for the poor, set up by a Mr Williams.

A workhouse, built by the Corporation about 1631, was erected to the west of Marlborough, but was demolished about 1709, when another was built in Hyde Lane, closer to the Town centre. When the almshouse on the Marsh site was being transferred to the churchwardens of St Mary's parish to house its poor, the workhouse in Hyde Lane was made over to the parish of St Peter's for the same purpose.[7]

By 1788, the almshouse was in a bad state of repair and its inmates were suffering from neglect. A proposal to have one workhouse for the two parishes was rejected and in 1790, St.Mary's workhouse was repaired and enlarged.[8]

Although the almshouse kept its name, its purpose became that of a workhouse, until 1860, when it was sold. According to the Charity Commissioners, the building was large, had an open area of 100 square yards at the back and, at the time of the enquiry, held forty-three inmates ('parish paupers'), fourteen of whom were old and infirm.

Notes:
1 Stevenson, 1983, 206.
2 Stedman, 41.
3 WSA Ref: G22/1/205/2 ff7, 74v.
4 Ch.Comm. vol.i, 704.
5 Hughes, 49.
6 Hobbs, 278.
7 Stevenson, 1983, 215.
8 Wiltshire Cuttings, xiii, 229. (Devizes Museum Library).
Charity Commission references:
1837:   1398
1908: 704, 739

Melksham   Fowler Almshouses   ST 902648
Back street off Bath Road, called The City

Fowler Almshouses, late 19th century CC

Founded and endowed by Rachel Fowler, in deeds of 1858 and 1864.
    By 1953, the foundation was endowed with £911 1s 11d stock and each resident was receiving 5s a week.

Constitution: For six widows or spinsters, over fifty years of age, with one or two married couples.

Six terraced tenements with gardens; they consist of a row of five houses, built on the site of Caroline Buildings in 'The City'.

The front wall is ashlar, but the back wall is of coursed rubble stone. The building is of five bays, with flush gables at each end. There are three small gables set in the front of the roof. There are six doors, set asymmetrically. The house and gardens are surrounded by a wall. The roof is corrugated tile and the windows are somewhat ecclesiastical in their design.

After some years of neglect and decline, the almshouses were reopened in 2014 for their original purpose.

Fowler Almshouses, 2012 SMT

Charity Commission references:
1908: 753-4

Mere   Poor House   ST 818327
On north side of Old Hollow

This almshouse, usually referred to as The Poor House, was a joint foundation by various parishioners but was never endowed. The expenses for erecting the building and maintaining the residents came from benefactors and Parish Stock.[1]

The seventeenth century Parish Book states: 'The next year following [1638] was all built and finished the almshouse of Mere, containing four rooms below and four rooms over the same, which was built with part of the estate of the poor then remaining in the hands of some of the parishioners and others, the which estate was heretofore given by the charitable benevolence of well-disposed people at their deaths and some otherwise, as may appear in a table at the end of this book; in which said year [1638] Ann Lucas, the daughter of James Lucas, died, a young maiden of the age of 18 years, and gave £5 to the poor of Mere, whereof £4 was bestowed towards the building the said almshouse for a memorial of her great charity towards the poor. The other 20s was bestowed on the poor at her funeral'.[2]

According to the Charity Commissioners' Report (1837), the almshouse had constantly been occupied by poor families, who, when their numbers were diminished by death, or by going out into service, were replaced by others more numerous, and thus more deserving and were maintained by other means. There was no estate belonging to the almshouse, so that upkeep was found entirely through the local rates.

In the 1851 Census returns for Mere, it appears that the almshouse housed seven poor families, each with at least four members. Unless extensions to the building had been made over the years, overcrowding must have been a severe problem.[3]

By 1877, the almshouse was ruinous and there was no money available for renovations. The Charity Commissioners, therefore, made an order in 1880 for the Charity Trustees to sell the site, together with all the old building materials, for not less than £20. It was sold for that amount in the same year to Alfred John Cross. The money was invested in consols and the proceeds presumably distributed among the existing town charities.

Constitution: Built for seven couples and two single men. In 1638 a list was made in the Parish Book of the current inmates who had been installed and it named seventeen people, fourteen of them married couples.

When first built, the almshouse consisted of two storeys, with four rooms on each floor. It is known from the account in the Parish Book that 6 tons of timber were used within the building, so it is most likely to have been timber-framed. Certain gentlemen of Mere gave ten trees between them.

Notes:
1 Rutter, notes.
2 WSA Ref: 9244/44.
3 Rutter, notes.
Charity Commission references:
1837: 767

North Bradley   The Daubney Almshouses   ST856548
North west of parish church, facing the village green.

The Daubney Almshouses, before demolition of chimney stacks, North Bradley CC

Grade 2

During the years 1808-10, Charles Daubney, Vicar of North Bradley and later Archdeacon of Sarum, built an 'Asylum' near the church in North Bradley for four aged people, together with a school. To these were added a row of three cottages in 1818 for twelve poor people maintained by the parish, known as The Vicar's Poorhouse. It is said that the village reading room, established by 1893, was held there.[1]

   Constitution: For four aged persons of good character and 'rather above the lowest classes'. The allowance was to be 4s a week each, together with the use of a piece of garden ground.

When he died, in 1827, the Archdeacon left £3,800 to the Warden and scholars of Winchester College, out of which they were to give £30 per annum to maintain Christ Church at Rode, then in the parish of North Bradley, to support the Sunday School there and to relieve regular attendees at the Christ Church, who lived in North Bradley. The rest of the income was to go to support North Bradley Asylum, school and poorhouses.

In 1881, another school was opened in North Bradley, the Daubney school was closed and Winchester College discharged from the Trust.

In 1903 the Vicar's Poorhouse was still occupied by people on parish support. In 1959 the name was changed to St Nicholas's Cottages and only one of the houses was occupied through the charity; the rest were let out. The Asylum had only two inmates and was in bad repair. It is now, however, fully functional again.

The Daubney Almshouses consist of a long, two-storeyed, brick building of seven bays with a middle pediment and two-light windows.[2] The roof is hipped and slated. It contained four two-storeyed and two-roomed houses, each with its own entrance. On the left of the central passage was the old schoolroom with accommodation for the teacher above.

The front entrance of the Daubney Almshouses SMT

Of the Vicar's Poorhouse, there remains only one cottage, called St.Nicholas's Cottages, brick built under a slate roof, comprising two semi-detached tenements with gardens. It is believed these are now in private hands.

The following inscription is on the outside of the Almshouse building:

North Bradley

Asylum

A 1810 D

Laus Deo

Above it are the arms of Daubney: Gules four lozenges conjoined in fess argent in chief a crescent of cadency

A plaque on the front of the remaining cottage of The Vicar's Poorhouse declares it to be: St Nicholas's Cottages

Notes:
1 Slocombe, I.,76.
2 Pevsner, 321.
Charity Commission references:
1837: 798-801

North Wraxall   Howell's Almshouses   ST818749

On the west side of The Hollow, leading from the A420 to North Wraxall church. Grade 2.

John Howell's Almshouses SMT

Mr John Howell, a native of the village of North Wraxall, the founder of the house of Howell & James, in Regent Street, London, built two almshouses in the parish in the 1840s; he endowed them with the interest of £300. The trustees were the rector at the time, and two persons nominated by him.

It is stated that of the four cottages in the deed of 1843, only two were ever appropriated for the uses of the Charity. The other two were treated as the private property of John Howell and devised, by his will, to one Isaac Holborow.

In 1908, the almshouses were inhabited by an old agricultural labourer and a widow, each receiving 1s a week from the Charity. They also received coal to the value of £1 and clothing to 13s a year. The man received poor-law relief of 3s a week.

The cottages are now private dwellings, known as 1-4 The Hollow.

Constitution: By indenture of 18 January 1843, John Howell of Rutland Gate, Knightsbridge, esq., and the Rev. Thomas J. Wyld, rector, Thomas Tuckey and Edward Mullins, gents., several pieces of land, formerly stone quarries, were conveyed to the use of John Howell for the erection of four messuages or cottages 'to settle eight poor, old and decayed persons', male or female; they were to be natives of the parish or long-standing residents.

John Howell's Almshouses SMT

The row consists of substantial, squared rubble-stone cottages of two storeys. Each cottage had a living room and good offices on the ground floor and two small rooms on the first floor. The buildings were erected close against a high rock face, the remains of the quarry. This was shored up by a wall, built at the expense of the Charity. This is just visible in the photo above. The low-pitched roofs are of slate, with coped gables, two ashlar ridge stacks and a south end stack. A connecting range runs to left and right of centre.

The windows are Tudor-style stone mullioned, with hoodmoulds and mullioned canted bays. There are three gable fronts, each with a 2-light upper window and a ground floor canted bay. The left-hand connecting range has an upper 2-light window and on the ground floor two C20 doors in Tudor-arched surrounds flanking a 2-light window, all with hoodmoulds. The range to the right has an upper 2-light and single light over 2-light and Tudor-arched doorway with plank door, all with hoodmoulds. The north end wall has an upper 2-light window and ground floor Tudor arched doorway with a single light to the right, all with hoodmoulds. There are three rear gables. Originally all the windows were fitted with small- paned casements.

Charity Commission references:
1908: 1037-9

Salisbury   **Blechynden's Almshouses**   **SU 147300**
Corner of Greencroft Road and Winchester Street (75 Winchester St.)
Grade 2.

Blechynden's Almshouses, 2013 SMT

These were founded by the will of Margaret Blechynden, dated 1682, who left over £500 to build an almshouse for six poor widows. Margaret Blechynden was described as being of St.Paul's, Covent Garden, London. Her nephew and executor, Samuel Eyre, purchased a site in 1684 and built the almshouse for considerably less, the residue moneys not being invested until 1752, when his grandson conveyed the almshouse and lands in Laverstock, Wiltshire, and Templecombe, Somerset, to a board of trustees. The details of this undertaking can be read in *Caring: A History of Salisbury City Charities* (SLHG).

The almshouses were rebuilt in 1857-8 and renovated in 1950.

In 1978, the Blechynden Almshouses were amalgamated with the Thomas Brown's Almshouses.

Constitution: Originally for six poor widows, to be at least fifty years old, receiving 12s allowance every three months for the repair of their dwellings. Funds were augmented by benefactors in 1755, 1778 and 1809. The original specification was not for widows from any particular place, but one of the benefactors asked for two of the widows to be selected from Whiteparish and Downton, whenever possible.

Allowances ranged from 4s a week to 4s 6d, depending on the time of year, with 3s on Christmas Day. By 1833, each widow was receiving 5s a week allowance and 3s at Christmas. This continued until 1956.

The present buildings are two blocks of single-storey cottages[1], at right-angles to each other, facing a small garden on the corner of Greencroft Road and Winchester Street. They are built of red brick under old tile roofs and it is believed that, externally, they resemble quite closely the original 17th century

Blechynden Almshouses, 20th century CC

buildings, having been sympathetically restored several times. Steps from Winchester Street lead to a small courtyard at the front of the building, which was formerly the garden. There was originally a room over the entrance gate, in which Samuel Eyre, Margaret Blechynden's executor, left instructions that all documents relating to the almshouses should be kept, the door being fitted with two locks; two of the trustees were to hold the keys.

Each unit has two windows facing onto the central courtyard, a single-light window on one side of the door, a 3-light window on the other, all with lattice casements. The doors are plain planked.

When first built, each woman in the almshouse had one room, a washhouse and a coal cupboard.

There are four plaques on the walls of the almshouses. One was originally over the entrance gate, but is now by the entry steps. It reads:

Margaretta

Thomas Blechynden, S.T.P. vidua,

Sam. Aldersey Mercat. Lond. Filia,

hanc domum

Deo et sex viduis

Pauperibus et honestis

dedicavit

Anno Salutis MDCLXXXIII

'S.T.P.' was the equivalent of the DD degree, but there is no trace of Thomas Blechynden having had a benefice in Salisbury. It is believed that Margaret's mother may have been an Eyre and perhaps that was her connection with Salisbury. The inscription is now almost impossible to read and the above was taken from the Salisbury Almshouse book.[2]

The next plaque is on the end gable of the house nearest the street. It is also badly worn:

REBUILT 1858

The third, near that of the founder's stone, reads:

THIS GROUP OF HOMES

WAS RESTORED BY THE GIFT OF

EDWARD WILKES GAWTHORNE

IN MAY 1950

And the last, facing Greencroft Street, reads:

BLECHYNDEN'S ALMSHOUSES

RESTORED 1980

BY

CLLR. MRS. JO BENSON, OBE, JP

CANON E.B. BROOKS, M.A.

H.C. HILL ESQ.

ALL OF WILTSHIRE

Notes:
1 RCHM, vol.1, p58a.
2 SLHG, 20.
Charity Commission references:
1837: 401-5

Salisbury   Brickett's Hospital   SU 145295
Corner of Exeter Street and Carmelite Way

Present day Brickett's Almshouses SMT

These were founded before 1533 by Thomas Brickett, a wealthy merchant and former Mayor of the City of Salisbury. In his will, written on the 25th September 1533, he says the following: Item I will that v almes howses that I have bylded in dragon streate be gevyn thuse of v poore men or wymen for christes sake to praye for me and that gifte ever to be doon by the mayer of this Cittie and he to have ev[er] at mydsommer xijd for his labour and every sergeaunte ijd Also I will that the mayer and his britherne take the Rent of two howses ioyning to the said almeshowses the whiche is by the yere xiiijs viijd to the chamber of the Cittie and they to see the said almshouses be well repaired and every yere to paye the quitterente.[1]

It would appear that at this date, though the houses had been built, they were not yet occupied. As will be seen from the above, two cottages adjoining the Hospital yielded 14s 8d annually in rent, which was used for the repairs of the Hospital. Further bequests were made during the 18th century, amounting to over £600 in all. In 1780, a rebuilding programme was carried out, financed mainly

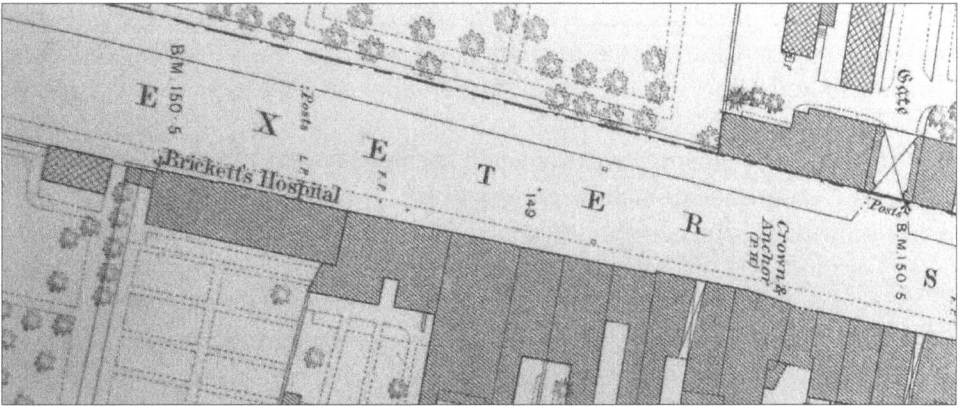

Site of the original Brickett's Almshouses OS 1:500 map 1880 WSA

by voluntary subscription and a grant from the Mayor and Corporation. At this time, the Hospital was intended for six poor widows or spinsters of Salisbury and the new building offered more commodious accommodation than the original. Each woman had two rooms and a weekly allowance of 3s 6d.

Brickett's – the 1780 building on Exeter Street CC

By her will of 1570, Joan Popley bequeathed her twenty houses in Basinghall Street, London, to be leased out and the rents used for the relief of the Salisbury poor. The houses were destroyed in the Great Fire of 1666, but they were rebuilt by Sir Thomas Clarges. Under his auspices, the charity brought in 6s a week to Brickett's Hospital, the remainder being allotted to the poor of Salisbury. About 1780, the allowance to the Hospital was doubled, £140 a year was given to the Salisbury Workhouse and £55 a year distributed to the remaining poor. In 1833, there were nine of these houses and the annual rent amounted to over £421. The Joan Popley Charity was amalgamated with the Salisbury Consolidated Almshouse and Other Charities Scheme of 1871 and its income was used to rebuild Eyre's Hospital [see below].

In 1895, the Hospital was yet again completely rebuilt as the building we see today. Accommodation now consists of a lounge, kitchen, bathroom and bedroom, with TV and central heating, and there is a central leisure room.

Constitution: Originally for five poor men or women. In the 18th century, it was for six poor women.[2] The Mayor was to select the almspeople who were to inhabit the Hospital and for this he was paid a small yearly sum. With the various rebuildings of the Hospital, the numbers have increased slightly.

The 1895 building is of two storeys in red brick with stone facings, tall chimneys and mock Tudor timber framing. There is a narrow yard and garden in front of the building, well-screened by trees and vegetation.

The original inscription on the wall facing Exeter Street has worn away and a new one has been erected beneath it, bearing the inscription:

Hospital for Six Poor Widows
Originally Founded by
Thomas Brickett
Mayor of this City in 1519

Brickett's through the gate SMT   *Old and new plaques on Exeter Street wall SMT*

Rebuilt by
Voluntary Contribution 1780
Rebuilt 1895

Notes:
1 TNA, PROB/11/25/92.
2 Returns to Visitation Queries, 1783. WRS vol. 27, 137
Charity Commission references:
1837:   374-6

College of Matrons, The Close, Salisbury SMT

Salisbury   The College of Matrons   SU 142297
South side of Choristers' Square, 39-46 The Close
Grade 1.

Built in the Cathedral Close, the College of Matrons was founded in 1682 by Seth
Ward, Bishop of Salisbury from 1667-89. He built, at his own cost, an almshouse
for the widows of priests ordained episcopally in the Diocese of Salisbury. The
endowment of the College was made by the gift of the former site of the Clun

Chantry and some land in the Close; also Whaddon Farm at Alderbury.

Thomas Glover of Harnham signed a contract in 1682 to remove buildings on the site and construct the College at a cost of £1193 12s.8d.[1] Glover was described on his monument as an architect. The total cost of the building to Bishop Ward, including the endowment, was £5123.[2]

The charity was augmented in 1693 by one Robert King and by the mid-1800s many rents were coming in from lands in Suffolk, Berkshire, Cambridge, Middlesex and London.

In 1793, William Benson Earle made a bequest of 2,000 guineas to the College and various other generous bequests and gifts were made thereafter.

In 1870, the building was improved to a design of T.H.Wyatt and further repairs and improvements were made in the 20th century.

Constitution: For ten Salisbury Diocese priests' widows. The matrons were to be at least fifty years old and to have an income of less than £10 per annum. They were to be made a weekly allowance of 6s each. In the event of a lack of numbers in the Salisbury Diocese, vacancies were to be made available to similar candidates from the Diocese of Exeter.

Matrons were to attend divine service in the Cathedral twice daily and were not allowed an absence of more than one month in the year.

Bishop Ward appointed candidates during his lifetime and afterwards, this right was invested alternately in the Bishop and the Dean and Chapter.

The Bishop was to be the College Visitor and the Dean and Chapter its governors.

In 1869 the number of matrons was reduced to eight, but could be raised to ten at the discretion of the governors.

The building is a red brick range of two storeys on a projecting plinth with moulded capping and with stone dressings and an ogee-moulded string.[3] The hipped roof is of old tiles. It has thirteen bays and there are projecting stone-

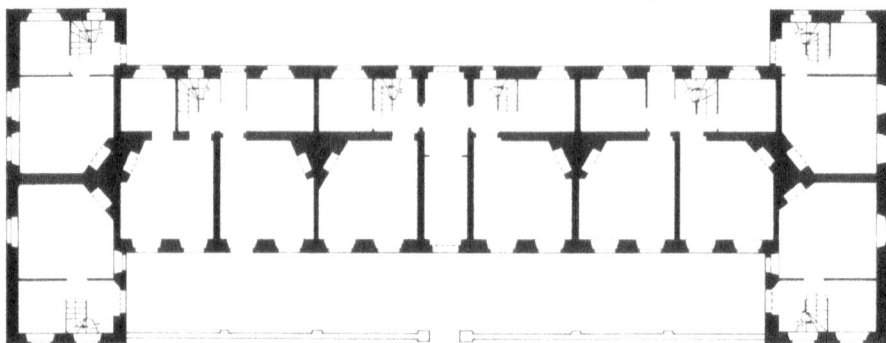

Reconstructed plan of the College of Matrons, 1682 RCHM

quoined wings at each end. The central attic dormers of the wings are circular with supporting scrolls and ball finials.

The door in the centre of the main block is beneath a wooden hood with a segmental pediment on brackets. Above it is a scrolled cartouche with inscription and above this is a steep top pediment with swags and coat of arms.

Originally there were ten houses, six with their own staircase and two pairs sharing an entrance and staircase; eight of the houses had four rooms each, but the two adjoining the centre had an extra room over the central passage, in front of, or behind the base of the cupola. The corner fireplaces are an early use of this feature. By 1833, each widow had two rooms. The windows are two-light casements, with wooden architraves.

The central entrance to the College SMT

In the front of the building is a small area laid to flower beds.

The royal arms of Charles I are borne at the top of the central pediment of the façade. Below this is a shield bearing the arms of the see of Salisbury impaling those of Seth Ward.

az. The Holy Virgin and Child, with a sceptre in her left hand, all or.

(for the see of Salisbury)

impaling:

az a cross pattee or (for Seth Ward)

all within a garter bearing the legend:

honi soit qui mal y pense

Stone plaque with dedicatory inscription SMT

Below this again is a black stone plaque inscribed:

COLLEGIUM HOC MATRONARUM

D° O° M°

HUMILLIME DEDICAVIT

SETHUS EPISCOPUS SARUM

ANNO DOMINI

MDCLXXXII

Notes:
1 RCHM, 1993. 152-3.
2 *ibid.*, 153.
3 *ibid.*
Charity Commission references:
1837: 409-18

Salisbury   Eyre's Hospital   ca. SU148301

Originally in Winchester Street, then rebuilt on the west side of London Road, at the junction with Winchester Street. This now lies beneath the Salisbury ring-road.

Position of the second Eyre's Almshouses. WSA: OS 1880 map SMT

The original almshouses were founded by the will of Christopher Eyre, merchant adventurer and Citizen of London, who had been born in Salisbury. His will was written in 1617 and proved in 1624. He was the son of one Thomas Eyre of the City of Salisbury and remembered the City generously in his will.

The almshouses were to be erected in brick on land to be purchased by the Mayor and Corporation, as near to Winchester Gate as possible, with accommodation for five or six poor couples from the City. The maintenance of the almshouses was provided by an endowment of at least £26 per annum, paid quarterly, from Eyre's estate, and to this effect he left a total of £600 for the erecting and maintenance of the establishment.[1] No land was actually purchased, but the almshouses were built on the north side of Winchester Street, near the end, with a quadrangle in front and a small piece of land behind, laid out as gardens.[2]

Various benefactors added to the endowment over the years and in 1871, they were included in the Consolidated Almshouses, Pensions and Charities Scheme and were rebuilt the following year.[3]

Constitution: For five or six poor couples, no longer able to work, known to be of honest disposition, capable of orderly living and with a fear of God.[4]

The original building was of brick. In 1872, it was rebuilt as a terrace of seven houses on the corner of the London Road and Winchester Street.[5] This can be seen to have been of two storeys with three gables, each with a window, paired doors and three-light windows along the length of the building, both on the ground floor and first storey. There were tall brick chimneys and a wall in front of the building, with little yards behind.[6]

Eyre's Almshouses, late 19th century CC

In the latter half of the 20th century, a ring road was planned for Salisbury and Eyre's Almshouses stood in the way. Eventually, it was agreed that the Council should buy the property and erect new almshouses on a site between Blackfriars Way and the new Churchill Way. After various delays, (including the necessity for installing double glazing against the noise of the Ring Road traffic) work on the new almshouses was completed in early 1971 and Eyre's House was opened later that year.[7]

By the terms of Christopher Eyre's will, a brass plate was to be attached to the front of the original almshouses bearing the following inscription:

The guift of Christopher Eyre Marchaunt adventurer sonne to
Thomas Eyre of this Citty

The present Eyre's House in Eyre's Way CC

And over that:

Dextram Domine lavabit me.

(The Lord's right hand will wash/anoint me)

In the event, it took the form of a small stone tablet over the door, bearing the legend:

DONUM DEI ET DEO

(a gift of God and to God)

CHRISTOPHER EYRE

ANNO.DOM. 1617.[8]

Notes:

1 TNA, PROB/11/145/28.

2 SLHG, 25.

3 *ibid.* 26

4 TNA, PROB/11/145/28.

5 SLHG, 26

6 WSA: OS map 1:500, 1880 .

7 SLHG, 26

8 *ibid.* 25.

Charity Commission references:

1837: 384-6

Salisbury (Fisherton Anger)   Hayter's Almshouses   SU139302

On the north side of Fisherton Street at the west end, just east of the railway bridge.

Founded by Sarah Hayter, the lady of the manor, before 1797. On 31 August 1797, by a tripartite indenture, Sarah Hayter of Carswell, Berks, conveyed to the trustees

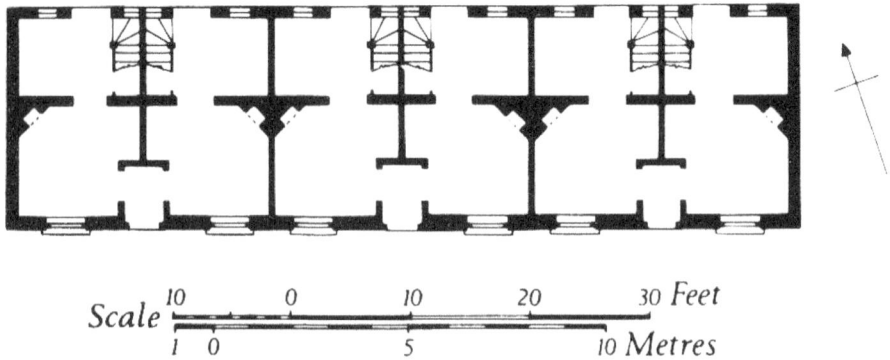

Plan of the original Hayter's building   Reproduced by permission of English Heritage

of the Almshouses she had already built, a number of pieces of land within the manor of Fisherton Anger, together with rents and profits of the manor, to ensure continued endowment of her foundation.[1] Sarah Hayter died in July 1822.

Constitution: For six, poor, unmarried women, over the age of fifty, named by Sarah Hayter during her lifetime and afterwards by the Dean of Sarum, the Minister of St.Thomas's, Salisbury, and the Rector of Bemerton. The women were not to have received parish relief within the previous five years and were to be drawn from the parishes of Fisherton Anger, Bemerton, St.Thomas's, Salisbury, and then from any other Wiltshire parish. But only Church of England members were to be admitted.

The two-storeyed, rendered buildings were under one tiled roof and contained six tenements of two rooms each, with a garden behind, divided into six plots.

They were demolished and replaced in 1964 with unimaginative block-type dwellings.

In 2000, these in turn were demolished and rebuilt, this time being replaced by a tasteful three-sided block in red brick, round a courtyard, with black iron railings across the fourth side of the courtyard.

A plaque on the wall was inscribed:

This Asylum
Built and Endow'd
For six poor women
By Mrs SARAH HAYTER
Lady of this Manor
1797[2]

This has now been inserted into the front of the far wall. A second plaque, on the right-hand end wall reads:

Sarah Hayter's Almshouses
Endowed 1797
Rebuilt 2000

Benefactors
Mr & Mrs Robert Hawkins
and
Salisbury City & Welfare Charities

Sarah Hayter's Almshouses, Fisherton Street (2010) SMT

Notes:
1 Pugh, 1962, 194.
2 RCHM vol.1, 58.
Charity Commission references:
1837: 473-77

Salisbury   Hussey's Almshouses   SU 143306
Set at right-angles to Castle Street, north end, west side, before the railway bridge.
Grade 2.

Founded in 1794 by William Hussey, who, by an Indenture, gave a plot of land in Castle Street to the City, with fifteen dwellings on it. Ten of these were to become the William Hussey Almshouses and the remainder were to be let and the proceeds used for the maintenance of the almshouse.[1]

Hussey's Almshouses, 2011 SMT

By 1833, the original ten houses had been made into thirteen, but the provision for them proved inadequate and they were found to be in a state of decay.[2]

Hussey's Almshouses OS map 1:500 1880. WSA

In 1874, the almshouses were demolished and completely rebuilt.[3]

Constitution: For ten aged and infirm poor residents of Salisbury, preference being given to married couples, the husband having been a manual worker. The survivor was to be allowed to remain until his or her death. The rents of the five houses were also to be used for food and clothing for the Almspeople and this was supplemented by a bequest in William Hussey's will.[4]

In the reorganisation of 1895, accommodation was made for seven married couples, six unmarried persons and a nurse.[5] The almshouse further expanded in 1984 and 1986, when a new house was built for the Warden, the old warden's house being used for almshouse accommodation. Community rooms were provided, along with a laundry room and central heating.[6]

Through the gate of Hussey's SMT

There are two parallel ranges, built of gabled Tudor-style brick, separated by an attractive courtyard. They are one-storey high with attics. The red brick has stone dressings and quoins. The roof line is broken up by steep gables with saddle stones and finials. The doors have pointed arches and decorative iron hinges.

The two gateposts have overhanging caps and an iron arch, with a lantern.

The ground-floor casements have stone dressings and the attics contain slit windows.

The ground at the back runs down to the millstream and is laid to lawn. A stone on the wall facing Castle Street bears the date of foundation, 1794, and William Hussey's coat of arms:

Barry of six erm and gu.

with a crest consisting of a

boot sa, spurred or, turned over erm.

A second stone records the 1875 rebuilding and consists of a shield of four bars (uncoloured); the supporters are two double-headed eagles.

A note in vol. vi of the VCH Wiltshire says that the east buttress from the Castle Street gate of the City was removed in 1906, when the coat of arms from it was built into the wall of Hussey's Almshouses. This is still visible, though the inscription is not easy to read, being badly worn.

Notes:
1 Crittall, 1962,171.
2 SLHG, 54; Ch.Com., 1908, 526.
3 *ibid.* 55
4 Ch. Com., 1908, 393.
5 SLHG, 55.
6 *ibid.*
Charity Commission references:
1837:   835-6.
1908: 393-5, 526, 536.

Salisbury   St.Nicholas's Hospital   SU139281
East side of St.Nicholas Road, opposite the junction with de Vaux Road

18th century view of the College of St Nicholas and Harnham Bridge, George Wainwright WBR

St.Nicholas's may have begun life as a simple hostel for travellers crossing the dangerous waters of the Avon at the ford nearby. However, the earliest reference to it is in 1215, when one Richard Aucher made a grant to 'God and the Hospital of St.Nicholas for the Master and Brethren who serve God in that place'.[1]

John Leland, in his Itinerary says: Richard Poure, Bishop of Saresbryi and first erector of the cathedrale chirch of New-Saresbyri, founded the hospitale of S.Nicholas hard by Harnham Bridge...' .[2]

St. Nicholas's avoided suppression at the Dissolution by the connivance of the Pembroke family at Wilton, who concealed the religious connections of the Hospital.[3] It was restored and reconstituted by James I in 1610.[4]

Constitution: Founded for eight poor women and four poor men, with a Master. Leland says it was for eight sisters and four brothers, who would have formed the staff for caring for the sick in the Hospital.

St Nicholas's Hospital residents, 1862 CC

A restoration was made by Butterfield in the 1850s, but much of the original medieval plan exists, including parts of the 13th century buildings, notably the twin chapels at the end of what was probably a double infirmary hall; this has led to the surmise that the building was divided into separate male and female 'wards'. The original stonework is still visible in the lower part of the walls. The foundations of the cells on the north side lie under the old courtyard, but those on the south, and the original arches, today form part of the Master's House and flats for some of the residents.

There are two irregular ranges at right-angles to the road, connected by a third range. The north range is two storeyed, in Victorian style, the ground floor

St Nicholas's Hospital Brethren CC

incorporating some old stonework. The roof is tiled, with hipped gable ends. There is a stone mullioned, cusped-headed window, which may be original. The doorway here has a four-centred head and a two-centred archway.

　　The south range contains several original features. On the north side is a five bay chamfered-arched arcade, built into the wall. This was originally the dividing arcade of the Hospital. Several lancet windows remain in what was the chancel area. There is a deep west porch and a blocked doorway, which led into

St Nicholas, Harnham WLSC

St Nicholas, Harnham WBR

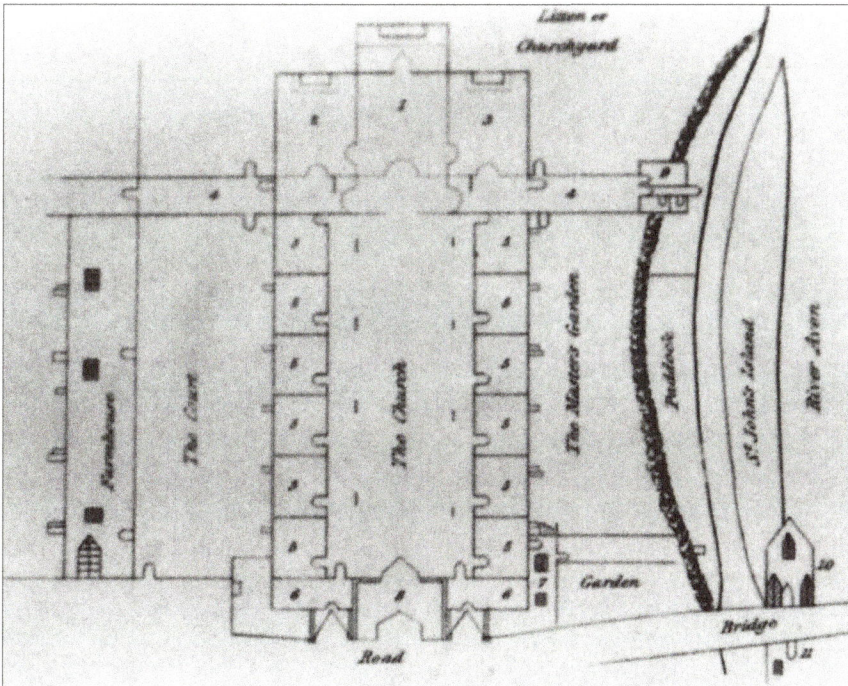

St Nicholas. Plan of 1843 CC

ST. NICHOLAS'S HOSPITAL

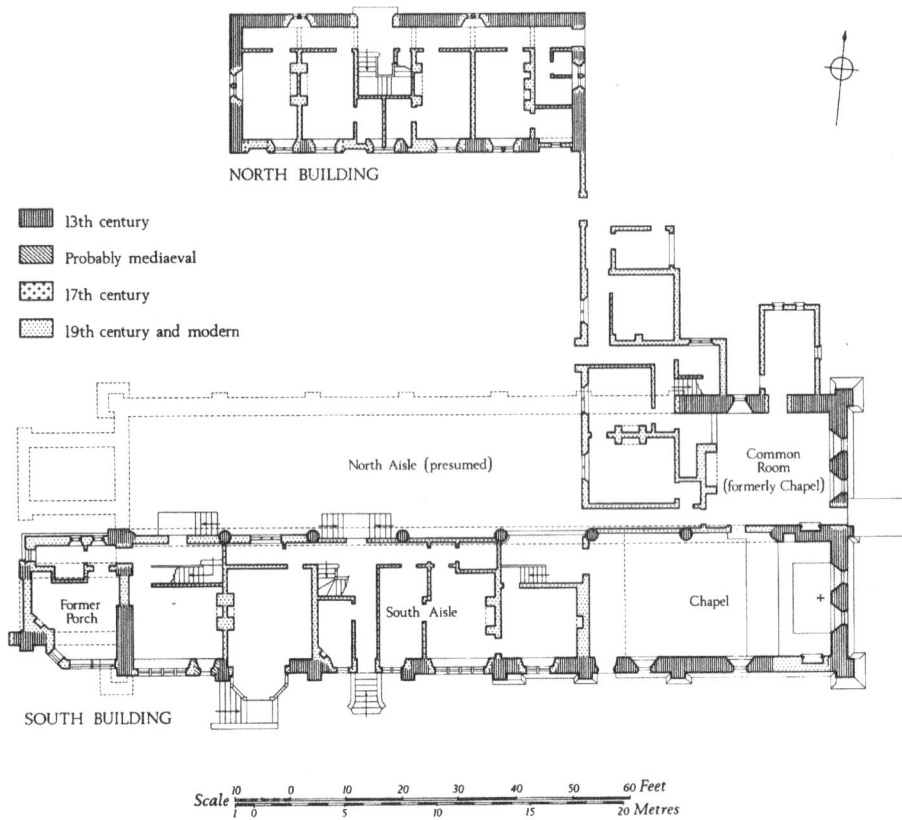

Modern plan of St Nicholas' Hospital Reproduced by permission of English Heritage

the south nave of the chapel, to which were added Victorian mullioned stone widows.

The linking east range is two-storeyed, of Victorian red brick, with a grey brick pattern and timber-framing to the first floor.

Three new blocks of self-contained flats were erected in the grounds during the 20th century and the original accommodation was modernised.

There are no plaques and no heraldry about the buildings, except in the Chapel, where there is an 18th century memorial to the Rev. Edward Emily, Master from 1782 – 1792. By his will he left all his estate to Bishop Barrington to invest for the benefit of the Hospital. This became known as the Barrington Trust.

According to the Cartulary of the Hospital, there was a seal of Ela, Countess of Salisbury, attached to a charter of 1226, the year she made her benefaction to the Hospital.

Blocked up medieval doorway WBR

Notes:
1 Pelly, 1.
2 Smith, vol. iii, 268.
3 Pelly, 8.
4 *ibid.* 10.
Charity Commission references
1837: 1415-31
RCHM vol.i, 26.

Salisbury   St.Paul's Home   SU139303
West end of Fisherton Street, SE of roundabout
Grade 2

Founded in 1863 by Francis Attwood, a Salisbury surveyor, when he gave land, buildings and an endowment of £2,700 for an initial almshouse building. In 1868 he provided for a second block with a similar sum of money; and £1,000 was left to the home in his will, after he died in 1871. His wife gave extra land to be let out for grazing and allotments, but this had all been sold off by 1930. The foundation fell on hard times, but in 1961, six of the houses were converted into twelve flats by the Salisbury Round Table. However, by the beginning of the 21st century, the whole establishment was dilapidated and it stood empty for some eight years. 2011 saw the launch of a new plan to convert the buildings to twelve one-person flats for rehousing some of the homeless people in Salisbury. The intention was to create a community, where people could be rehabilitated and

St Paul's Home CC

have an address in order to find jobs. In November 2012, the restored building was reopened and there are now twelve flats for homeless people from the Salisbury area.[1] A far cry from Francis Attwood's original plan; but no doubt he would have been pleased with such a worthy cause.

Constitution: Originally for three Anglican gentlewomen of 50 years or more. Their annual income was to be between £25 and £70, but no more and they were to have been at least five years resident in the Diocese of Salisbury. Later, accommodation was made for six single women. The almshouse was open to widows, sisters and daughters of clergymen and they received a stipend of £30 p.a. In 1906, the stipends stood at £28; by 1955 there were none.[2]

The Trustees were the Mayor and Dean of Salisbury, together with the incumbents of the three ancient parishes of Salisbury and Fisherton Anger.[3]

There are six houses under one roof, built in two rows of flint and grey brick, in a free Tudor style. The two ranges are connected by screen walls. The gable ends have a pierced quatrefoil parapet.[4]

Notes:
1 Salisbury Trust for the Homeless: www.stfh.org.uk
2 Pugh, 1962, 184.
3 *ibid.*
4 DoE Listed Buildings, Wiltshire.
Charity Commission references:
1908 1002-7.

Salisbury   Taylor's Almshouses   SU 147305

Corner of Bedwin Street and St.Edmund's Church Street
Grade 2.

Thomas Taylor, Alderman, left £1000 in his will of 1695 to build an almshouse of six rooms and garden plots, with permission to cut ten oaks from his estate at Bramshaw in the New Forest.

Taylor's Almshouses, showing the building along St Edmund's Church Street SMT

Matthew Best's will of 1733 bequeathed £10 for the purchase of greatcoats of a light-blue colour for the almsmen. Each coat was to be handed down to a successor for up to three years, after which time it was at the wearer's disposal. 6d was to be paid to each man every Friday. These gifts came from the rents of two houses in the High Street.

By 1833 each almsman received 3s 6d per week.

In 1886, the almshouses were rebuilt.

Constitution: For six poor, single men. In 1906 there were six widowers under the care of a nurse. By 1956, widows and single women were also allowed places in the almshouse. At present, there is a warden and seven units of accommodation for five women and two men.

Taylor's Almshouses, about 1896 CC

The almshouses are comprised of an L-shaped, two-storeyed block in dark red brick with ashlar dressings, on a raised stone plinth, built round a garden court. The doorway and windows have heavily moulded surrounds and the stone quoins are noticeably chamfered. Just below the roof is a big Dutch gable, with moulded coping and stone side scrolls supporting a small pediment and finial. There is a one-storey wing at the back.

The windows are narrow, six on the first floor have stone bolection frames; the two double windows on the ground floor are similar and there is a wide central door. Outside there are two inscriptions. One is on the ornamental gable and reads:

Endowed by Thomas Taylor

Alderman of this City

1698

The second is on a cartouche, over the entrance door:

Rebuilt by the

Municipal Charities

Trustees

Wm. Fawcett

Chairman

1886

Inscription on gable SMT

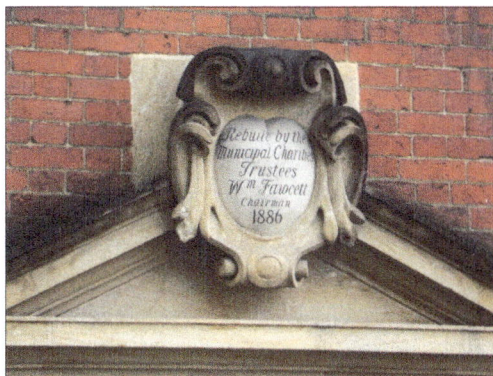

Inscription on cartouche over the entrance SMT

Inside, in the tiled entrance hall, are two more plaques. One, on a large square stone reads:

The gift of
Mr.Thomas Taylor
late Alderman of
this city and built
by his Executors
Mr.Wm.Antram
Mr.John Bushell[1]

The second plaque, a cartouche, reads simply:

T.T.
1698[2]

Notes:
1 SLHG, 28.
2 *ibid.*
Charity Commission references:
1837: 376-9

Salisbury   Trinity Hospital   SU 144298
North side of Trinity Street
Grade 1.

Traditionally the Hospital was founded by Agnes Bottenham in about 1370. It is said that she originally kept a brothel on the site and that when she saw the error of her ways, founded a charitable institution in reparation for her sins.

In 1394, John Chaundler, Agnes's executor, took out letters patent for the Hospital and he then claimed to be the founder. He was the Master in 1383.[1]

Trinity Hospital SMT

The Hospital escaped the Dissolution, as it was a secular foundation. Over the centuries it has continued to adapt, so that today it is a thriving almshouse in the centre of the City.

Constitution: Originally the Hospital was to give succour to twelve poor men, who were permanent, and eighteen temporary resident poor. Later, assistance was given to many more. In the 18th century, the almshouses were under the direction of the Mayor and Corporation.[2] Under the terms of John Fricker's Charity (will proved 1701), twelve inmates of the Hospital were to receive 5s weekly. In each of the years 1833, 1905 and 1957, £3 was paid to the Hospital from the Charity.

When the accommodation was modernised in 1950, the number of residents was reduced to ten men and one nurse.

Plans to rebuild the Hospital were afoot as early as 1699, when Robert Sutton, the founder of Sutton's Almshouses, left £100 towards the rebuilding. In

1702, these plans were produced and the Brothers (as the residents were termed) had to find temporary accommodation. The new building consisted of a chapel, a common hall, thirteen separate rooms, with another hall and a garden to the rear, divided into twelve plots. In the early 18th century, the rooms were provided ready furnished and in 1908 the chapel was renovated. Modernisation took place in 1950 and new plans were produced in 1987 to expand the Hospital, by building seventeen more flats and a warden's house.

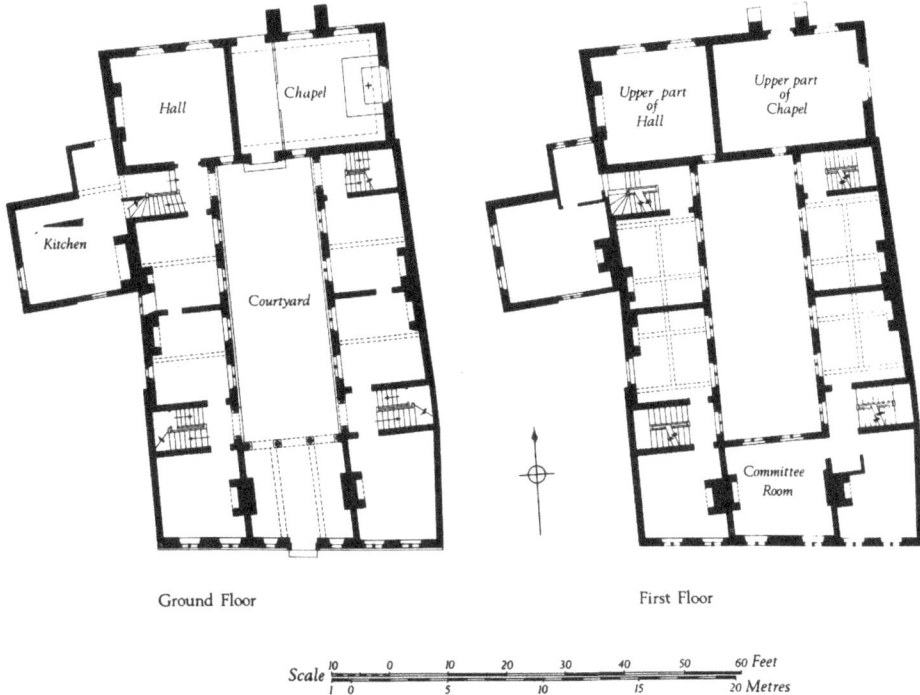

Ground and first-floor plans of Trinity Hospital Reproduced by permission of English Heritage

The present building of 1702, is of seven bays, built of brick with stone dressings. It is two-storeyed with attics and the roof is hipped and tiled. There are two tall chimney stacks.

The two hipped dormer windows have latticed leaded casements and tile-hung sides. On the first floor are six 2-light stone mullioned windows, with central panel and sundial. On the ground floor are six similar windows and a central door. The windows flanking the door are of one light only.

The outside door opens to a paved courtyard with three arches and stone Doric columns, with seats ranged round the walls.

At the entrance to the building are two modern, oval shaped plaques, one on either side of the doorway. They read as follows:

Founded by
Agnes Bottenham circa 1370
Rebuilt 1705 Modernised 1988
Courtyard and Chapel
open to the public
9 am to 5 pm

Salisbury City
Almshouse and
Welfare Charities The Corporation
of the Master and Poor of the
Hospital of the Holy Trinity
Now known as Trinity Hospital

The courtyard of Trinity Hospital SMT

Inside the courtyard, on the left and right-hand walls, are two boards, bearing the names of the benefactors.

There is a very old stone altar slab supported on a carved base, which may have been part of a chest. Its central motif is the Star of David.

There are also two old pieces of glass in the windows, one depicting the Crucifixion, the other containing a coat of arms. These are the arms of England

Ancient altar slab supported on carved base SMT

under the Stuart kings, though the contents of the lower dexter quarter are obliterated.

Out in the courtyard, above the entrance to the chapel, is a painted shield of the arms of Sir Stephen Fox. Sir Stephen had a charity in Salisbury, but the connection with Trinity is not known. The arms are:

erm. on a chevron az. three foxes' heads couped or.;

on a canton az. a fleur de lys or.

The Fox arms above the main door   SMT

Notes:
1 Parsons, 357.
2 Ransome, 1972, 137.
Charity Commission references:
1837: 368-374

Salisbury, St.Edmund   Bedwin Row   Presumably   located   on Bedwyn Street

There are few records of this almshouse, but from the ones that do remain it would appear that whatever form the almshouse took, it housed a large number of almspeople.

Wiltshire Record Society's vol. 31, entitled 'Poverty in Early Stuart Salisbury', is a transcription of registers and surveys of the poor in Salisbury from 1598 – 1669. On p6 it speaks of the listing of the parish poor in St.Edmund's in 1645:

'[the listing] surveys the poor by chequer, ending with the names of the old men and women in the alms-house in Bedwin Row'.[1]
This list appears on p78 and names forty-five individuals, including a number of offspring. The ages of the adults range from 40-90 years.

Early spellings of Bedwin Row are 'Bedden rowe' and 'Beaden-Row'; it is interesting to speculate if this name arose from the number of 'bedesmen' or almsmen residing there, or whether it was named for the villages of Great and Little Bedwyn in this county.

The burial register for St.Edmund's names five deceased as coming from 'the Bedden rowe' in 1626. Then in 1629 and 1630 there are two entries which state 'of the new Almshouse'. It is difficult to say which almshouse this would be, since most were built after this date. It might have been Eyre's, built in 1617, though it is more likely that Eyre's almshouse came under the parish of St.Martin. There is no further reference to almshouses or almspeople in St.Edmund's until the late 18th century (see Frowd's and Trinity).

Notes:
1 Slack, 6.

Salisbury, St.Martin   Culver Street Almshouses   SU 148299
West side of Culver Street, but this area has been all but obliterated by construction of the Salisbury Eastern bypass.

These almshouses lay in the parish of St.Martin and were said to date from the reign of Elizabeth I, but it is not known who founded them. The later buildings,

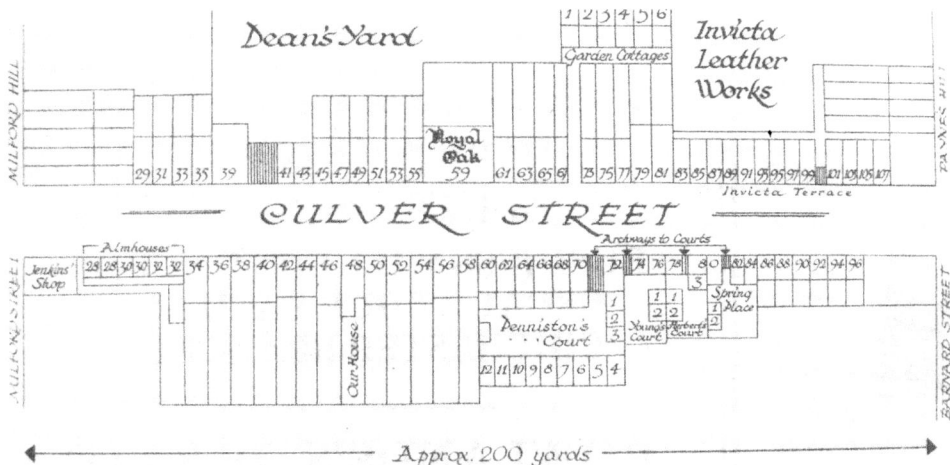

Street plan showing the position of Culver Street Almshouses CC (North is to the left)

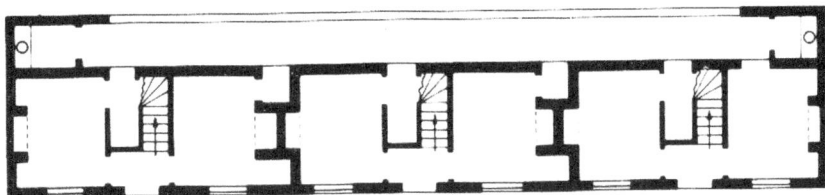

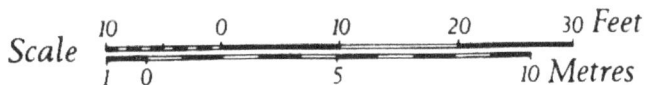

Elevation and ground plan of Culver Street Almshouses Reproduced by permission of English Heritage

erected in 1842 to replace the Elizabethan structures, comprised Nos. 28-32 Culver Street and were of two storeys, brick-built, with slate-covered roofs.[1] They were demolished in 1972 to make way for a car-park.

Constitution: The original almshouses provided accommodation for six almswomen; and although no founder is known, a number of named benefactors left legacies and gifts for the maintenance of the almshouses and stipends for the residents.

Notes:
1 RCHM vol. i, 58.
Charity Commission references:
1837: 424-6

Salisbury   **Frowd's Hospital**   SU 146302
Corner of Bedwin Street and Rolleston Road
Grade 2.*

Frowd's Almshouses SMT

By his will of 1719, Edward Frowd left £7500 to buy a piece of land near St.Edmund's Church, on which were to be built twenty-five almshouses, with little gardens to each. The residue was to provide incomes for the almspeople. He also instructed pews to be made for the almspeople to sit in together, to listen regularly to the service in St.Edmund's. Further money was invested in land to pay for the service.

The will went to the Court of Chancery and was not finally proved until 1773, when much of the money had been lost in legal costs. However, the almshouses were built in 1750 and further bequests were made over the following years.

In 1950, the building was restored and improved, using money from a bequest of Edward W.Gawthorne.

Back of Frowd's Almshouses SMT

Constitution: Originally for twenty-four almspeople, poor relatives of the founder, or parishioners over fifty years of age. After the Chancery case closed, the numbers were reduced to six unmarried men and six spinsters, all over sixty years old when admitted, except for relatives of the founder.

The residents were to be single; if they married, they were to leave the almshouse within ten days.

A coat for each of the men and a gown for each of the women were to be supplied every two years, and every year the men were to receive a new shirt and the women a new shift. New shoes and stockings were also supplied, once a year. Attendance at church was to be twice on a Sunday and on the first Friday of each month, for which two pews were supplied. A weekly allowance of 4s 6d was made to each individual, with extra at Christmas and Candlemas.

Doorway of Frowd's CC

Inscription over the doorway of Frowd's
Almshouses SMT

A long, two-storeyed building of nine bays, extending along Bedwyn Street, of dark red brick with brick quoins on a raised plinth, with a small garden laid out behind.[1]

The central door has Doric pilasters with a small Palladian window above. The door is of dark oak, with Tuscan pilasters above it. Higher up, under a pediment, is a Palladian window, and on the tiled roof is an octagonal lantern with a lead cupola. The windows are small, broad and widely-spaced, four-segmental headed 2-light casements, with 3-pane top lights. At the back of the building is an arched colonnade, with arched windows, which used to open onto the men's apartments. Above this is a row of round windows, which used to open onto the women's apartments. Some of the windows contain leaded lights.

Within the segment over the doorway, there is a panel with a rococo carved border, inscribed:

> *Built and endow'd*
> *by the Liberality of*
> *Mr.Edward Frowd,*
> *Merch't late of this City,*
> *1750*

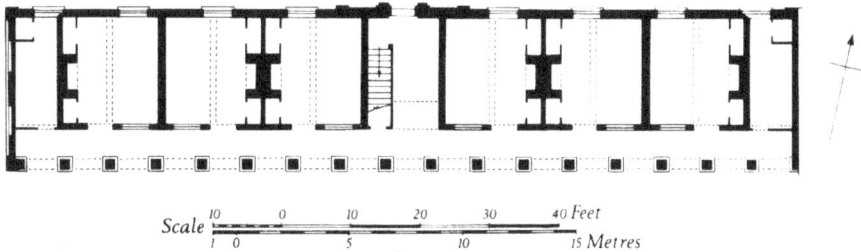

Scale

Plan of Frowd's Almshouses Reproduced by permission of English Heritage

In 1974 the building was much altered within and is now used as a hostel.[2]

Notes:
1 Pevsner, 404.
2 RCHM, vol. I, 59.
Charity Commission references:
1837:   418-22
RCHM (Salisbury) 1980: 58b

Salisbury   Sutton's Almshouses   ca. SU147297
St.Ann's Street, between Dolphin Street and the eastern bypass.

These were founded in 1700 by the will of Robert Sutton, a clothier. The site comprised three messuages in what is now St.Ann's Street, but was then Tanner Street.

His will makes provision for poor weavers. '. . . And whereas I am lawfully possessed to me and my heires of and in foar messuages or tenements and gardens with the appurtenances scituate lying and being in Tanners Street within the Citty of New Sarum . . . one of which . . . I doe hereby give devise and bequeath unto the said Joseph Albin my wifes kinsman . . . and putt into the said three tenements with the appurtenances in Tanners Street aforesaid three poor Weavers living within the said Citty . . .'[1]

After the decease of his executors, he gives the tenements into the hands of the vestry and churchwardens of St Martins, advising that they shall, from time to time: '. . . make choise and permit and suffer three poore Weavers of the said Citty to dwell and inhabit rent free in the said three tenements and gardens and theire widdowes after theire decease for soe long time as they continue Widdowes and noe longer and to these uses I give the same for ever. . .'[2]

In 1719, the almshouses came into the possession of St.Martin's parish and the selection of places rested with the Vestry.

Until 1833, the accumulated rent was spent on bread for the almspeople, but after this date it was used for repairs to the buildings.

The almshouses were closed and sold in 1876 and the proceeds invested in stock, which then went to the combined charities of Salisbury.

When the estate was put up for sale, the following description was employed: A piece or plot of land situate in St Ann Street, Salisbury, with the baker's shop, dwelling house and outbuildings and the three adjoining cottages known as Sutton's Almshouses thereon erected, having frontage to St Ann Street of 66 ft. and extending with garden in the rear about 121 ft.[3]

Although today there is no mention in any records of the existence of these almshouses on the ground, they are almost certain to be the four terraced houses of similar build to be seen today on the north side of the east end of St Ann's Street. In plan, they are seen to have little gardens running back from the houses and the RCHM gives a building date of about 1700, also adding that originally, the four dwellings were of uniform build.[4]

The four similar houses at the far end of the row are almost certainly those which formed the original Sutton's Almshouses SMT

Constitution: The provision was rent-free accommodation for three poor weavers and their wives, already living in the City, and for the weavers' widows after their husbands' decease. The rent from a fourth house in the same street paid for the maintenance of the almshouses.

Notes:
1 TNA, PROB 11/459/172.
2 *ibid.*
3 WSA Ref: PR/Salisbury St Martin/1899/126.
4 RCHM vol.i, 121 (no.278).
Charity Commission references:
1837:   426-7

Salisbury   Thomas Brown's Almshouses   ca. ST 143305
North end of Castle Street, west side.

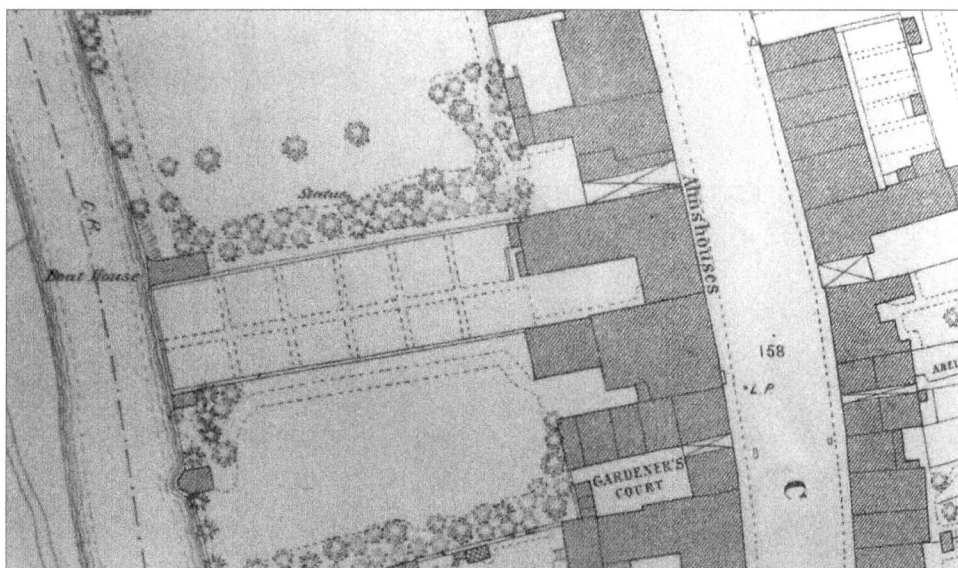

Site of Brown's Almshouses   OS map 1:500 1880   WSA

In 1857, an Almshouse Trust was set up by Thomas Brown, a wealthy currier, who died unmarried and childless in 1872. After his death, some of his nephews became trustees of the Trust. The piece of land on which the original almshouses were founded was on the west side of Castle Street, at its northern end, not far from Hussey's Almshouses.

Constitution: The seven cottages existing on the land were adapted as six almshouses for six married couples, who had to be Salisbury-born, over fifty years of age and with a maximum income of 2s 6d per week. The survivor of the couple would be allowed to remain until death, provided he or she was of good conduct.

A list of rules was drawn up for the residents and the occupiers of Cottage No.3 were to keep the keys to the houses and that of the gate to the river.

The original cottages dated from about 1800 and were of red brick with tiled roofs.[1] Three faced Castle Street and three stood at right-angles to it. Each contained a small sitting room with a bedroom above. A water supply, a communal wash-house and one privy served all and were located outside. A piece of garden ran down to the river.

Over the years, the buildings fell into a parlous state and money was not available for their upkeep. They were demolished in 1971 and in 1978 the Thomas Brown Almshouse Trust was amalgamated with the Margaret Blechynden Charity

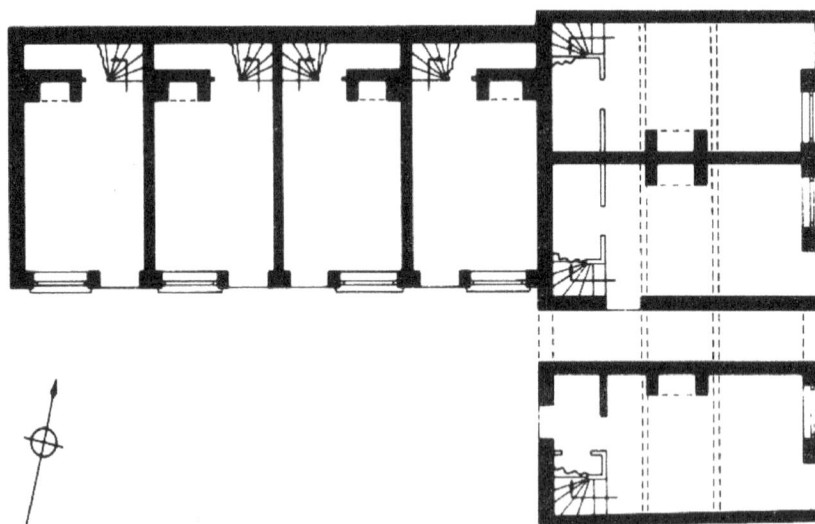

Ground plan of Thomas Brown's Almshouses Reproduced by permission of English Heritage

Notes:
1 RCHM vol.1, 58.
Charity Commission references:
1908: 551-4

Stockton   Topp's Almshouses   ST 980383

West side of downland lane, running south from Stockton main street.
Grade 2.

Topp's Almshouses JAT

Founded by the 1642 will of John Topp, merchant, of Stockton, the almshouses were built in 1657.

Constitution: Built originally for eight unmarried poor people, four from Stockton and four from Codford St.Mary, the adjoining parish, of which the Lord of the Manor of Stockton was also Lord of the Manor.

Each almsperson was to have two rooms, the use of the wash-house, enjoyment of an orchard, the cultivation of one of eight plots of garden, a yearly supply of wood for fuel, and an allowance of 4s 6d per week. The men were also to have a cloak and the women a blue gown. A nurse was to be provided at an allowance of 3s per week and was to reside with whoever needed her most. According to the Vicar in 1783, the endowment was about £70 per annum and the allowance for each person was 2s a week, a garment annually and the use of garden, orchard and a supply of firewood.[1]

The manor of Stockton, held by the Topp family, included part of Codford St Mary and they also leased the manor of Codford St Mary from the Mompesson family.

Small, stone-built, round three sides of a little forecourt. One storey high, with dormers. A simple front wall with a gateway set in the centre. The garden

Copy of the Topp's Almshouses Constitution and rules SMT

Topp's Almshouses with residents CC

plots are at the rear. There has been some internal modernisation during the 20th and 21st centuries.

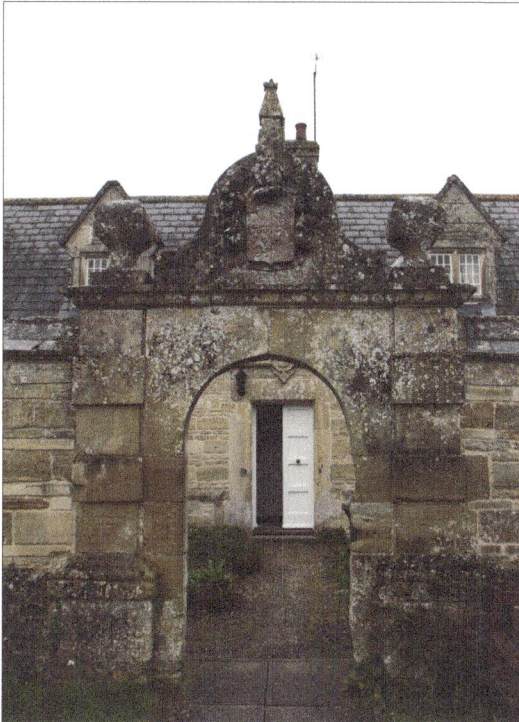

Gateway to the Almshouses   JAT

On a pediment over the gateway is the Topp coat of arms in stone relief:
ar. on a canton gu. a gauntlet clasped or.
(quartered with, presumably, the arms of his wife)

Notes:
1 Ransome, 1972, 188.
Charity Commission references:
1837:   731-6

Swindon   Christchurch Almshouses (also known as Anderson's Almshouses)   SU 157839
Cricklade Street, next to Christchurch

The almshouses were built in 1877 as a result of the will of Alexander Anderson, dated 6 May 1865, proved 21 April 1874, in which he bequeathed £1636 for the benefit of the poor. A further sum was added to this by the local board and the

Christchurch (Anderson's) Almshouses WBR

almshouses were erected in Cricklade Street. Administration was to be in the hands of the Vicar and Churchwardens.

Constitution: For four almspeople, men or women, over the age of sixty, widowed or single, but resident in Swindon for over three years and not to be in receipt of poor relief. Preference was given to those who had seen better days, but were now reduced by misfortune. The residents in houses 1 and 2 received small weekly pensions of 2s 6d and in 1897 a further pension was made available to the resident of house No.3. House No.4 was reserved for the latest-elected almsperson, and, as this resident received no pension, there was little demand for admission.

The buildings are of stone with north-facing windows, overlooking Christchurch churchyard. By 1970 each house had a living room and pantry on the ground floor and a large bedroom above.

There is an inscription on the end wall of the building facing the road:

A.D.1877

FROM A BEQUEST LEFT BY THE LATE

MR. ANDERSON OF THIS TOWN FOR THE

BENEFIT OF THE SECOND POOR OF SWINDON

THE TRUSTEES HAVE ERECTED THIS HOSTEL.

THEY HAVE ALSO INVESTED FIVE HUNDRED

POUNDS TO PROVIDE AN ANNUAL ENOWMENT

AND ONE HUNDRED POUNDS AS A REPAIRING

FUND FOR THE SAME.

HENRY GEORGE BAILEY A.M. VICAR
JOHN CHANDLER}
ROBERT SMITH EDMONDS} TRUSTEES
WILLIAM HENRY READ ARCHITECT

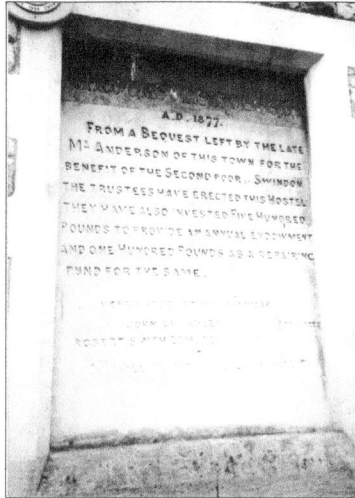

Inscription stone on wall of Christchurch Almshouses   SMT

Charity Commission references:
1908: 931-35

Teffont Evias   The Almshouse   ST990313
On west side of the high street
Grade 2.

The almshouse was built in 1883 under an indenture between William Fane de Salis, his wife Emily and others.[1]

It stood on about a quarter of an acre of ground, with some garden at the back and front and was on a ninety-nine year lease from 29 September 1884 at £1 10s 0d per annum, plus stocks. Endowment consisted of £450 Metropolitan Consolidated £3 10s % Stock, which produced annual dividends of £15 15s.

By 1984, the buildings, which were part of the Teffont estate, were leased as private dwellings, known as Acacia Cottages.

Constitution: Provision was made for two sets of occupiers, widowed, single people, or elderly couples, and they received 2s 6d per week, out of the income.

This was a tiny almshouse, consisting of two tenements built of local stone, in Gothic style,[2] situated in the main street of the village, each tenement

Former Teffont Almshouse SMT

consisting of a living room and kitchen, with a bedroom above. The building is two-storeyed, of rubble stone, with an ornamental tiled roof, ceramic ridge crest and ashlar chimney stacks. The upper storey has three windows, the lower storey two, with a central, four-panelled door, which has a transom light. The porch is gabled with a pointed arch opening. The windows either side are of three lights, mullioned, with hood moulding; those on the upper floor are of three lights with hood mouldings and small gables over. At the rear there is a single-storey integral outshut. Internally there is a central lobby with doors off to either side, which would have led to the separate almshouses.

Over the central window is a shield-shaped tablet of stone, with the wording:

ERECTED

BY

W and E.FDS

1883

Notes:
1 Stevenson, 1987, 195
2 *ibid.*
Charity Commission references:
1908 vol ii 694-6.

Tidworth, North   Dr.Pierce's Almshouses   SU 235490

Just past modern Post Office on west side of A338

Founded by Indenture dated 4 September 1689. It appears that the endowment was met from the proceeds of Sir Stephen Fox's manor and rectory of Maddington, though the building was the brainchild of Dr Thomas Pierce, Dean of Sarum.

In 1691, the almshouses were conveyed from Robert Pierce, son of the founder, to 'Speaker' John Smith, in whose family the maintenance and repair of the almshouses remained until the death of Thomas Assheton Smith in 1858.[1]

From 1901 onwards, the houses were sold off to private buyers. They are believed to have been demolished during the 1970s. Unfortunately, no photograph of these almshouses has come to light.

Constitution: The four residents were to be selected from Tidworth Moiles and Tidworth Zouch and they were to be old widows or widowers. They were to be paid 2s a week on a monthly basis and there were to be a Master and a Deputy. That memories of the old religious foundations had not gone away completely, is borne out by the fact that the almshouses were originally called a Hospital and the residents were to attend daily prayers, twice a day, on pain of a 6d fine.

Dr Pierce and his heirs were to have the selection of the residents and when these heirs became extinct, the nomination was made by the successive owners of the Tidworth Zouch estate.

By the beginning of the 20th century, the residents could be married, widowed or single, so long as they were aged and deserving.

The almshouse building consisted of a terrace of four cottages of red brick with tiled roofs, built at right angles to the Salisbury Road (A338), just past the present North Tidworth Post Office, on the west side, and just south of Zouch Farm. Each tenement consisted of one room up and one down. At the back was a small garden for each house and two lavatories for the use of all residents. There was also a communal woodshed behind and a courtyard in front, edged with a wall and palisades.

Notes:
1 Croman,
Charity Commission references:
1837:   716-9

Till Valley Flood Charity   The Flood Charity Almshouses

The five separate sets of cottages which made up the Flood Charity dwellings of the Till Valley cannot be truly called almshouses in the traditional sense of the word. They were not founded by an individual with a wish to perpetuate his or her name for posterity, nor were they founded by an establishment endeavouring to help the poor of a parish or town. But they arose from an immediate need in the most tragic of circumstances and some were even changed to almshouse status later in their existence.

In early 1841, there had been a bitterly cold spell, in which the ground was frozen solid. A heavy snow storm was followed by a thaw, which set in on the night of 16th January. The water had nowhere to run, owing to the ground being frozen and so it overflowed the banks of the river Till, which then caused flooding to a depth of six or seven feet in places. Some seventy or more cottages down the valley, mainly of mud and cob, were washed away, three people were drowned and several hundred rendered homeless. A fund was raised by public subscription and the various contributions went towards a Flood Charity to alleviate the distress of those who had suffered loss in the flood. Details of the disaster were recorded in the Devizes and Wilts Gazette for 21 January 1841.[1]

In the ensuing twelve months or so, public subscription raised enough money to build a number of replacement cottages in each of the five villages affected by the flood and the rents from them were used to provide the victims of the flood with clothing, fuel and bedding, most having lost everything. Sheets seem to have been the main item supplied over the following years.

An indenture of 5th September 1842 for £20 from John Maton, gave a plot of 20 perches of land at Maddington, facing the turnpike road from Shrewton to Maddington, now the High Street. On this were built two cottages. They were later used as almshouses. In 1904, some of the income from the cottages was used to provide twenty-seven sheets for the poor.[2]

A second indenture, of the same date, made by Stephen Mills for £40, gave a plot of land of 40 perches in Orcheston, bounded on the south by the turnpike road, on which were to be built four cottages. Rents provided income for fuel, clothing and bedding and sheets were distributed to the needy. In 1991, the cottages were transferred to a housing association.[3]

Of the same date, a third indenture for £20 from John Simpkins, gave a plot of land of 20 luggs in Tilshead, bounded in front by the turnpike road from Tilshead to Devizes which was to support two cottages. Again, rents from the cottages were used to support the residents of the cottages. In 1901, in common with the other flood villages, sheets were provided for forty-five people. During the 20th century, the income from the rents was mostly used to repair and maintain the cottages and in 1991, it was proposed to convert them to almshouses.[4]

An indenture of 3rd June 1843 for £49 19s from Ann Windsor and two others, gave a plot of land of 25 perches in Shrewton, bounded on one side by the road leading from Shrewton to Winterbourne Stoke. In 1843, they were transferred to trustees who regulated the income from the rents and in 1863 they supplied ninety-eight people with a pair of sheets each. Between 1889 and 1904, sheets were regularly distributed every year until the 1920s, when vouchers, each worth 2s 6d, were issued. During the 20th century, the cottages were occupied by needy parishioners until in 1984, a scheme converted them into almshouses.[5]

A final indenture of 9th September 1863 from the Rt.Hon.William Bingham gave a plot of land of 32 perches at Winterbourne Stoke, bounded on the west by the turnpike road, on which were to be built two cottages.[6]

In so far as the charity can be said to have been founded, the five people listed above might be called the founders, since they supplied the land on which the cottages were to be built: John Maton, Stephen Mills, John Simpkins, Ann Windsor and the Rt.Hon.William Bingham. When the cottages were built, the funds raised were vested in twelve trustees, who were responsible for the upkeep of the cottages and for distributing material succour to those in need.

A declaration of the Trust was made on 9th September 1863 and enrolled on 22nd December 1863. It decreed there should be:

4 cottages in Shrewton
2 cottages in Orcheston St.Mary
2 cottages in Orcheston St.George
2 cottages in Tilshead
2 cottages in Maddington
2 cottages in Winterbourne Stoke

Each set of cottages was to bear an inscription of its foundation. In reality, the following were erected, each with a board bearing a common inscription:

4 cottages in Shrewton
4 cottages in Orcheston St Mary
2 cottages in Tilshead
2 cottages in Maddington
2 cottages in Winterbourne Stoke

By 1904, each tenement contained a living room, pantry, two bedrooms and a small garden. In the 20th century, the cottages at Winterbourne were sold to Shrewton, who immediately demolished them. The remaining cottages were handed over to a housing association, who let them to the deserving poor in association with the District Council, who administer the cottages.

Constitution: In 1882 it was agreed that the available funds should be distributed yearly in the form of fuel and clothing and a scheme of two clauses for the distribution of the Charity was drawn up:

The Charity shall be given to necessitous poor persons of good character of the labouring classes only, inhabiting in the parishes named in the deed.

The clergymen and churchwardens of each of the parishes shall be requested to supply to the trustees, on or before the 1st December in each year, a list of persons whom they may recommend to the trustees as fit objects for the Charity.

N.B. Master tradesmen, shopkeepers, landlords of public houses or beer houses, owners of property in the said several parishes or elsewhere, and inhabitants of one or other of the parishes for less than three years, should not be recommended for the Charity, except under special circumstances to be stated to the Trustees for their consideration.

By 1904, the distribution of sheets had taken the place of fuel and clothing and strict guidelines were laid out for the provision of such.

Originally built at Maddington, Orcheston, Tilshead, Shrewton and Winterbourne Stoke, the remaining cottages are now at Maddington, Orcheston, Tilshead and Shrewton.

Each of the remaining sets of cottages carries a large inscription board on the front wall in the centre of the block. The wording on each is identical.

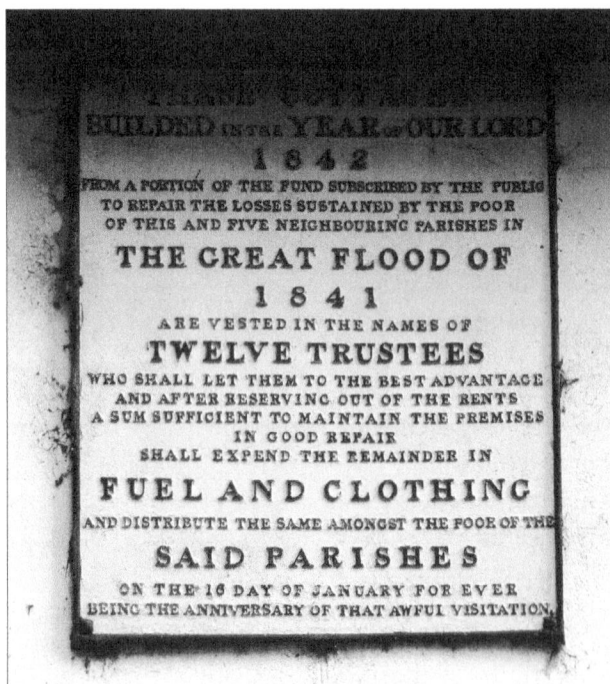

THESE COTTAGES WERE
BUILDED IN THE YEAR OF OUR LORD
1842
FROM A PORTION OF THE FUND SUBSCRIBED BY THE PUBLIC
TO REPAIR THE LOSSES SUSTAINED BY THE POOR
OF THIS AND FIVE NEIGHBOURING PARISHES IN
THE GREAT FLOOD OF
1841
ARE VESTED IN THE NAMES OF
TWELVE TRUSTEES
WHO SHALL LET THEM TO THE BEST ADVANTAGE
AND AFTER RESERVING OUT OF THE RENTS
A SUM SUFFICIENT TO MAINTAIN THE PREMISES
IN GOOD REPAIR
SHALL EXPEND THE REMAINDER IN
FUEL AND CLOTHING
AND DISTRIBUTE THE SAME AMONGST THE POOR OF THE
SAID PARISHES
ON THE 16 DAY OF JANUARY FOR EVER
BEING THE ANNIVERSARY OF THAT AWFUL VISITATION

Dedication board at Orcheston Flood Cottages SMT

Maddington   Flood Cottage   SU 066440
On the north-east side of Maddington Street

The building is a semi-detached pair of cottages, built in the same style as those at Orcheston, with rustic porches and a foundation board high up on the centre of the façade. It has recently been re-roofed and the chimneys have been removed.

Orcheston   Flood Cottages   SU059453
On the northeast side of the high street

Flood Cottages, Maddington High Street SMT

Flood Cottages, Orcheston SMT

The cottages at Orcheston are in two blocks, each containing two semi-detached cottages, probably of rendered brick. The front doors, each with a small rustic porch, are situated at either end of the front façade and open directly onto the road. The casement windows are arranged with two on the ground floor and two on the first floor, one being above the front door. The roofs are of slate and the central pair of chimney stacks is of brick, in a mock-Tudor style. The gable-end bargeboards are of an engrailed pattern. Both blocks bear the foundation board in the centre of the front wall of the block.

Shrewton   Flood Cottages   SU 069436
On the west side of Salisbury Road, running from Shrewton to Winterbourne Stoke

Flood Cottages, Shrewton SMT

At Shrewton, the four tenements are all in one terraced block, with the foundation board in the centre of the facade. The whole block has been refenestrated in fairly recent times, with two windows on the ground floor and two above and the façade presents a modern-looking build. The doors are situated one at each end of the terrace and two more adjoining in the centre. The walls are now painted and possibly rendered, but it is assumed the building is of brick. The roof is of dull red tile and the two chimneys, of brick, are positioned over the centre of each half of the building. Like the barge-boards at Orcheston, those at Shrewton are also patterned.

Tilshead   Flood Cottages   SU 031479
South side of the high street, near the west end.

Flood Cottages at Tilshead, with benefaction board in centre SMT

The Tilshead Flood cottages are a semi-detached pair. An end wall collapse in 2014 revealed cob construction under render. The façade is symmetrical, with four casement windows set about the plain doorway. The roof is slated and the centrally placed pair of chimney stacks are of brick in a mock-Elizabethan style. The standard Flood benefaction board is placed in the centre of the front wall. The cottages open straight onto the road, but there appear to be gardens extending behind.

Notes:

1 Devizes and Wilts.Gazette, 21 January 1841, p.3 [WSA].

2 Freeman, 1995, 213.

3 *ibid.*, 1995a, 234.

4 *ibid.*, 1995b, 275.

5 *ibid.*, 1995c, 252.

6 *ibid.*, 1995d, 284.

Tisbury   Vicar's Cottages   ST 944291
Church Street, on west side of parish church yard

Vicar's Cottages, near the parish church, were established as an almshouse in the 17th century.[1] In 1649 the property belonged to Tisbury Rectory and was occupied by one William Rogers.[2] It comprised a tenement at the south end of the Church House, with five lower rooms and four rooms over them. At the south end were a little stable and other outhouses and a garden. The stone building was thatched. At the south west end there was a further cottage. On the north side of 'Parsonage Close' there were two little outhouses for glovers, called water houses, with yards, watercourses, etc.

The row was at one time known as 'The Rank' and later 'The Glove Factory'.[3] It was in poor condition in 1887, when a brick top floor was added. In this room, known as the 'Long Room in the Rank'. In the early 20th century it was used as an annex to the nearby Primary School and girls' subjects were taught here for some twenty years or more – cookery, laundry, dairy work and cottage gardening, with water being fetched in buckets from a tap in Church Street and waste water carried down again. In the 1930s sinks and drains were installed.[4] In the early 1970s, gloves were being manufactured in this upper room.[5] In 1981 there was a planning application to turn the property into flats.[6] The row was fully restored in 1985 as individual houses, let for a term of 999 years from that date. The builder received a Conservation Award.[7]

Vicar's Cottages, Church Street, with inscription WBR

It is not known what the constitution was.

Stone terrace with a brick upper storey, along the front of which is the following inscription: 'As for me and my family we will serve the Lord'

Notes:
1 Cheetham & Piper, 168
2 Bristol Record Office Dean & Chapter's Estate: Ref: DC/E/3/2.
3 Info. from Tisbury Local History Society.

4 Rex Sawyer, pers.comm.
5 Jackson, et al, 21.
6 WILBR: B634.
7 Sale particulars for 2 Church Street, WBR Ref: WILBR/B634.

Trowbridge   **Lady Brown's Cottage Homes**   **ST 859579**
South west side of Polebarn Road
Grade 2.

Lady Brown's Cottage Homes, Polebarn Road SMT

Founded some time before 1901 by Sir Roger Brown in memory of his deceased wife. The premises were conveyed to trustees by indenture, dated 28 May 1901.

   Constitution: For six women, widows or spinsters, of good character and 'moral worth' in reduced circumstances, their religious beliefs to be no bar. Aged sixty or more; born or resident in Trowbridge or Hilperton. While funds permitted, they were to receive 7s per week. Vacancies were to be nominated by the founder while he was still alive.

   The original constitution is at the WSHC.

   Applications were to be made bearing name, address, age, marital status, late husband's name and date of death, how long resident in Trowbridge or Hilperton, and means of support.

   The buildings consist of two single-storey, semi-detached blocks, each of stone, roofed with tiles. Each block has two gables and tall, thin chimneys.

There is a yard at the back and the premises are backed by a public park.

There are two stone relief plaques on each building. On the left-hand block the left-hand plaque reads:

PEACE
WHEN THOU COMEST
AND PEACE
WHEN THOU GOEST
MAY
THY FOOTSTEPS
ECHO PEACE

The right-hand plaque bears the arms of Brown. They are:

Party of three palewise, each pale per fess ar a bee prop az, a cushion ar, all counterchanged.

Motto: Fortuna et Labore

On the right-hand block, the left-hand plaque reads:

LADY BROWN'S
COTTAGE HOMES
AD ERECTED 1900
IN LOVING MEMORY
BY
SIR ROGER BROWN

The right-hand plaque reads:

LO
MINE HELPMATE
ONE TO FEEL
MY PURPOSE
AND REJOICING
IN MY JOY

Charity Commission references:
1908: 989-92

Trowbridge   Union Street Almshouses   ST 857582

Corner of Union Street and Church Street
Grade 2.

Union Street Almshouses from Union Street, with St James's Church beyond, early 20th century. WLSC

The Reverend J.D.Hastings had some land in Back Street conveyed to him in 1859 and in 1861 he built on this, partly at his own cost and partly by subscription, eight almshouses. These fronted onto Union Street and became known by that name. In 1868, the almshouses were conveyed to trustees.

Each occupant was to receive 5s per week, as long as funds permitted. Various donors gave large sums of money over the years and one such sum was donated expressly to raise the weekly allowance to 6s. The names of some of the donors are to be found in the VCH volume for Trowbridge.

Constitution: For eight men, unrelieved by parish funds, incapable of earning their own living and to be aged sixty or more. The almsmen were to be chosen by the trustees. They were to be paid 5s a week, as long as funds permitted.

The architect was H.Blandford & Smith. The ground floor is of stone and has arcades; the upper floor has a timber balcony with gables.

Union Street Almshouses, taken from St James's churchyard SMT

Charity Commission references:
1908: 977-8

Trowbridge   Tabernacle Cottages (United Reform Almshouses)
ST856582
North side of Church Street, end on to the road, facing onto a path.
Grade 2.

These four cottages were erected during the mid-19th century, but were never registered as a charity or an almshouse. Until the 1990s, qualifying members of

United Reform Almshouses, 21stC   SMT

the United Reform Church next door were allowed to live there free of charge, with additional support from the Sunday offerings of the congregation. The cottages were run by a committee of elders and stewards of the church.

United Reform Almshouses (Tabernacle Cottages), possibly early 20thC   WLSC

As the Church was originally known as the Tabernacle, the cottages were called Tabernacle Cottages, as can be seen on the accompanying map.

1886 map of Trowbridge   WSA

Constitution: No constitution is known, but residence was open to single or married members of the church. Today, the residents are paying tenants of the church. A stone plaque in the middle of the front wall records:

Plaque on the front wall of the Tabernacle Cottages   SMT

THESE TABERNACLE COTTAGES
WERE RECONSTRUCTED IN 1938
BY C.INGHAM HADEN
IN LOVING MEMORY OF
ROSA M.INGHAM HADEN
WHO PASSED TO HER REST JULY 4 1937

Trowbridge   Palmer's (New) Almshouses   ST 858586
West side of Islington, just before Downhayes Road
Grade 2.

Palmer's Almshouses WLSC

Founded in 1893 by Brigadier General G.L.Palmer in memory of his father. No longer an almshouse, though it is not clear when it ceased to function; possibly about 1995.[1]

Constitution: For aged couples. By 1939, each occupant received £1 monthly.

Red brick and mock timber-framed. Two big gables at either end. A red tiled plaque on the front wall over the central doorway reads:

Palmer Institute
These
Almshouses were
Erected and endowed by
George Llewellen Palmer
In 1892 in memory of his
Father Michael Palmer
Who died November 20 1891
Aged 77

Notes:
1 Information from Mr Kenneth Rogers.

Trowbridge   Salter's Almshouses   ST 858582 and ST 857582
To west of Baptist Chapel built off Church Street (originally Back Street)

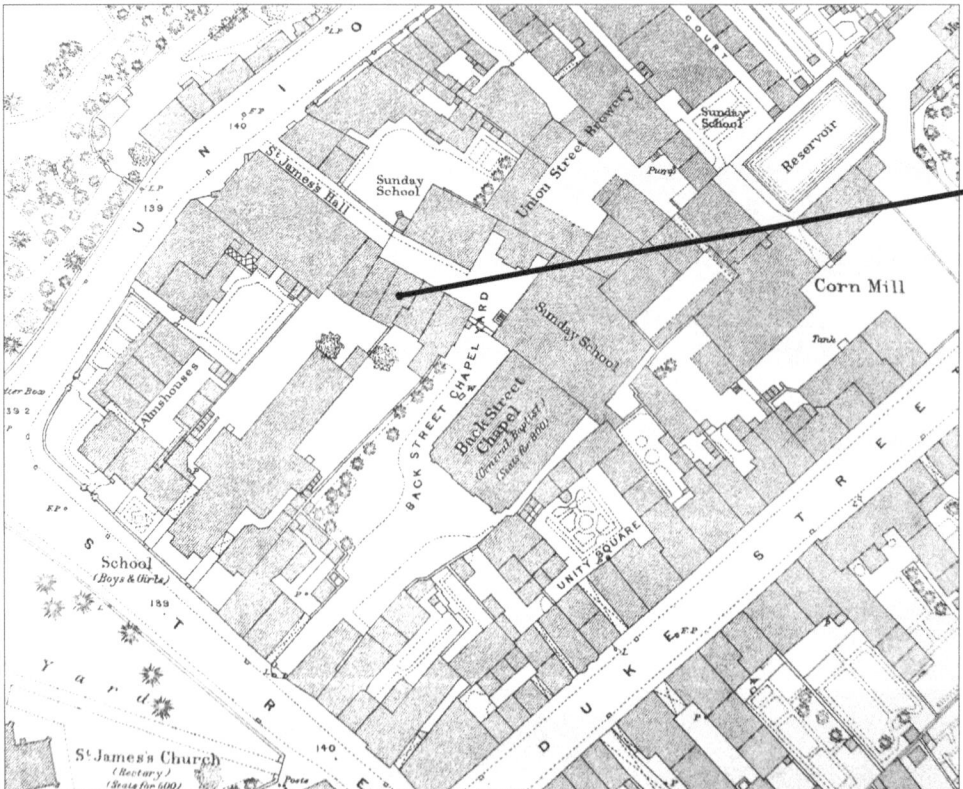

1887 1:500 map of Trowbridge, sheet xxxviii 7.10 WSA

Salter's Almshouses began life as seven houses adjacent to the Emmanuel Baptist chapel, which was called new-built in 1829[1]; they were conveyed by indenture in 1851 to trustees for the deceased Samuel Salter, a cloth manufacturer. In 1884, two of the houses were pulled down and the site used to facilitate the approach to the chapel and school. At the same time, part of the school was converted into two replacement almshouses. The remaining old almshouses were pulled down and rebuilt as a row of red-brick cottages in Chapel Yard. In 1903 there were ten widows in the almshouses.[2]

Believed to be part of Salter's Almshouses PW

Constitution: Five of the houses were to be used for poor widows or widowers, chosen by the chapel deacons from communicants of the congregation.

Plaque from the original Sunday School building PW

SUNDAY SCHOOL
EXTENSION
THIS STONE WAS LAID BY
C.W.DERBISHIRE ESQ. M.P.
JULY 11TH 1923

Notes:
1 Chandler, 1985 , 121.
2 Pugh, 1953a, 169.
Charity Commission references:
1908: 1000-3

Trowbridge   Terumber's Almshouse (Old)   ST 858582
North east side of parish churchyard

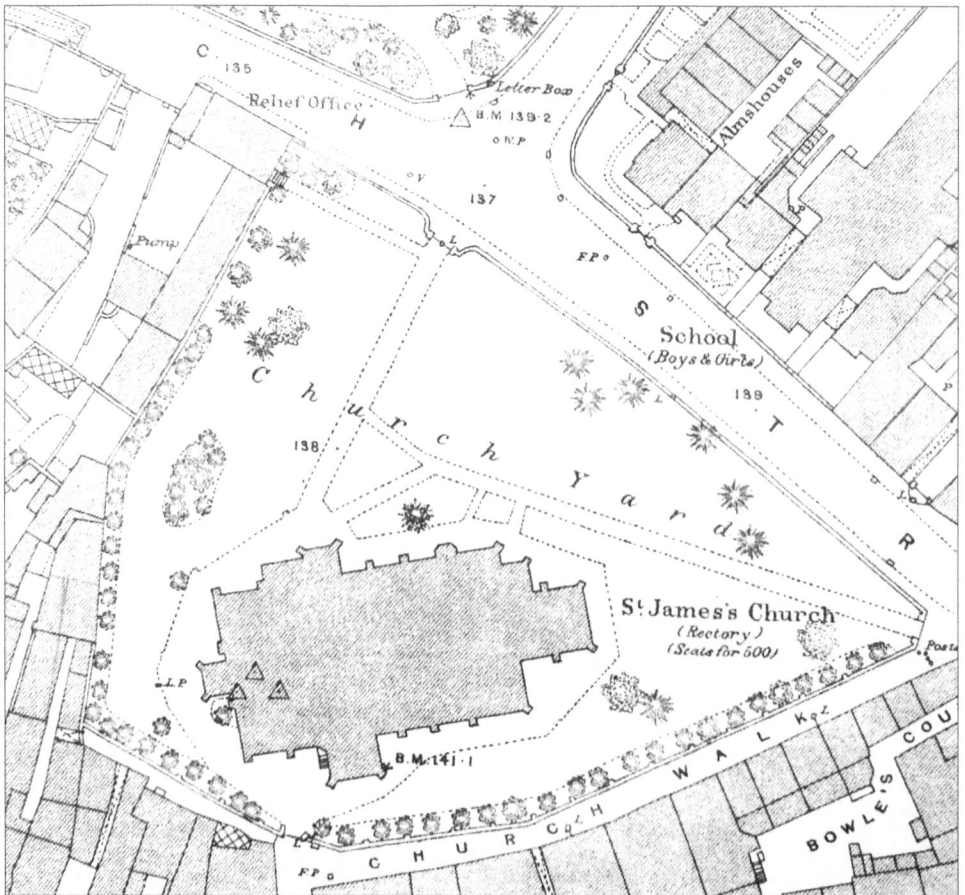

St.James's Churchyard OS map 1:500 1887 WSA

The Old Almshouse was founded prior to 1483 by James Terumber. He was the wealthiest Trowbridge clothier of his time. As he had no children, his enormous wealth was endowed upon the people of the town.

In 1479, Terumber and his wife, and others in the town, took of the lord of the manor a piece of ground in the churchyard. It measured 116ft by 33ft and the almshouse was built on it. To this was added the reversion on another plot of ground, held by the rector; this was to become the garden for the almshouse.

At the Reformation, rent charges on the Terumber lands were used to support the almshouse. Being a secular foundation, it escaped dissolution.

In 1763, it was proposed that the old almshouse should be pulled down, which caused a great uproar. There were said to be twenty-seven people living below stairs at the almshouse and seventeen above, such was the plight of the poor in the town at that time.[1] It was eventually demolished in 1811.

Constitution: For six poor men or women. They were to pray twice a day for the soul of the founder and his two wives, Joan and Alice, and then proceed to the parish church to recite the Psalter of Our Lady. Each almsperson was to have a separate room and to enjoy the common garden.

In 1483, a deed of enfeoffment gave the almspeople a 3d weekly allowance, until 6 marks had been spent (about £4).[2]

A priest had a room on the north side of the almshouse with a little garden attached. He was to govern the community, with the oversight of the feoffees and churchwardens.

Leland, writing in the 1540s, says: 'This Terumber made also a little almose house by Throughbridge chirch, and yn it be a 6. poore folks having a 3. pence a peace by the week towards their finding'.[3]

Accounts for repairs in 1669 and 1670, show that the almshouse was a timber-framed building. There were six small rooms up and six down. Evidently part of the building had collapsed at this time and had to be supported while repairs were carried out. A number of local workmen and tradesmen were mentioned by name.

Notes:
1 Rogers, 1984, 54, 73.
2 WSA Ref: 206/38
3 Smith, vol.i, 136.
Charity Commission references:
1837: 354-5
1908: 952-3, 1010

Trowbridge   Yerbury Almshouses   ST 859581
South-east side of Roundstone Street, at junction with Yerbury Street

Yerbury Almshouses, 2010 SMT

Grade 2.

Founded in the late 17th century. The will of Dr Henry Yerbury, proved in 1685, left money to his three brothers, William, John and Richard, and to the Bishop of Oxford, for charitable purposes. The brothers in their turn endowed the almshouses, which were probably erected after their older brother's death. William's will of 1698 bequeathed £50 towards the enlargement of the almshouses and £200 towards the maintenance of the residents. In 1700, Richard bequeathed £100 for maintenance and Edward and William, his sons, also gave large sums for the upkeep of the foundation.

In 1724, all money for the maintenance of the almspeople was vested in trustees, who also purchased land in Trowbridge and North Bradley and the income from leasing this land was used for the repair of the almshouses and the maintenance of its residents.

Constitution: For six Church of England widows.

Originally built of stone, consisting of six tenements, each of two rooms, with a garden plot behind each tenement. Rebuilding took place in 1914 and the present building is of red brick with gables.

On the front of the present building, on a stone lozenge, is the following: [the date following is unclear]

Yerbury Almshouses
1914

On the corner of the building is a very worn stone coat of arms, (which may have come from the original building) depicting what appears to be: A horse rampant impaling a chevron between three ?apples. However, the General Armory for 1883 gives for Yerbury, Trowbridge: per fess or and ar a lion rampant az. Another Wiltshire version is: per fess or and sa a lion rampant counterchanged. It is, therefore, something of a mystery as to whom this coat of arms belongs. It may be that of the rebuilder of 1914.

Yerbury Almshouses ca. 1910 WLHS

Charity Commission references:
1837: 349-354
1908: 949-52, 964-8

Trowbridge   **Zion Chapel Almshouses**   ST 858582
Behind the Chapel in Union Street

Founded by Indentures of lease and release, dated 21 and 22 June 1816. They were rebuilt in 1893, when William Applegate conveyed land and property in Union Street to trustees for the use of the Chapel.

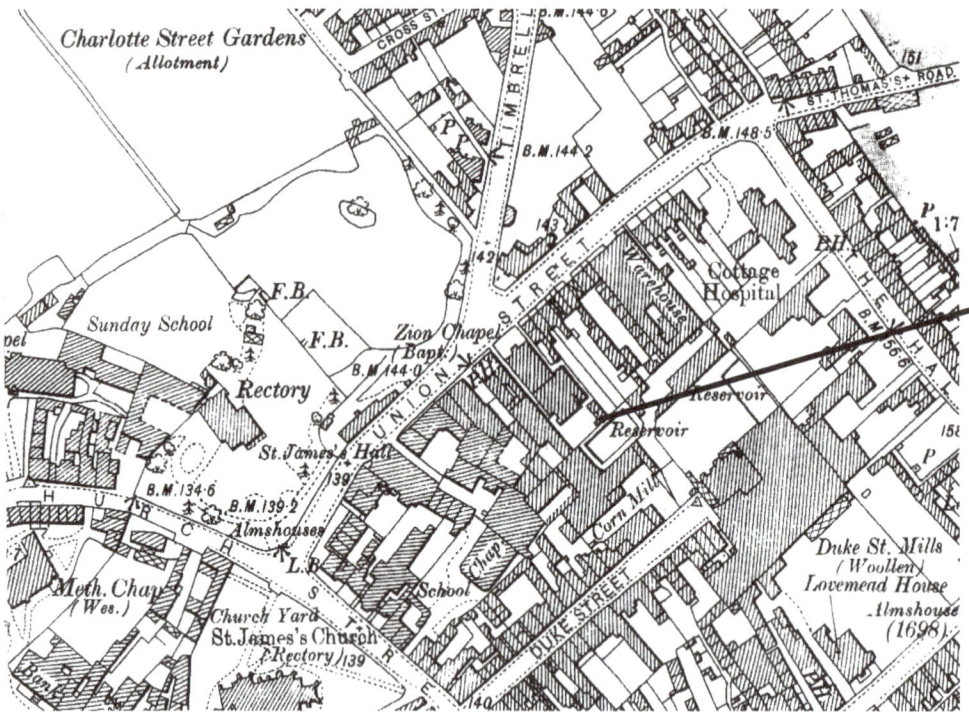

1899 1:2500 OS map, showing possible location of Zion Chapel almshouses

The almshouses are believed to have been down this passageway. The Zion Chapel is on the right. Photo 2012 SMT

The Zion Chapel, Trowbridge, 1903 CC A narrow passageway can be seen between the two buildings and this is probably the passage leading to the almshouses behind.

Constitution: The almshouses were to be occupied by two members of the Zion Chapel, of either sex, aged sixty years or over; or, failing this, they could be from elsewhere, as long as they were of the same faith, i.e. Calvinists or Particular Baptist. In 1903, there were two women in the cottages.

The almshouses were probably closed before the Second World War and have since been demolished.

These almshouses consisted of two cottages in the back yard of the Zion Chapel in Union Street. Each had two rooms, one up, one down.

Charity Commission references:
1908: 1006-8

Warminster   Warminster Almshouse   ST 875452
South end of Portway, facing onto George Street.

There was an almshouse in Warminster by the mid-16th century and there are several references to Almshouse Bridge, to which it gave its name. Colt Hoare says it was formerly on the river side, 'as appears by the Church Records', and that it fell into decay and was demolished about 1750.[1] John Daniell, in his book of Warminster history, was more specific; he placed the almshouses on the bank of the brook on the west side of the Organ Inn, which lies on the south side of George Street. He goes on to say that several poor male and female persons were lodged here and received alms from those passing over the adjacent bridge.[2]

The Parish Book[3] records that in 1607 Clement Abath, a leading citizen of the town, gave by deed £5 to the inmates. The building was still in use early in the 18th century, when the Parish Book records that in 1705-6, 13s were paid for repairs to the almshouse. It eventually became ruinous and was demolished about 1750.[4]

In 1765, a timber merchant called Thomas Marsh, took a lease on the ground on the west side of Portway, from Portway House down to Almshouse Bridge. This bridge carried the road over the little River Were, as it ran north to south across what is now George Street. Originally it was a wooden bridge. It was replaced by a two-arched stone bridge, the first stone bridge in Warminster.[5] It now lies beneath George Street.

Constitution: This is not known, but the burial registers for Warminster, between 1556 and 1642, give numerous entries for almshouse residents. There were men as well as women living there.

Notes:
1 Hoare, vol.4, 40.
2 Daniell, 120-1.
3 WSA Ref: 2144/71, 6
4 Daniell,107.
5 Phillips, 24, 25.
Charity Commission references:
1837: 415

Warminster   Louisa Warren's Almshouses   ST 873452
East side of Portway, before railway bridge

Warren's Almshouses, early 20th century CC

Founded in 1873 by an Indenture between Louisa Warren, widow, and others, 25 January, enrolled 1 February 1873, in memory of Louisa Warren's late husband. The endowment was £2500. [1]

Constitution: For four Protestant widows or spinsters, of Warminster, over sixty years of age. Louisa Warren had the sole right of appointment during her lifetime. There was an allowance of 6s per week to each resident.

Four tenements in brick under one slate roof, with gables to right and left. In each of the gable faces is a pentagonal plaque; the left-hand one bears the inscription:

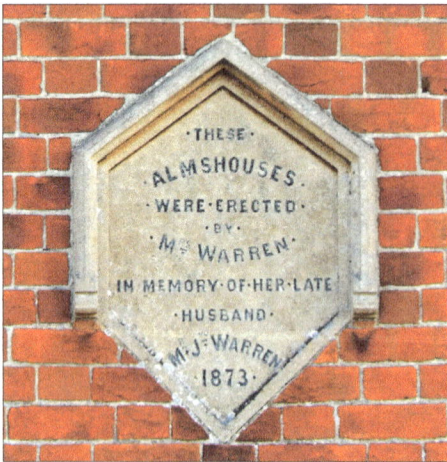

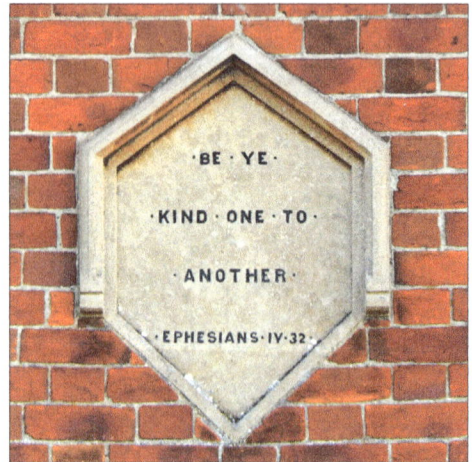

Inscription in left-hand gable SMT   *Inscription in right hand-gable SMT*

These Almshouses were erected by
Mrs.Warren in memory of her late husband
Mr.J.Warren 1873

The right-hand plaque reads:

Be ye kind to one another.
Ephesians iv 32

In the twenty-first century, the almshouses were sold and completely renovated.

Warren's Almshouses, 2014 SMT

Notes:
1 Rogers, 1965,135.
Charity Commissions reference:
1908: vol. ii 768

West Lavington   Alderman Dauntsey's Almshouses   SU 008530
East side of Church Street, at right-angles to the road.

Founded in 1543 by the will of Alderman William Dauntsey, in which five poor men or women were to pray for his soul, to receive 6d. a week each and to be in the almshouse 'by Michaelmas next'.[1] A piece of empty ground on the north side of the Vicarage, belonging to the parish church of West Lavington, was purchased and a school and a block of eight almshouses were built.

Constitution: The almshouses were to be for five poor, aged impotent men, to be called the Beadsmen of West Lavington. Two Beadswomen were later admitted. The

The former Alderman Dauntsey's Almshouses, now Dauntsey Court SMT

residents were to receive ten guineas quarterly.

The foundation was later entrusted to the Mercers' Company of London, who made payments in 1824-1830 of 6s a week to each of the five beadsmen and two women. From 1830 there were five men and five women in the almshouses, receiving 8s a week and £3 per annum for clothing.

Standing: Mr Baker, Mr Kyte (ex-policeman) Mr Saunders
Seated: Mr Merritt, Mr Baker.
'These are all bedesmen wearing their red waistcoats' CC

Originally built in 1553, the almshouses were rebuilt in brick, with some original remains, in 1810, with a central timber clock turret. Each dwelling consisted of a sitting room, bedroom and buttery, with a common room for all. The clock turret has now gone.

West Lavington Almshouses, pre-1914, with the original timber clock tower   CC

As one faces the row, on the left-hand side is a circular plaque. Within it is set a coat of arms with crest and mantling. The arms are difficult to distinguish, but with the aid of the General Armory, they can be confirmed as those of Dauntsey: Per fess dancettee or and gu a lion rampant seizing upon a wyvern erect counterchanged, a border engrailed erm.

Plaques on façade of Almshouses, West Lavington   SMT

To the right of the row is another circular plaque with the head and shoulders of a woman. She has shoulder-length hair and wears some sort of coronet, which may be of feathers.

On the west gable end, facing the road, is yet a third circular plaque with the following inscription:

ALDERMAN DAUNTSEY'S
ALMSHOUSES AND SCHOOL
ENDOWED
AD 1642
THE LORD OF THIS MANOR
PATRON
THE MERCERS COMPANY
TRUSTEES
WEST WING ERECTED
1831
G.R.H.SURV[R]

Notes:
1 Horn, 224
Charity Commission references:
1837: 372
1908: 622-4, 626-7

Plaque on end gable of Almshouses, West Lavington
SMT

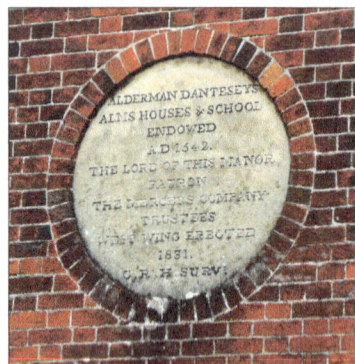

North front of Alderman Dauntsey's Almshouses, before renovations, ca.? 1960s. CC

West Lavington   West Bank Almshouses   SU006531
In Church Lane at junction with Church Street, just north of Church

West Bank Almshouses, 2014 SMT

Endowed by the then lord of the manor in 1499. The original must have been rebuilt, maybe several times, but a short row of cottages dating from 1831 still stands on the site, though now converted to a private dwelling.

The Crowe Collection of photographs refers to this as William of Lavington's Almshouses.

Constitution: For three residents, usually women, all to be receiving poor relief. This is unlikely to be the original constitution, but it was in practice for many years. 1s a week was paid out to each resident from the manor of West Lavington.

A line of single-storey cottages divided into three, rebuilt in 1831. Each had a sitting room, bedroom and buttery. A bakehouse and wash-house was attached for communal use.

On the front of the building was the following inscription:

Endowed by the Lord of the Manor 1499

Rebuilt 1831

C.R.H.Surv[r]

This is no longer present.

West Bank Almshouses, 1912 CC

*Miss Hilderbrand, outside West Bank
Almshouses, 1930s. CC*

Charity Commission references:
1837: 372
1908: 625

Westbury   The Laverton Almshouses   ST875511
Prospect Square, south east side of Bratton Road
Grade 2.

Abraham Laverton was a radical mill owner and twice stood for election in
Westbury; on both occasions he was defeated, but he petitioned Parliament
that the electorate had been intimidated: the other candidate threatened to evict
people if they voted for Laverton. As a result, Parliament passed the Ballot Act of
1872, which ensured a secret vote.[1]

Laverton wanted to both compensate those who had suffered at the hands
of his opponent and to house his own old and disabled mill workers. Prospect
Square was built, with thirty-nine houses surrounding a green. It was known at
the time as 'Laverton's City of Refuge'. It was completed in 1869 at a cost of £200
per house and in celebration, Laverton and the architect, W.J.Stent, paid for a
grand dinner, which was held on the central green.[2]

It was Laverton's wish that the seven houses at the top of the rise, on
the south-east side of the green, should be set aside as almshouses. He made
provision for this in his will, and his nephew, William Henry Laverton, carried
out his uncle's wishes in 1886, conveying the remaining thirty-two houses in
trust. The rent from these was to provide maintenance for the seven almshouses.

The central almshouses at the top of Prospect Square SMT

In 1983, all the Prospect Square houses were sold for private use and the proceeds used to build the present Laverton Court Almshouses on another site.

Constitution: Married or single couples, usually former employees at the Laverton Mills. A weekly allowance of 5s was made.

The almshouses consisted of a row of brick and stone dwellings. Two of the almshouses had five rooms, the rest four rooms. They stand at the top of the rise which forms Prospect Square and command a magnificent view across the valley to the north-west.

A plaque set in the wall above the middle of the block reads:

THESE SEVEN HOUSES
HAVE BEEN DEDICATED AS
ALMSHOUSES
FOR THE USE OF OLD OR DISABLED
FACTORY OPERATIVES
AND THEIR WIDOWS
AND THE NEIGHBOURING THIRTY-TWO
HOUSES AND LAND
HAVE BEEN ASSURED AS AN ENDOWMENT
FOR THE ALMSHOUSES

View from the top of Prospect Square   WBR

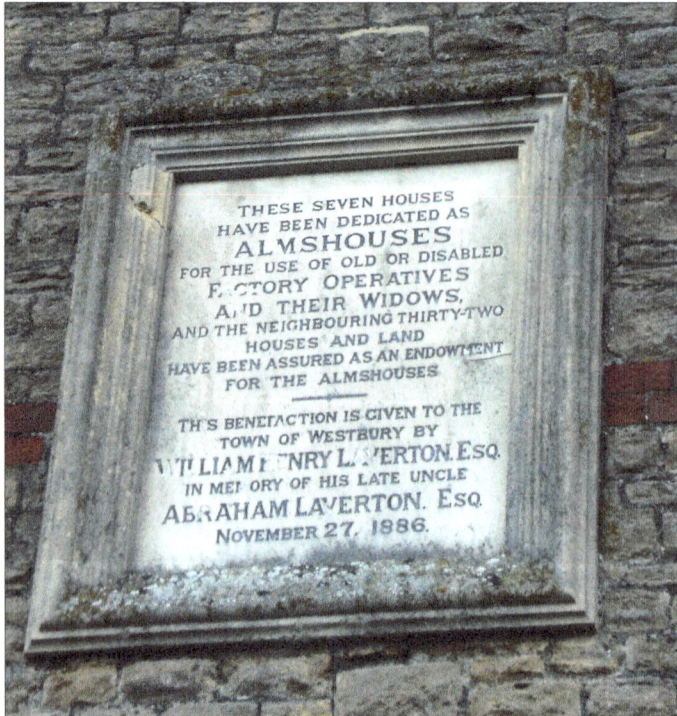

THESE SEVEN HOUSES
HAVE BEEN DEDICATED AS
ALMSHOUSES
FOR THE USE OF OLD OR DISABLED
FACTORY OPERATIVES
AND THEIR WIDOWS,
AND THE NEIGHBOURING THIRTY-TWO
HOUSES AND LAND
HAVE BEEN ASSURED AS AN ENDOWMENT
FOR THE ALMSHOUSES

THIS BENEFACTION IS GIVEN TO THE
TOWN OF WESTBURY BY
WILLIAM HENRY LAVERTON. ESQ.
IN MEMORY OF HIS LATE UNCLE
ABRAHAM LAVERTON. ESQ.
NOVEMBER 27. 1886.

Plaque on wall of Prospect Almshouses   SMT

THIS BENEFACTION IS GIVEN TO THE
TOWN OF WESTBURY BY
WILLIAM HENRY LAVERTON ESQ.
IN MEMORY OF HIS LATE UNCLE
ABRAHAM LAVERTON ESQ.
NOVEMBER 27 1886

Late 19th century burial registers rarely, if ever, give the abode of the deceased as being an almshouse. However, earlier Westbury burials produced some interesting entries:

1705 almschild, Borough; almsman, Town; almsman, Leigh

1706 almswoman, Leigh

1709 almswoman (2)

These entries imply that there may well have been an earlier almshouse in Westbury or at Westbury Leigh. On the other hand, one must also accept that perhaps these individuals were in receipt of alms, but remained in their own dwellings.

Notes:

1 Wood, 84-5.

2 *ibid.*

Westbury   Stafford Brown Almshouses   ST873512

Ivy Court, near junction of Edward Street and Warminster Road

By a Deed Poll of 1890, Mary Brown, daughter of Stafford Brown, Vicar of Westbury from 1845 to 1847, conveyed, in trust, fourteen cottages on this site. Four of the cottages were to be let and their rents used to maintain the rest of the property, which were to be known as the Stafford Brown Almshouses, Ivy Court. Four of the cottages adjoined the Warminster Road, while the other ten adjacent cottages formed Ivy Court.

In 1937, four of the cottages were sold and converted into a house and shop. During WW2, they housed evacuees for a while, but gradually became ruinous. In 1955 the whole site was sold. Nothing remains of the almshouses and shops now occupy the site.[1]

Constitution: For poor parishioners of Westbury, members of the Church of England. The inhabitants of the cottages were to be over sixty years of age, married couples, widows or single women. The Charity was to be managed by the Vicar and Churchwardens.

A double row of two-roomed dwellings in a small court extending back from the Warminster Road.

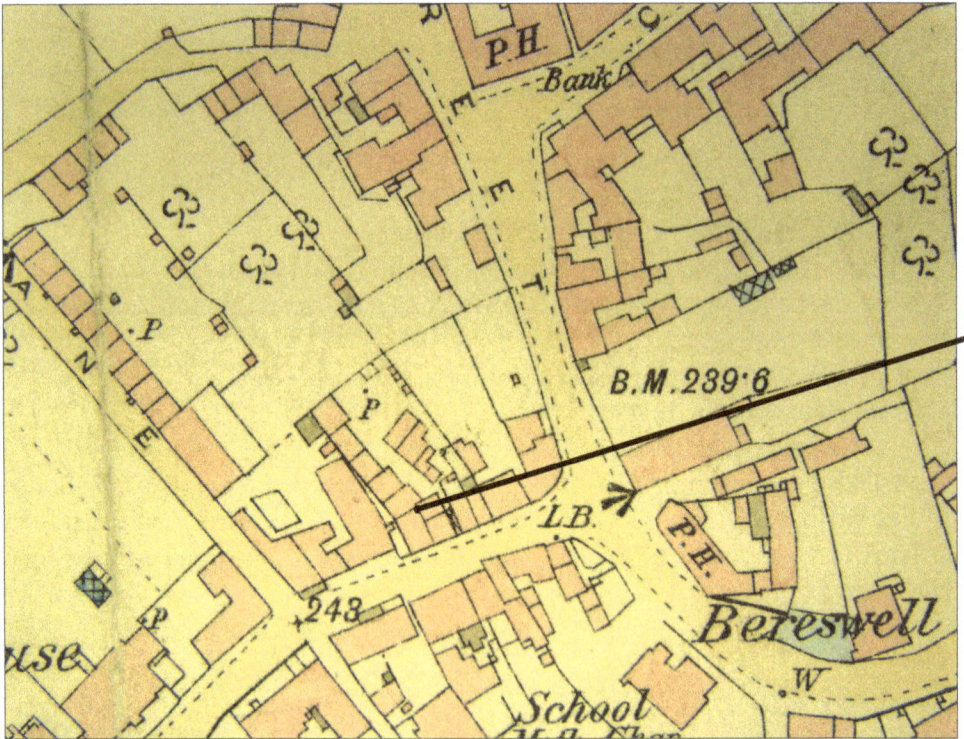

1:2500 OS map of 1884, showing position of Stafford Brown Almshouses   WSA

Notes:
1 Wood, 84-5.
Charity Commission reference :
1908 : vol.ii 808-9.

Wilton   Hospital of St.Giles   SU 101315
West side of King Street
Grade 2.

Founded some time before 1135, it was originally a leper hospital and tradition
has it that it was founded by Queen Adeliza (or Adelicia) of Louvain, the second
wife of King Henry I. Whether or not she had leprosy herself, or whether the
Hospital was founded for a maidservant of hers with the disease, is not known.
But the King gave her land in Wilton on which to build a lazar house and it was
endowed with tithes of the King's rents in Wilton.[1] Henry II confirmed the grant
by a Charter given at Clarendon, Wiltshire, and King John also confirmed it by
grant on 23 May 1206. In 1247, Henry III issued a deed of Royal Protection for
the Hospital, brethren and lands.[2]

Originally it stood in the grounds of what is now Wilton House, just behind some disused gates alongside the old Quidhampton road.

The Queen was buried in the graveyard of the Hospital Chapel and a 17th century historian recalled that her grave was still identifiable in that century.

The Hospital had lands in Quidhampton, in whose parish it stood, as well as Bemerton and Burdensball. There is still an old building on the south side of Quidhampton village street which used to be known as Hospital Farm. It was rebuilt in 1677, but had ancient connections with St.Giles's.

St.Giles' Hospital CC

During the 19th century, the Chapel was converted into two cottages and remains of these could still be seen in 1909. It is doubtful if anything remains today.

In 1830, the Hospital was rebuilt on its present Fugglestone site in King Street.

Constitution: It is believed that the original Hospital consisted of a Prior, brethren, sisters, two poor men and two poor women. In the 18th century, it housed two poor men and two poor women, until 1796, when one additional poor man was admitted from then on.[3]

The almshouses now contain employees from the Wilton House estates, three men and two women.

In 1909, the Prior still received a corody of £4.[4]

Today's Hospital is a row of terraced cottages in brick under a slate roof, two storeys high. There are three gables facing the road. There is one bay window in the central gable; the outer windows are mullioned. The chimneys are tall and slender. There are gardens at the front running down to the pavement.

The string coursing along the front of the building bears the following inscription, carved in relief in the stone, in Gothic lettering:

Hospitium S:Egidii Adelicia Reg.Hen Fund.

(The Hospital of St.Giles, Adelicia, Henry's Queen, Foundress)

Inscription CC

There are two seals in existence. One dates from 1275, showing a cloaked figure with a staff in his hand: B M Catalogue of Seals, I, no.4339; illustrated in Hoare's Modern Wiltshire: Hundred of Branch and Dole, p 130; casts at Wilton House and the Wiltshire Museum.

The other seal is 15th century and shows the legendary wounded hart seeking refuge with St.Giles: it bears the legend:

s' * domus * elimosinare * sci * egedi * iuxta * wilton *

The seal is believed to be in the possession of Wilton Borough .

Notes:

1 Stratton, vol.i, lii-liii.

2 Ransome, 1972, 91; Stratton, vol.i, lii.

3 Pugh and Crittall, 1956, 364, quoting Charity Commission, 1908, 857, 884.

4 Stratton, vol.i, lii.

Charity Commission references;

1837:   479-81

Wilton   Hospital of St.Mary Magdalene   SU101310
Junction of King Street and The Avenue, just east of St.Giles' Hospital
Grade 2.

The origins of the Hospital are unknown. There was a chantry chapel of St.Mary Magdalen in Wilton Abbey and this, together with a named chaplain, was mentioned in the Register of Simon de Gandavo in 1302; though there is no evidence for the Hospital having been founded around this time. However, it was well established by 1420, when a contemporary poem refers to it.

It originally stood on the south side of Minster Street, in the parish of Wilton, a little to the north west of Wilton House, just east of the present Pembroke Arms. It is now on a site at the junction of King Street and The Avenue, in the ecclesiastical parish of Fugglestone.

Various lands and properties came to the Hospital between the 14th and 16th centuries and records of the leasing out of many of these exist among the Wilton House deeds. Hospital property was often known as 'Maudlins Mead', 'The Maudlins' and 'Morlands'.

On the eve of the Dissolution, the nuns of Wilton Abbey were making an annual payment to maintain thirteen poor magdalens to pray for the souls of the Wilton Abbey founders.

Hospital of St.Mary Magdalene, Wilton SMT

After the Dissolution, the Pembroke family succeeded to the Abbey's interest in the Hospital; between 1717 and 1833, Maudlin Money of £18 was paid out every six months by the Earls of Pembroke.

Constitution: It is thought to have been originally endowed for twelve poor bedesmen, who were to pray for the soul of St. Edith. At the Dissolution, it was refounded for thirteen poor women, 'magdalens', to pray for the souls of the founders. The 16th century Pembroke Survey speaks of the Brothers and Sisters of the Magdalene:

27 March 10 Eliz (1568)

Idem Henricus Boddenham pro una pecia prati jacente in

Orientali parte pertinente fratribus et Sororibus

Magdalene extendente ad orientem nuper Johannis Walle   ijs.[1]

[The same Henry Boddenham gives for a piece of pasture lying in the east part of the appurtenance of the brothers and sisters of the Magdalene extending eastwards to the late John Walle's, 2s]

Originally founded for men, women are also recorded living in the Hospital before the Dissolution. Though the Sisters are known to have eked out a living selling 'horse loaves' (made from beans and peas), it is not known what the Brothers did. The Abbey Roll of expenses, 1328, has an entry which reads:

'To Robert the Granger of the Abbey of Wilton for the purchase

of bread from the Magdalene Sisters for the Abbey Cart horses

24s 6d by one tally......' .[2]

In 1720, there were twelve inmates; by 1788, only six. In 1826, the will of the 11th Earl of Pembroke refounded the Hospital for six old men or women, who had served the Pembroke family; they were to be nominated by Wilton House.

St Mary Magdalen's in the early 20th century CC

There were originally five old Maudlin houses and gardens, situated at Almonry (or Armoury) Corner. These were pulled down in 1831 and were rebuilt in 1832 by Catherine, Countess of Pembroke, as six two-storey, brick-built cottages under a single slate roof, on the present Fugglestone site. Three gables face the road, two of them adjoining. The chimneys are tall and slender. Most of the windows are mullioned. The two outer ground floor windows are bays. The land is a little higher here than that on which St.Giles is built. Gardens run down to the pavement.

In the the east gable is a fancy-shaped iron plaque, bearing the following inscription:

This Hospital of Saint Mary Magdalen
of Wilton was rebuilt on this present site
in fulfilment of the intentions of
George Augustus XIth Earl of Pembroke & Montgomery
by
Catherine his Widow and sole Executrix A.Dm. 1831

There is a seal of the Hospital, found near the original site and possibly used by the foundation. It shows Christ rising from the tomb with two stars to the left and a crescent on the right. Below is an arch, containing a clerk holding a chalice on an altar. The legend reads:

svrrexit dns de sepvlcro
(the lord is risen from the tomb)

A cast of the seal is kept at Wilton House; the whereabouts of the original is unknown.

Notes:
1 Stratton, vol. i, 185.
2 *ibid.* introduction, lii, liii.
Charity Commission references:
1837: 482

Wilton   The Hospital of St. James, later St.John   SU 094314
North end of West Street, opposite turning to Ditchampton
St John's Chapel Grade 2*, 4 and 8 St John's Sq. Grade 2; 5 St John's Sq. Grade 2*; 10 and 12 St John's Sq. Grade 2.

The origins of the Hospital are obscure, but it would appear from Feet of Fines that in 1195 the Prior of the Hospital of St.James held lands in Ditchampton and Bemerton. In order to maintain a permanent bed in the Hospital, one Gervaise quitclaimed to the Prior 16 acres of arable land and one acre of meadow in Ditchampton and Ugford. A chapel in the Hospital is supposed to have been dedicated in 1217.[1]

The Chapel and adjacent buildings of St John's CC

When the Hospital was rededicated to St.John is not known, but the church
of St.Michael, Wilton, was confirmed to the Hospital by the Bishop of Salisbury
at the request of King Henry III. From then on, St.John's makes a number of
appearances in documents. It is thought that there may have been connections
with the Knights Templar, though there is nothing to confirm this.[2] 14th century
documents refer to sisters as well as brethren.

St John's, showing the tall chimneys still present in 1889 CC

Bequests were made by a number of prominent figures including Henry III in 1223 and 1235, and William Longspee, Earl of Salisbury, in 1225. Other benefactors can be found listed in the VCH Wilts. Vol.iii, 365.

At the Reformation, the commissioners of 1548 found that the Master received the value of the Hospital for himself and that no poor persons were maintained. The foundation was held to be charitable, but not superstitious.[3] It survived the vicissitudes of the remainder of the Reformation.

The Hospital fell into decay and was rebuilt in 1851, the chapel being restored in 1868.

Constitution: By 1821, two poor men and two poor women were provided for and the Master (Prior) was a clergyman selected by the Dean of Salisbury. The original constitution may have provided for a similar number of poor, together with brethren.

The Prior had first vesture of some meadow lands in the vicinity and the tenants in Netherhampton were required to cut and carry his hay.[4]

The chancel of the chapel remains, with late 13th century east windows and Decorated and Perpendicular side windows. The nave and north transepts are used as dwellings.[5] The chapel was restored in 1868 and enlarged in 1902.

By 1825 the Hospital was in a state of decay and was rebuilt in 1851 as a block of almshouses, in flint and stone with some brick: these were built by Charles Pearson, the Prior of the Hospital at the time, and in the late 1980s, further dwellings were added to the site. In the 21st century, there have been further restorations and additions.

St John's, early 21stC, the chapel to the right SMT

In each of the front-facing gables of the 19th century block are low-relief shields, set slightly into the wall, within an ecclesiastical-style surround. The left-hand shield depicts an Agnus Dei, while that in the right-hand niche displays the following: Per fess embattled gu and az and three suns in splendour or, for Charles Pearson, impaling the arms of his wife, which appear to be: or a chevron vert.

There is a seal, described in WAM xix, 362. It depicts an Agnus Dei (Lamb of God), with the legend: Sigillum hospitalis sancti iohannis ivxta wilton. This is an 18th century copy of an original and is still used by the Hospital.

Notes:
1 Chettle & Crittall, 364, quoting WAM xix, 261.
2 Stratton, Pembroke Survey,liii.
3 Chettle & Crittall, 366, quoting PRO E 301/58/87 and Hoare.
4 Stratton, Pembroke Survey, liii.
5 Pevsner, 522.
Charity Commission references:
1837: 489-94

Zeals   Chafyn Grove Almshouses   ST 782318
On the northwest side of High Street, NE of the village, just beyond the church
Grade 2.

Chafyn Grove Almshouses SMT

Built in 1865 with money given by William and Elizabeth Julia Chafyn Grove in memory of their mother, Eleanor, neé Michell. William died in 1865, aged just twenty-five, and his will was proved in 1866, with its codicils, in which he bequeathed to the Vicar of Mere, the Incumbent of Zeals and the owner of Zeals House, £3 % stock, to be invested to produce £50 per annum, in trust, for support of the poor.

Elizabeth Chafyn Grove, by her will in 1880, gave money for repairs to be carried out. The almshouses were not endowed as such and money for their upkeep is now derived from the rent paid by the four residents.

Constitution: For two old men and two old women. In 1908 they were all women, who were paid £1 a month and an extra £1 at Christmas.

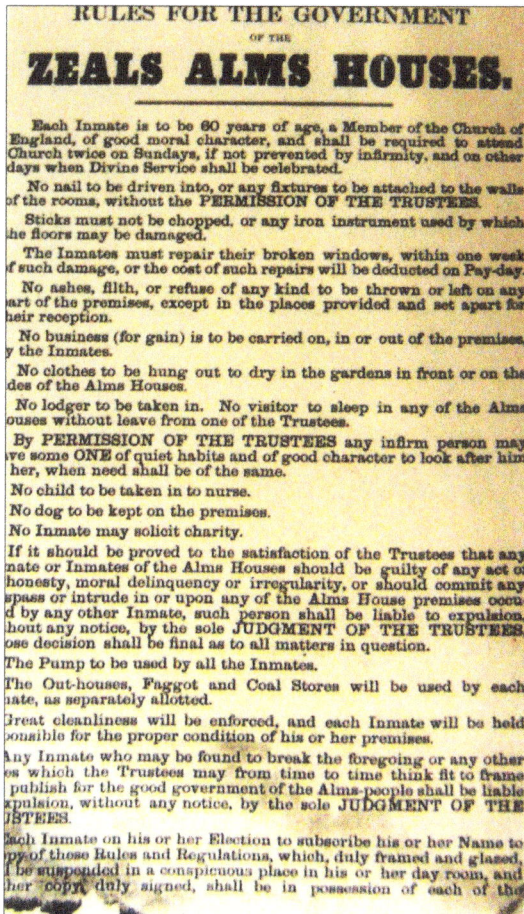

RULES FOR THE GOVERNMENT
OF THE
ZEALS ALMS HOUSES.

Each Inmate is to be 60 years of age, a Member of the Church of England, of good moral character, and shall be required to attend Church twice on Sundays, if not prevented by infirmity, and on other days when Divine Service shall be celebrated.

No nail to be driven into, or any fixtures to be attached to the walls of the rooms, without the PERMISSION OF THE TRUSTEES.

Sticks must not be chopped, or any iron instrument used by which the floors may be damaged.

The Inmates must repair their broken windows, within one week of such damage, or the cost of such repairs will be deducted on Pay-day.

No ashes, filth, or refuse of any kind to be thrown or left on any part of the premises, except in the places provided and set apart for their reception.

No business (for gain) is to be carried on, in or out of the premises, by the Inmates.

No clothes to be hung out to dry in the gardens in front or on the sides of the Alms Houses.

No lodger to be taken in. No visitor to sleep in any of the Alms Houses without leave from one of the Trustees.

By PERMISSION OF THE TRUSTEES any infirm person may have some ONE of quiet habits and of good character to look after him or her, when need shall be of the same.

No child to be taken in to nurse.

No dog to be kept on the premises.

No Inmate may solicit charity.

If it should be proved to the satisfaction of the Trustees that any Inmate or Inmates of the Alms Houses should be guilty of any act of dishonesty, moral delinquency or irregularity, or should commit any trespass or intrude in or upon any of the Alms House premises occupied by any other Inmate, such person shall be liable to expulsion, without any notice, by the sole JUDGMENT OF THE TRUSTEES, whose decision shall be final as to all matters in question.

The Pump to be used by all the Inmates.

The Out-houses, Faggot and Coal Stores will be used by each Inmate, as separately allotted.

Great cleanliness will be enforced, and each Inmate will be held responsible for the proper condition of his or her premises.

Any Inmate who may be found to break the foregoing or any other Rules which the Trustees may from time to time think fit to frame and publish for the good government of the Alms-people shall be liable to expulsion, without any notice, by the sole JUDGMENT OF THE TRUSTEES.

Each Inmate on his or her Election to subscribe his or her Name to a copy of these Rules and Regulations, which, duly framed and glazed, shall be suspended in a conspicuous place in his or her day room, and another copy duly signed, shall be in possession of each of the

The Rules of Chafyn Grove Almshouses CC

This is an attractive brick building of Flemish bond on a rubble stone plinth, divided into four, in the Tudor style, with gables, tiled roofs and front gardens, with diaper work in vitrified headers. The tiled roof has coped verges and diagonally-set brick stacks. The plan of the two-storey building is asymmetrical and there are three windows on each storey. To the left of the centre, there is a recessed porch with a moulded doorway with a 4-light ovolo-mullioned casement with a hoodmould on either side; and a similar casement with 3-lights to the right. The first floor has three 3-light ovolo-mullioned casements. On the left is a single-storey range with a gabled porch containing an arched doorway, 4-light ovolo-mullioned casement and a second arched doorway to left. Attached to the right is a single-storey wing projecting to the front with a Tudor-style arched doorway in a gabled porch, a 3-light mullioned casement in the gable end and a large external stack on right return. There is a rear lean-to with mullioned casements, and a single storey range with a large stack to the rear.

Chafyn Grove Almshouses, possibly early 20th century CC

On the front wall is an inscription tablet, gabled over with a coped verge, which reads:

To the dear memory of
His Mother
These Alms Houses were Erected and Endowed by
William Chafyn Grove
AD 1865
Blessed is the man that considereth the poor
The Lord will deliver him in time of trouble. Psalm XLI

Over the main entrance is a coat of arms in relief. It does not appear to be the Chafyn arms, but may be one of the Groves', whose arms are: on a chevron engrailed gu three escallops or, with, for a crest, a Talbot.

A tablet in the south chantry chapel of Mere church, placed there in 1893 by Miss C. Bazeley states:

Entrance porch to Chafyn Grove with plaque above and inscription tablet on the right   SMT

'To the Rector and Churchwardens of Zeals £400 in trust,
the interest to be applied as required for keeping the Alms
Houses at Zeals and the fences, gates and walls in repair
and order.' [Quoted in WAM xxix, 314]

Charity Commission References:
1837: 333-34

Appendix

The following are buildings which have traditionally been thought of as almshouses, but for which no evidence has been found. In most cases they were cottages built by an estate or farm to house their retired workers.

Compton Bassett   14, 15, 18 Compton Bassett

Almshouse Cottages, Compton Bassett WSA

There is a record of these cottages being referred to as almshouses in sale particulars for the Compton House estate. They look like farm workers' cottages, which in 1868 is what they were. They consist of a row of cottages in red brick with ashlar dressings, with Tudor-style windows and dormers. In 1898 they appear to have housed estate pensioners, when the building was referred to as almshouses. But they were never registered as such and there is no reference to them in the Charities Commission reports.
(Freeman, 20, 149; WSA 2904/53; 1409/185)

Crudwell   Limetree Cottage and The Kennel, The Street.

The Department of the Environment description lists this as 'Former almshouses, now two cottages'. There is a date stone in the west gable with the inscription: WM/AD/1847. This may refer to the Rector of Crudwell, William Maskelyne, born 1808 in Purton, who came to the parish in 1839 and died there in 1866.

Cottages at Crudwell WBR

The Charities Commission Report cites Robert Jenner's foundation, as it appears in Camden's Britannica; but this is a description of Jenner's foundation in Malmesbury. Jenner's will contains no mention of Crudwell.
(Crudwell PRs; Alumni Oxoniensis; Camden)

Horningsham   73-75 Church Street.

73-75 Church Street, Horningsham SMT

A thatched stone row of one build with grouped chimneys, referred to by the DoE as former almshouses. There is a short description of the cottages in the online site for Wiltshire Community History. This says that these three 'one up, one down' cottages were built in the 17th century and that in 1910, they were rented out at 1s a week each. The range certainly looks like almshouses, but no records in the Charities Commission reports have been found.
(history.wiltshire.gov.uk)

Ludgershall   15, 17, 19 Castle Street

The buildings identified as almshouses still stand, but are now private dwellings and have probably been so for a very long time. The cottages were built about 1690 and are of flint and brick with a thatched roof, each being single-storeyed with an attic. Photographs and references to them are made in Barbara Humphrey's book on Ludgershall, where they are referred to as almshouses. However, there are no entries in the burial registers, nor in the Charities Commission reports to suggest that any almshouses ever existed in Ludgershall.
(Humphrey)

Pewsey   Phoenix Row, Pewsey Market Place

The Department of the Environment lists these buildings on Phoenix Row as former almshouses, but they look most unlikely candidates and there are no records in the Charities Commission reports of any almshouses having been established here. The VCH states they were erected in 1823 and incorporated shops, as part of the new market place. The buildings are three storeys high, of colour washed brick with thatched roofs.
(Crowley, 1999, 181-207)

Short Biographies
of Almshouse Founders

The main sources of information are acknowledged at the end of each entry and further details and portraits of individual founders may be found on many of the websites listed.

ANDERSON, Alexander
Founder of Christchurch Almshouses, Swindon

Alexander Anderson appears to have remained a lodger and bachelor all his life and it is not known what trade or occupation he followed. In the 1861 census returns, he was lodging in Prospect Place, Swindon, with the Riddlestorffer family. According to this census, he was born in Southwark, in about 1811. The head of the family, with whom he lodged, Edward Riddlestorffer, was also born in Southwark (1813) and was a clerk on the Railway. It is possible that Alexander moved to Wiltshire with this family. There are other Alexander Andersons in the census returns, but none in the Swindon area. The will of an Alexander Anderson, who died in Swindon on the 9 April 1874, was proved on 21 April 1874, with effects amounting to £5,000. This would seem to be the Alexander Anderson who founded the Christchurch Almshouses. *(UK census returns; Ancestry.co.uk; Nat.Prob. Calendar for 1874)*

APPLEGATE, William
Founder of Zion Almshouses, Trowbridge

William Applegate was born about 1819 in Westbury Leigh. He seems to have begun life as a maltster, which is how he is recorded in the Bradford on Avon Directory of 1848; he was living at Widbrook at that time. Over the years

William Applegate and his wife (By kind permission of Michael Marshman)

he became a successful wine merchant, eventually owning the Roundstone Hotel in Trowbridge, where, in 1881 he was living with his wife, Mary Ann, and three of their children. His eldest son, William Selfe Applegate followed in his father's footsteps as a wine merchant, living in Hilperton Road, Trowbridge, at the time of the 1881 census, with his wife, three children and two servants. His youngest son, Frederick Selfe, was a brewer. But on 3 February 1887 a notice appeared in the London Gazette to the effect that the Appplegate business, hitherto run by the partners William Applegate, William Selfe Applegate and Henry Applegate (his second son), would henceforth be run by William senior and Henry only. Whether there had been a difference of opinion or whether William Selfe wanted to set up independently, we may never know. In 1893, William senior built, at his own cost, the vestry for the Zion Chapel in Union Street. He also gave them an organ and erected three new schoolrooms.

(Pugh, 1953: 160, 169; UK census returns; London Gazette, 23 Sep 1881; www.freshford. com (2014)

ATTWOOD, Francis
Founder of St.Paul's Homes, Fisherton Anger

Francis Attwood was a Salisbury surveyor and magistrate, living in The Close, quietly serving his home town. He took a great interest in the Cathedral and was treasurer of its restoration appeal. He was a benefactor of other charities,

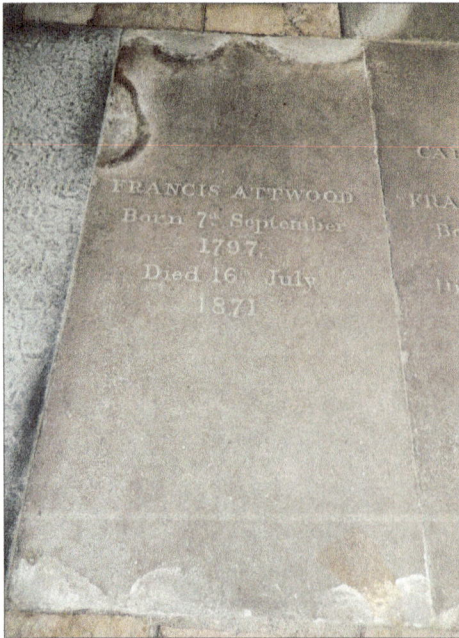

Grave of Francis Attwood in the floor of Salisbury Cathedral cloister SMT

as well as the St Paul's Homes, which he founded, including the Infirmary. According to the 1851 Census Returns, Francis was born in The Close in 1797, the son of Richard Attwood and his wife, Elizabeth, who were sub-tenants of 16 The Close from about 1817 until after 1837. On 29 May 1828, Francis married Caroline Mary Rigden, daughter of John and Mary Rigden, in All Saints Church, Maidstone. Caroline had been christened in 1801 in Lenham, Kent, some ten miles south east of Maidstone. There were no children of the marriage. In 1841, Francis and Caroline were sharing a house in The Close with Richard and Elizabeth, Francis' parents, and Caroline's brother, Richard Rigden, then aged 25. This may have been No.16. Ten years later, Francis' parents had died, but his brother in law, Richard

Rigden, was still living in the house, as was Mary Reed, a niece. By 1852 Francis was leasing 20 The Close from the Dean and Chapter. He died in 1871 and was buried in the south cloister walk of the Cathedral, close to his parents. Caroline died in 1884 and was buried next to her husband.
(Pugh, 1962: 184; RCHM 1993, 105, 115; UK Census Returns; familysearch.com)

AUCHER, Richard
Early founder of St Nicholas's Hospital, East Harnham (see also Bishop Poore and Bishop Bingham)
In 1242-3, Richard son of Aucher was a tenant in demesne of the manor of Fisherton, which at that time had two overlords, the Earl of Salisbury and the Earl of Arundel. The parish eventually took its name from the family, which went through the forms of Aucher – Aunger – Anger, which name it retains today. The manor descended through the Auchers to the mid-14th century, during which period, one of the family, Sybil Aucher, became Abbess of Wilton.
(Crittall, 1956: 241; Pugh, 1962:18)

BARRETT, William (see also SMYTH, Cleophas)
Co-founder of Devizes Old Almshouses
The old annals of Devizes relate that Mr William Barrett, Citizen and Grocer of London, and Mr Cleophas Smyth, Citizen and Draper of London, both born in the Borough of Devizes, each left £5 in their wills towards the rebuilding of the Old Almshouses, which took place between 1615 and 1616. There are two baptismal entries for a William Barrett in the registers of St John's, Devizes, but since the fathers are not named at that time, it is difficult to decide which one is the William Barrett in question. One entry was for a William Barrett baptised on 14 January 1559/0, the other on 18 October 1564. From his will, made in 1619 and proved in 1621, we learn that William was a citizen and grocer of London. He had been born in Devizes and left £5 to the poor of his birth town. He married Elizabeth Stile, daughter of Julian Stile, and by her had ten children, all under 21 years in 1619. He also mentions a brother, Nicholas, and two cousins, Maurice Abbot and Johanne Walker, the wife of John Walker; but where these individuals resided is not known. William asked to be buried in St Alban's Church, Wood Street in London. He probably died during the latter part of 1621.
(will TNA, PROB 11/138; Cunnington; parish registers of Devizes St John)

BAYNTON, Sir Henry
Founder of the College of the Poor, Bromham
Born about 1572 at Bromham House, he was the son of Sir Edward Baynton. He was sometime MP for Devizes Borough and was elected High Sheriff of Wiltshire in 1597. In about 1593, he married Lucy, the daughter of Sir John Danvers of Dauntsey and they had two sons and a daughter. In 1601, Henry was

knighted. In 1606, he and some of his servants were prosecuted for illegally taking deer and timber, removing boundaries and enclosing a park in Pewsham and Blackmore forests. During the slump in the cloth trade in the early 17th century, many workers were impoverished and it was for six poor weavers that Sir Henry built six cottages in 1612. He died in 1621 and was buried in St Nicholas's Church, Bromham, though no memorial to him exists. His wife was buried in Westminster Abbey.

(www.bayntun-history.com (2012))

BINGHAM, Bishop Robert

Official founder of St Nicholas Hospital, Harnham.

Although both Bishop Poore and Richard Aucher were doubtless early founders of St Nicholas Hospital, Bishop Bingham is regarded as the official founder, since the Hospital was probably rebuilt by him, some time after 1229, when he became Bishop of Salisbury. The surviving medieval structures of the building date from around this time. In 1231 and 1235, timber was granted by royal licence for the building. He was also responsible for building Ayleswade Bridge and linking it with his Hospital, thus opening up direct trade and transport routes with the new City of Salisbury. Of Somerset origins, Robert was a learned and erudite man, with a certain holiness about him, similar to his predecessor, Bishop Poore, to whom he was an assistant in his early years. He spent much time in the schools

Bishop Robert Bingham, from his tomb in the North Choir, Salisbury Cathedral　SMT
(By kind permission of the Dean & Chapter, Salisbury Cathedral)

of the Diocese, though most of his life was as a resident of the Salisbury Chapter and, like Richard Poore, he was responsible for a number of reforming statutes. He died in 1246 and was buried in Salisbury Cathedral.
(Edwards, 344)

BLECHYNDEN, Margaret
Founder of Blechynden's Almshouses, Salisbury
Margaret Blechynden was the widow of the Rev.Thomas Blechynden, DD, a Prebendary of Canterbury Cathedral. Thomas was baptised in Aldington in Kent in 1592 and married Margaret Aldersley at St.Gregory's, London, in 1635. Margaret was the daughter of Samuel Aldersley and Mary van Oyrel and was baptised in 1617 at St Olave's, Southwark. Her husband, Thomas, died in 1663, seised of the manor of Ruffins Hill, Kent, and was buried in the chancel of Aldington church, near his father. Margaret was not known to have had any connections with Salisbury, her will of 1682 describing her as being of St Paul's, Covent Garden; but her nephew, Samuel Eyre, the son of her sister Ann and Robert Eyre of Chilhampton and Salisbury, was himself a Salisbury man. He it was who was entrusted with the legacy to buy land for Margaret's foundation. This is almost certainly why the almshouses were built in Salisbury.
(SLHG, 20-2; Hasted, 314-327; will TNA, PROB11/375)

BOTTENHAM, Agnes
Founder of Trinity Hospital, Salisbury
Traditionally, Agnes was the keeper of a brothel on land now (2013) occupied by the Raie d'Or restaurant and Trinity Hospital, at the corner of Brown Street and Trinity Street. The story is that Agnes eventually saw the life she was living for what it was and as an act of reparation (she was presumably a fairly wealthy woman) had a hospital for the poor erected, the Trinity Hospital, where the residents would say constant prayers for her and her family. Another version tells of Agnes building the Hospital on the site of a brothel – with no other connection with it. However, there is strong evidence that Agnes was the widow of a Salisbury citizen, John Bottenham, and a conveyance of tenancy naming him was drawn up in 1399. Certainly the Hospital was on the site before 1379. John Chaundler (vide infra) was mentioned as Master of the Hospital in 1383 and was an early benefactor of it, if not a re-founder.
(Parsons, 357; Baker, 376-7)

BRICKETT, Thomas
Founder of Brickett's Almshouses, Salisbury
Brickett was a wealthy Salisbury merchant and a one-time mayor of the City. Little has been written about him, but his will, written and proved in 1533, reveals much about the man. The early spelling of his name is Brickhed, and this is

consistent throughout his will. He married at least twice, since he referred to his
first wife's sister. His present wife's name was Mercy and they lived within the
parish of St Edmunds, Thomas bequeathing money for the repair of the church
and desiring to be buried there. He was also pious, leaving bequests to chantries,
to church repairs for all churches in Salisbury, to various religious houses and
for diriges and Masses for his soul, this being on the eve of the Reformation.
Brickett had two sons and two daughters, one of whom was married to a William
Brian and he had several Brickett kinsmen about the county. The description of
his clothing legacies indicate that he was indeed wealthy, with satin, fur, velvet
and leather being among the items. Brickett died between the 15th September
and the 11th December 1533 and was, presumably, buried in St Edmund's. That
church and churchyard have long been de-consecrated and the site of his grave
is now lost.
(Crittall, 1962: 168; will TNA, PROB 11/25)

BROWN, Mary dau. of Rev.Stafford

Founder of Stafford Brown Almshouses, Westbury
Mary was the daughter of the Rev. Stafford Brown, Vicar of Westbury (1845-7),
and his wife, Caroline. Her parents married on the Isle of Wight in 1839 and
Mary was born at the end of the following year (1840) on the Island, though in
later Census returns, she gave her place of birth as Calne, Wiltshire, the place
where she spent her childhood. Her father did much for the church when he
became Vicar of Westbury, increasing its congregation dramatically; and he set
about its restoration. Unfortunately, he saw little of his work completed, for he
died in 1847, aged only 31. Mary's mother and Mary's two siblings lived on in
Westbury, first in Church Street and then in Alfred Street. Caroline died in the
summer of 1889, aged 73. In 1890, Mary was able to found the almshouses
in Westbury to commemorate her father's work in the parish. By 1911, she had
moved away to Hampstead in West London and was living with one servant in St
James's Mansions, West End Lane. On census night she had a visitor, Lucy Mary
Eagles Harston, aged 61, born in Ireland. At the end of that year Mary died; her
will was proved the following January and probate was granted to Lucy Harston
and Lionel de Courcy Eagles Harston. This may have been Lucy's brother, or else
a son. Mary's effects amounted to just over £14,030.
*(Crittall, 1965: 191; Capes & Drew, 28; Nat.Prob.Calendar for 1912;UK Census
Returns)*

BROWN, Sir William Roger

Founder of the Lady Brown Cottage Homes, Trowbridge
William Roger Brown was born at Bath in about 1831. He began his career
as a clothier, building up from a small business, which he took over in 1853;

*Sir William Roger Brown, from The Illustrated London News 15 June 1889, donor of the new
Jubilee Townhall, Trowbridge (By kind permission of the WSHC, Chippenham)*

eventually, it became the largest business in Trowbridge and Brown invested in
property, both in the town and neighbouring villages. In 1857 he married Sarah
Elizabeth Brown (born in London in 1833) and the following year they moved to
Highfield House in Hilperton. They do not appear to have had any children and
by 1881, they were living in Highfield House with four servants, and at some
point, Sir William bought the manor of Cutteridge, North Bradley. In 1855 he also
built a shooting box at North Bradley, known as Brokerswood House.

Sir William became a JP and did much for Trowbridge, in particular,
building the Town Hall in 1889, the year of Queen Victoria's Golden Jubilee,
which he presented to the town. On the 16 January 1890, he was installed as
a Mason at the Lodge of Concord, number 632, in Trowbridge and there exists
an impressively-bound scrap book of items from his inauguration and from his
first year with the Masonic brotherhood. In 1898 he was made High Sheriff of
Wiltshire. He was also involved in charitable works – founding a local school,
and giving money to the deserving poor, as well as founding the almshouses in
Polebarn Road. A charity in his name still exists today. He died in 1902 and is

buried, with his wife, in a pink granite mausoleum in Trowbridge Cemetery.
(*www.history.Wiltshire.gov.uk; Rogers 1986, 120; WSA 3649/5/2*)

BROWN, Thomas
Founder of Brown's Almshouses, Salisbury
Thomas was a Salisbury man, probably born in about 1783, in the parish of St
Martin. He was a currier by trade and his workshops were in Castle Street. He
lived not far away, further along Castle Street, but outside the limits of the old
City, just inside the Milford area. He never married, but lived comfortably with
two or three servants in a house with coach-house, stable, gardens and a cottage.
In the 1851 Census, he was recorded as a currier, aged 68, living in Milford, with
Hannah Whitlock, a female servant, and Nathaniel Simmends, a servant, who
was also registered as a currier. Twenty years later, in 1871, Hannah was still his
servant and there were Thomas Sheppard and Jessie Marton, servants, and their
address was given as 143 Castle Street, Milford. Thomas made his money by wise
investment and owned at least five other properties in Castle Street, including the
Rising Sun Inn, and there was another property in High Street. At his death, on
18 October 1872, many of his nieces and nephews were beneficiaries of his will
and some of his nephews became trustees for the Almshouse Trust, which he
had set up. Three of his nephews were his executors – Henry Brown, a Salisbury
bookseller, Thomas Brown of Salisbury,
gentleman, and William Pickford, like
his uncle, a Salisbury currier.
(*Nat.Prob.Calendar for 1872; SLHG, 70;
UK Census Returns*)

CHAFYN GROVE, William & Julia Elizabeth
*Founders of the Chafyn Grove Almshouses,
Zeals*
The parents of William and Julia were
William Chafyn Grove and Eleanor
Michell, who were married in 1819
at South Stoneham, Hampshire.
William Chafyn Grove was the son of
another Chafyn Grove, who was MP
for Shaftesbury from 1768-74 and for
Weymouth and Melcombe Regis from
1774-81. His time in parliament was
unremarkable and fairly cursory, but
nevertheless he was painted by the
celebrated portrait painter, George

Julia Elizabeth Chafyn Grove CC

Memorial erected in Mere Church to William Chafyn Grove SMT

Romney; and he served as High Sheriff of Wiltshire in 1784. His son, William, and Eleanor had at least four children: John, born in Hampshire in 1820, Julia Elizabeth, born in East Knoyle in 1825 and Hugh, also born in East Knoyle in 1828. Some sources suggest a Marie, born in 1838, and a Henry, who died in 1862, though these cannot be verified, and there may have been others. William Chafyn Grove, the younger, was probably their last child. He was born in 1840 in Clifton, Bristol. He joined the Wiltshire Rifle Volunteers and served as a Captain. He fought in India and was killed in Poonah, in the Presidency of Bombay, aged 25, on 13 November 1865; his will was proved the following year, when his effects were just under £35,000. There is a memorial to him on the wall of the Chafyn Grove chapel in St Michael's Church, Mere, and a window erected to his memory by his sister.

The family had lived at Zeals House for many years and Julia continued to live there, unmarried, a generous benefactor, both to Zeals and Mere. When a missionary church was decided upon in Mere, it was Julia who provided the site for what became St Matthew's Church, opened in 1882. In 1883, she restored the altar in the south chapel of Mere church. And in the year of her death, she paid for an extension to the National School, now the Grove Building, and gave the playground opposite. She died on 27 November 1891 and by her will left money for a new Church roof and paid for a chaplain for the new church of St Matthew. She also left money to the Dorcas Society of Mere, for the needs of poor women when lying-in. Being childless and having no living siblings, she left Zeals House to a close cousin, George Troyte Bullock, originally of Sedghill, Wiltshire, but later of North Coker in Somerset. George's name is to be found in several of the Chafyn Grove probates and the bulk of Julia's effects went to him.
(*timberlake.webtrees.net; Longbourne, 30, 72, 76, 88, 100, 140; Nat.Prob.Calendar for 1892; familysearch.com*)

CHAUNDLER, John
Co-founder of Trinity Hospital, Salisbury
John Chaundler was a Salisbury citizen and derived his wealth from the textile industry. He was probably born in the 1320s. It is thought that he raised the illegitimate John Swyfte, who later became the chief beneficiary of Chaundler's will and changed his name to that of his foster father. Swyfte became the well-

known Bishop John Chandler of the early 15th century. John Chaundler the elder was granted letters patent in 1394 to found Trinity Hospital, but there is documentary evidence to show that it was already in existence some time prior to this, almost certainly at the instigation of Agnes Bottenham (*vide supra*); and so it is more likely that Chaundler refounded the Hospital, having been the executor of Agnes Bottenham's will. In 1400, Henry IV granted him a licence to assign a number of properties to the master of the Hospital for its upkeep.
(*DNB online; Baker, 376; Parsons, 357*)

COVENTRY, Thomas & William
Co-founders of Devizes New Almshouses
Devizes, long the dower of the Queen consorts of England, was acquired by Henry IV's second wife, Joan of Navarre, in 1405 and she had the Castle renovated and made habitable, living there from 1411-12. The Coventry family oversaw these repairs and alterations. Thomas Coventry was one of this well-established Devizes family who, in the 14th and 15th centuries were closely connected with the churches in Devizes and their chantries. Between them they founded and endowed three chantries in the 15th century and a long-standing charity, the Coventry Dole, arose from the benefaction of the family. Thomas was probably born towards the end of the 14th century, perhaps the son of William Coventry, who was elected Mayor of Devizes in 1388. John, William's son, was Mayor in 1398 and again in 1415; he may have been a brother of Thomas, but there is no evidence for this. There was certainly a William jr., who flourished in the 1420s and 30s, who may well have been Thomas's brother. In 1430, Thomas was elected Mayor of the town. Thomas is known to have founded an almshouse on the north side of St John's church by 1451; it was later known as the 'New Almshouse'. In 1451 he made his will and died soon after. In it, he mentions his wife, Alice, to whom he leaves lands, tenements and gardens, some of which were to sustain Alice herself in her widowhood, but others were for the maintenance of the poor in the almshouses, and it is on condition that Alice maintain ten beds in the almshouse that Thomas leaves her his Devizes lands. On her death, Thomas makes provision for his lands to pass to the Mayor and Corporation, with the same condition attached. Thomas and Alice appear to have had no children, but one of his executors was Thomas Smyth, the son of his friend, William, whose family was also of importance in the town during the next two centuries at least and who were responsible for founding the 'Old Almshouses' in Devizes.
(*will TNA, PROB 11/1; Kite, 250-256; Pugh, 2001: 236*)

DANVERS, Henry, Earl of Danby
Founder of Earl Danby's Almshouses, Dauntsey
Henry was the second son of Sir John Danvers of Dauntsey and the Hon. Elizabeth, daughter of John Neville, 4th Baron Latimer. He was born at Dauntsey in 1563,

Henry Danvers, Earl of Danby, mezzotint by Valentine Green, ca.1638, after van Dyck
© National Portrait Gallery, London

became a page to Sir Philip Sidney, and was probably with the latter at the Battle of Zutphen in 1586, where Sidney was killed. Henry and his brother Charles were both distinguished soldiers. A long-standing feud with the Long family of Draycot Cerne, led to the murder of Henry Long in 1594 and both brothers fled the country. Henry was employed in the service of the French army and returned to Britain via Ireland, where he was very active in military engagements. He was an extremely wealthy man, unmarried, and a public benefactor and bought the extensive and beautiful Cornbury House and Park at Charlbury, Oxfordshire. In Oxford, he bought the site of the Jews' Burying Ground, opposite Magdalen College, and created Oxford's now-famous Botanic Garden on the site. During the Civil War, he sent £3,400 to the king for the Royal cause, but this may well have been a strategy to ensure favour with the king, so that when he, Danvers, died his estate should not pass to his Parliamentary brother. In Oxfordshire, he made himself unpopular. A local landowner accused him of enforcing forest laws and there was a long-standing legal wrangle on the subject. Eventually, Danvers lost the case and ended up in the Fleet Prison and was fined. He died in 1644, aged seventy, and was buried at Dauntsey. He was related to both John Aubrey and George Herbert.

(DNB online; Waylen, 257-8; Jessup,63, 119; Mee,1949:56)

DAUBENY, Archdeacon Charles
Founder of North Bradley Almshouses
Charles was the second son of George Daubeny, a wealthy Bristol merchant. He was educated at a private school in Norton St.Phillip and was Head Boy at Winchester. But following a bout of severe illness in his youth, he remained frail all his life. He graduated from New College, Oxford, and became Fellow there. When his father died, he inherited a fortune. His poor health drove him to spend some time abroad, taking the waters, and in 1771 came under the influence of the Princess Dashkow and was presented at Court at St Petersburg, where he studied Greek Catholicism. He returned to England in 1772 and was ordained the following year, being offered the College living of North Bradley soon

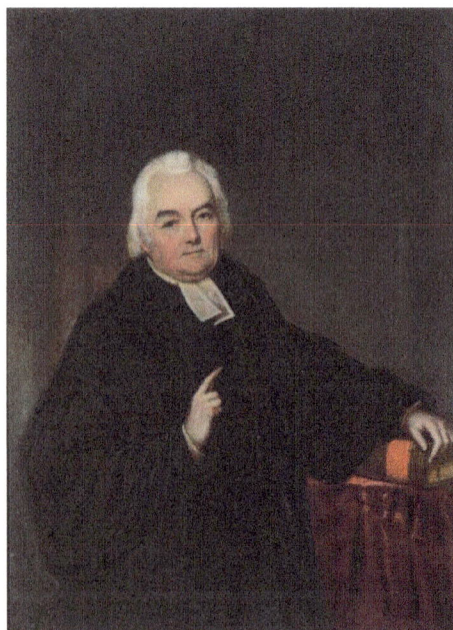

Archdeacon Charles Daubeny, Maul & Paulbank, after miniature by Jagger (Internet image from Christies sale catalogue,2005; further provenance not found)

after. He married Elizabeth Barnston and they lived at Clifton until the vicarage at North Bradley was in a fit state of repair. There followed four children, two sons, George and Henry, and two daughters, Elizabeth and Mary. Despite poor health, he restored the church, rebuilt the vicarage and started a Sunday School in Rode, which was then in the parish of North Bradley. He also founded the first Free School at Walcot in Bath. He went abroad again for his health and was in Versailles at the outbreak of the French Revolution. In 1804, he became Archdeacon of Sarum and much of his time was given to literary work. In 1808 he suffered a paralytic stroke, but continued to devote his remaining energies to his flock. He built the almshouses, supervised the Poorhouse and contributed towards the church at Rode. His wife predeceased him and he died in 1827, being buried in Christchurch at Rode, now in Somerset, where there is a monument to him. The church is now redundant and is used as the home and workshop of a violin dealer and repairer, Andrew Hooker (2014).
(DNB online)

Grave of Archdeacon Daubeny SMT

Memorial to Charles Daubeny in Christchurch, Rode. SMT

DAUNTSEY, Alderman William
Founder of Alderman Dauntsey's Almshouses, West Lavington

Born about 1480, William was the youngest son of Sir John Dauntsey, esq. of West Lavington, and his wife Margery, and was apprenticed to a liveryman of the London Mercers' Company. In 1504, he married Agnes Tenacres, the step-daughter of his master. He rose quickly in esteem in the City and in 1522

purchased the lease of the manor of Lavington Bayntun in Market Lavington, from Sir Edward Bayntun. He made further acquisitions in Enford and Tidworth and in 1527 acquired the lordship of the manor of Kennington in Surrey. He survived a brush with religious reform, the Mercers' Company having a number of Lutheran cells within its ranks, and he was elected Sheriff of London in 1530-31 and Alderman of Faringdon Without in 1535. He undertook much trade across the Channel and became a merchant of the Staple in Calais. There were no children of his marriage and his wife predeceased him. He died in 1543 and was buried in the Church of St Antholin, Budge Row, in the City of London.
(DNB online)

EYLES, Sir John
Founder of Eyles' Almshouses, Devizes
The son of John Eyles, mercer, woolstapler (and shopkeeper in Devizes from 1640 until his death in 1662), and his wife Mary. The younger John carved a career for himself in London, though there are no records of his life there. He became an agent and broker for the sugar and slave trades to Barbados and acquired the principal farming of the alnage (the assize of woollen cloth). At various times he was an Alderman of London, Lord Mayor of the City, a JP for Wiltshire, Deputy Lieutenant for the County and MP for Devizes. He was a Whig collaborator in James II's reign and was knighted in 1687. He married Sarah Cowper and they had two sons and five daughters. He acquired an estate in Southbroom, Devizes, where he probably spent some of his time when not in London, and he seems to have kept in contact with his old home town, for in 1670, he gave £60 and a house for the poor of Devizes St John's. However, John appears to have been a strict Baptist and when he drew up his will in 1703, he left considerable sums to the Baptist church, both in Devizes and London. He died the same year and was buried in the family vault at St Helen's Church, Bishopsgate.
(DNB online; www.historyofparliamentonline.org; will TNA, PROB 11/470; Phillipps, 365)

EYRE, Christopher
Founder of Eyre's Almshouses, Salisbury
The inscription on Christopher's monuments reads:
In ye Parish Church of St Stevens, in Coleman Street, London lieth Buried ye Body of Mr Christopher Eyre, 4th Sonne of ye Worthy Thos. Eyre, Esq., Alderman of this Cittie, who Attained Prosperously to be an East India Merchant Adventurer, and Committee of ye Honourable company of ye East India Merchants, & Upper Warden of ye Worthy Company of Leathersellers, & one of ye Common Councell of ye Honourable Cittie of London, & Also to this Cittie for ye erecting of an Almeshouse in this Cittie, and Maintenance Thereof for ever, & for A weekly Lecture in this Parishe for ever. & being of ye Age of 47 Years, Departed this

Christopher and Esther Eyre, St Thomas's Church, Salisbury SMT

Life in ye Year of God Hating Idolatry. His late Loving Wife, Daughter of George Smithes, Alderman of ye Honourable Cittie of London erected this & ye Opposite Monument according to his Will.

Christopher was the fourth son of Thomas Eyre (a Salisbury Alderman) and his wife, Elizabeth Rogers, who had fifteen children. He was born in 1577 and baptised in St Thomas's Church, Salisbury, in 1578. The family lived at what is now 31 Cheesemarket. It was sold to Robert Eyre in 1541, together with a garden, separated from it by the river behind. It was originally a modest town house, but a later family member, Sir Samuel Eyre, the heir of Margaret Blechynden (vide supra), built a large house in its back garden (29 Cheesemarket) and drove a carriageway through the ground floor of the old house. Christopher became an Alderman of the City of Salisbury but spent most of his working life in London, for that was where prosperity lay, Salisbury's heyday being now over. In 1603 he married Hester (or Esther) Smithes, the daughter of a London Alderman. He became a Merchant Adventurer and was a co-Founder of the East India Company; he was an Upper Warden of the Leathersellers' Company and a member of the City of London Common Council. He died in the City in 1624 and was buried in the Church of St Stephen Coleman. There is an elaborate monument to Christopher and his wife in the north corner of the Lady Chapel of St Thomas's

Church in Salisbury and another to his parents in the south corner. Both were moved from the chancel some time during the 19th century.
(Crittall, 1962: 169; monument in St Thomas's Church, Salisbury; will TNA, PROB 11/145; RCHM, 59)

FANE DE SALIS, William & Emily
Founders of Teffont Evias Almshouses

William Fane de Salis, and Emily Fane de Salis (neé Mayne) (Internet images)

William Andreas Salicus Salis was born in Marylebone in 1812, the third son of Jerome, Count de Salis-Soglio. His father was, by all accounts, a colourful character, 'an Anglo-Grison-Irish noble, visionary, vegetarian and landowner'. Jerome married three times, his third wife being the mother of William. She was Henrietta Foster, the daughter of an Irish cleric and she and Jerome were married in St Thomas's Church, Dublin, in 1810. She had nine children by Jerome, of whom William was the second. The couple must have travelled a great deal, since the children were born variously in Dublin, London, Florence, Paris, Bath and Pisa. In 1809, Jerome received a licence from the King, allowing him to use the title of Count of the Holy Roman Empire and sometimes William, too, is entitled 'Count', though he never inherited the title. Jerome and Henrietta lived at Dawley Court, Hillingdon, and are buried in ornate tombs in the church of SS Peter and Paul, Harlington, West London. William, known later as William Fane de Salis, was a businessman, a colonialist and a barrister, being called to the

The tombs of Jerome and Henrietta de Salis, the parents of William Fane de Salis, in the sanctuary of St Peter's Church, Harlington, Middlesex JS

Right-hand side of a triptych, commemorating members of the de Salis family, St Peter's Church, Harlington. William's and Emily's names are on the right-hand panel. JS (Courtesey of Rev.Marian Smith)

Bar in 1836. He then worked at the Inner Temple, the Court at Northampton and that at Nottingham. He followed his brother Leopold to Australia for some time, establishing a firm in the wool industry. He returned to England and became involved in the Grand Junction Canal Company. He was Chairman or Director of various institutions and, in 1859, married Emily Mayne of Teffont Evias. Having lived at various locations about London, William and Emily settled in Teffont Manor, both dying, childless, in August 1896, within ten days of each other. They were buried with the rest of the de Salis family in St Peter's Church.
(R. de Salis, 2003; R. de Salis, 1934; Burke, 1976; Skinner, 1830)

FOWLER, Rachel
Founder of the Fowler Almshouses, Melksham
Born in 1797, Rachel Fowler was a Quaker and a member of a prominent business family in Melksham and for much of her life lived at 1 Bank Street, now a chemists and community Health Centre (2013).

She was, by all accounts, a dominant, and determined spinster lady, who, despite her belonging to the Society of Friends, recognised the importance of other Christian churches, particularly those within the town of Melksham. One of Rachel's family members, John Fowler, born 1826, was an engineer and the inventor of the steam plough. As well as founding her almshouses, Rachel also

New Hall, Market Place, Melksham   SMT

Rachel Fowler SMT
By kind permission of the Rachel Fowler
Centre, Melksham

Top part of Rachel Fowler's gravestone SMT
Rachel Fowler Centre

Rachel Fowler's home is believed to have been the central part of this building. SMT built and gave to the town of Melksham a New Hall, for meetings of a non-political nature, reading and lectures.

She was buried in the Quaker churchyard in King Street, the building recently occupied by the Melksham Spiritual Church. The Church presented the stone from her grave to the Rachel Fowler Centre.
(*www.rachelfowlercentre.org*)

FOX, Sir Stephen

Founder of Sir Stephen Fox's Hospital, Farley

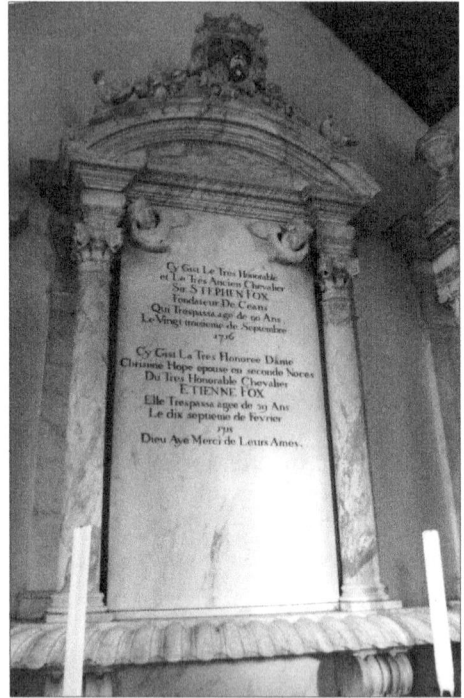

Sir Stephen Fox's memorial stone, written in French, in Farley Church SMT

Born at Farley, Wiltshire, in 1627, he was the seventh son of William Fox and his wife, Elizabeth Pavey, a very modest family, who could not afford to send their son to university or to Law School. But he became a member of the Salisbury Choir School, paid for by an uncle. He then followed his brother John to Court as a pageboy, (John's place being recommended by the Dean of Salisbury) finding favour during the years of the Civil War, serving the Prince of Wales at home and in the Netherlands. On his return to England, he married Elizabeth, daughter of William Whittle of London and they had nine children. He saw service with the Duke of Devonshire and built up his estates and wealth with a balanced portfolio of investments. He became the longest-serving Treasury commissioner of the age. He stood for Parliament on numerous occasions, representing Salisbury, Westminster and Cricklade. In 1655 he was knighted and three years later was granted arms and some estates in Hampshire. In 1668, the diarist, John Evelyn, dined with Fox and later wrote of him: 'He is believed to be worth at the least £200,000 honestly gotten, and unenvied, which is next to miracle, and that with all this he still continues as humble and ready to do a courtesy as ever he was; nay, he is very generous, and lives very honourably, of a sweet nature, wellspoken and well-bred, and so very highly in his Majesty's esteem and useful that being long since made a knight, he is also advanced to be one of the lords commissioners of the Treasury. .. In a word, never was man more fortunate than Sir Stephen; and with all this he is an handsome person, virtuous and very religious, and for whom I have an extraordinary esteem'.

Elizabeth died in 1696, in her seventieth year and Stephen, then well-advanced in years, married a second time to Christine Hope from Lincolnshire, a much younger wife, and produced a further four children. Stephen died in 1716, aged ninety, and was buried in Farley Church.
(*DNB online; www.historyofparliamentonline.org*)

FROWD, Edward
Founder of Frowd's Hospital, Salisbury
Edward Frowd considered himself to be of the parish of St Bartholomew in the City of London, though he originally came from Salisbury and remembered his home town in his will, requesting to be buried in the family vault in the churchyard of St Edmund's parish church. He was a wealthy lace merchant, one of his bequests being to his manservant, to whom he bequeathed a stock of Mechlin and Brussells lace, as well as a monetary gift. When not in London, he had a house and estate in Mitcham in Surrey, where his property and household goods included a diamond ring, a gold watch, silver plate, a 'chariott' and a team of horses, all of which was to be sold to raise some £8,000 for his bequests. £1,000 of this was to allow poor children to be apprenticed and a further £7,000 was to be used for the establishment of his almshouse. This was not built until the 1770s, following Chancery proceedings from the disputed will, although the will itself was proved in 1720. Frowd died in 1720 and was buried in St Edmund's Church, Salisbury, with his father, mother, brothers, sister and a niece, his one remaining sister, Lydia Guest, surviving him. It is interesting to note an entry in the London Gazette of March 1723 which announces that, pursuant to a decree in the High Court of Chancery, the sale of 'a parcel of Flanders Lace', late the goods of 'Edward Frowd of London', is to take place on 12 March at 5.0 p.m. One wonders whether this was the stock of lace originally bequeathed to his manservant, which had to be sold to meet the expenses of other bequests.
(*will: TNA, PROB 11/574; London Gazette, 5 March 1723*)

GROBHAM, Sir Richard
Founder of Grobham Cottages, Great Wishford
Richard Grobham was born in 1551 and in 1602 married Margaret, the daughter of William Whitmore, esq., of London. Richard was steward to Sir Thomas Gorges of Longford; Sir Thomas wished to build a new mansion there, demolished the old building and began a new one. He was Governor of Hurst Castle at the time of the Spanish Armada and his wife begged of the Queen the wreck of a Spanish galleon. This was granted and the hold was found to be full of silver bars. The value was enough to complete the edifice at Longford and to enrich Gorges' steward, Richard Grobham, who then procured a knighthood for himself. Sir Richard died in 1629, a very wealthy man, leaving a fortune which almost matched that of his master. He was buried at Great Wishford, where he was Lord

Sir Richard Grobham, Great Wishford   JAT

of the Manor. Sir Richard is said to have been the last man to hunt and kill a wild boar in Groveley Forest and his monument shows him with his feet resting on a gilded boar's head.

(information from text at side of monument in Great Wishford Church; Mee,1964: 95)

HALL, John

Founder of Hall's Almshouses, Bradford on Avon

The Halls were a prominent family at Bradford-on-Avon from the 12th to the 18th centuries. The first recorded Hall was the town miller and the family kept control of the mills on the River Avon. John, the last of the line, was the son of Sir Thomas Hall who was born in 1601 and married Katharine Seymour, daughter of Sir Edward Seymour of Berry Pomeroy Castle, Devon. Thomas was a Royalist, knighted for his support of the king but forced to compound for his estates in 1647. He died in 1663. John was born about 1630 and in 1670 married Susan Cox of Wells, Somerset. The same year he was Sheriff of Wiltshire. His father's title was not inheritable. His second marriage was to Elizabeth Thynne, sister of Thomas Thynne of Longleat, a rake nick-named 'Tom o' Ten Thousand' because of his wealth. Although Thomas Thynne married Elizabeth Percy, daughter of the Duke of Northumberland, he died childless when he was murdered in 1682 in Pall Mall. John Hall as his executor was left Monkton House, Broughton Gifford, and erected a monument to him in Westminster Abbey. He died in 1710 and his various estates were left to Rachel Baynton of Little Chalfield, aged 15, thought to have been his illegitimate daughter. In 1711, the year of probate, she married William Pierrepont, later 1st Duke of Kingston. The descendants of John Hall's sister Bridget, who married William Coward of Wells, Somerset disputed the will but it was confirmed by a Special Act of Parliament.

(P.Slocombe, 8-9)

HASTINGS, Rev.J.D.

Founder of the Union Street Almshouses, Trowbridge

During the second quarter of the nineteenth century, St James's Church in Trowbridge was found to be in a parlous and dangerous state of repair. The Rector, Francis Fulford, made some rash and unpopular moves towards the building of a new church, but it was to be his successor, the Reverend John David Hastings, who raised almost £7000 to restore and partly rebuild the church, beginning in 1846. John Hastings was born in 1801 in Melksham. His incumbency at Trowbridge was to be a long one, from 1841 to 1869 and during this time he not only restored the church, but also built the National Schools and adjoining cottages, opened up the churchyard and widened Church Street. By 1856, Hastings was Rural Dean. Before he

Rev.J.D.Hastings
(By kind permission of Michael Marshman)

died, Hastings bought the gift of the living from the Duke of Rutland, who then owned it, and presented it to the Church Patronage Society; this ensured that the church was served by rectors with an evangelical leaning and set the tone of the clergy for many years to come, even into the 20th century. He died in April 1869 and Letters of Administration were granted to his widow Ellen. He is buried in a fine mausoleum in Trowbridge Cemetery.

(Rogers 1984: 99; Crockfords)

Sarah Hayter's memorial, Salisbury Cathedral   SMT
(by kind permission of the Dean & Chapter)

HAYTER, Sarah
Founder of Hayter's Almshouses, Fisherton Anger

The Hayter Almshouses were founded on a family's wealth and a manor, all descending on a sole unmarried daughter. Sarah Hayter was descended, on her mother's side, from the old-established Harris family of Salisbury. James Harris was an early occupant of the house in The Close, later known as Malmesbury House and his son, also James, was a well-known leader of musical festivals and concerts in the City. James the younger inherited Malmesbury House in 1733 and is believed to have entertained Handel there.

His son, a third James, became the 1st Earl of Malmesbury. Sarah's grandfather was William Harris, almost certainly a cousin of the second James Harris, (in his will, James refers to his 'kinsman William Harris of The Close') and her mother, also Sarah, was born to William and his wife, Frances, in about 1726. The family lived in Symondsburgh House in The Close, now The Deanery, though it may have been the same William Harris who owned 17 The Close until his death in 1746. In 1747, the manor of Fisherton Anger came into Frances' hands, as William's relict; it had descended to her from the Ashley family, Gabriel Ashley having married the first James Harris's aunt, Margaret Harris. In due course, this descended to Frances' younger daughter, Sarah. This Sarah also inherited a considerable fortune from William Pinckney, her maternal grandfather, which descended, along with the manor of Fisherton Anger, to her daughter, Sarah. Sarah Harris, the younger, married firstly William Hayter of Hayes in Kent in 1746 and they had two children, William and Sarah. A branch of the Hayter family occupied Mompesson House in The Close throughout the 18th century, though how they were related to William is not obvious. When William Hayter sr. died, his widow married Henry Southby from Hampshire. Her son by her first marriage inherited the manor of Fisherton Anger, but died in about 1797, insolvent and insane. His sister, Sarah Hayter, succeeded to the estate in 1797 as the sole heir and together with her mother's inheritance, she thereby had adequate funds for the foundation of her almshouses in Fisherton Anger. She died in 1822 and was buried in the north transept of Salisbury Cathedral. (Pugh, 1962: 194; wills TNA, PROB 11/805, 362, 647, 138, 361, 750 & 471; RCHM 1993,98-109, 131, 162)

James Harris, the younger, from his memorial stone, Salisbury Cathedral SMT (by kind permission of the Dean & Chapter)

HOWELL, John
Founder of Howell's Almshouses, North Wraxall

John Howell was born in North Wraxall in 1776. He began life as an assistant to a bookseller in Bath, but then moved on to Harding's linen drapery firm in Pall Mall. There he became a lace buyer and eventually a partner in the firm of Howell & James. By the early 1820s, he owned his own shop in Regent Street, lately built by Nash. It sold all kinds of haberdashery and material furnishings, silk, furs and lace. In 1825, John Howell bought the lease of 10, Charles Street, Westminster, which backed onto his Regent Street premises. During the next decade, Howell employed an eminent architect, J.B.Papworth, to renovate and redecorate both buildings and eventually the two premises were made to connect. By 1847, Howell had expanded the business to include millinery and dresses for court- and ball-wear, and even jewellery and perfumes. He died in 1872. (Whitlock, 33; Sheppard,159, 289)

HUNGERFORD, Lady Margaret
Founder of the Hungerford Almshouses, Corsham

Margaret was the daughter of Alderman William Halliday, a wealthy London merchant, from whom she inherited a vast amount of money; she was also step-daughter of the Earl of Warwick at that time. William was chairman of the

Lady Margaret (Halliday) Hungerford, from her tomb at Farleigh Hungerford Castle Chapel
SMT

East India Company and married Susannah, daughter of Henry Rowe, (of the Worshipful Company of Ironmongers and later Lord Mayor of London). William and Susannah had two daughters, Anne and Margaret, the latter being born about 1603. In 1621 Margaret married Sir Edward Hungerford and they took up residence in Corsham House, now Corsham Court. Sir Edward was, in turn, the owner of a great deal of land and property in Wiltshire, London, Somerset and Berkshire and commanded Cromwell's troops during the Civil War. When he died in 1648, he left Margaret a wealthy, childless widow and she used her money for the benefit of the poor and destitute, building a school and almshouses in Corsham. She died in 1673 and was buried next to her husband in the chapel of Farleigh Hungerford Castle. The elaborate tomb, erected over both of them, between 1658 and 1665, may have been designed by Lady Margaret herself, costing the then huge sum of £1,100.
(Thomson, 2011: 1; Kightly, 26-7; Hird, 1997; Badeni, 30, 33)

HUNGERFORD, Lady Margaret (nee Botreaux)
Refounder and endower of St John's Hospital, Heytesbury
Margaret, daughter and eventually sole heiress of William, Lord Botreaux, was born about 1410. By 1421 she was married to Robert, 2nd Lord Hungerford when a modest jointure was made over to her. They produced three sons and

two daughters. Their eldest son, Robert, was wounded and captured during the battle of Châtillon in 1453, and his parents mortgaged much of their estate in securing his ransom and release. Robert died in 1459 and Margaret endowed the almshouses in Heytesbury which her father in law, Sir Walter Hungerford, had founded, in honour of him and of her husband. However, in re-establishing the statutes of the almshouse, she deviated considerably form the original plans and wishes of her father in law.

Her innovations were no doubt due to her extreme piety; she even banned married men from taking up vacancies in the almshouse. It would appear that she wanted to model the

Seal of Margaret Botreaux
(By kind permission of the WSHC, Chippenham)

establishment on Christ and his Apostles. She it was who ordained that the almsmen were to wear white gowns with badges bearing the initials JHU.XRT

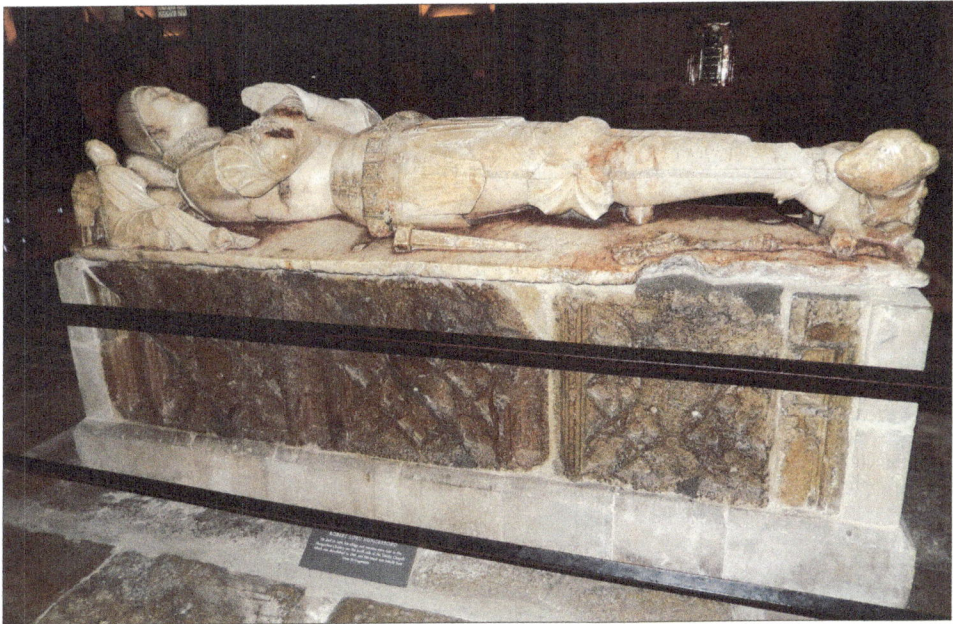

Robert, 2nd Lord Hungerford, husband of Margaret Botreaux   SMT
(By kind permission of the Dean and Chapter, Salisbury Cathedral)

Margaret Hungerford's signature, from her will of 1476 SMT (By kind permission of the WSHC, Chippenham)

(Jesus Christ) in black. She died in 1478 and was buried in the Chapel of the Annunciation in Salisbury Cathedral, along with her husband; but when the chapel was later reorganised and the monuments re-sited, her tomb was lost. Robert's now stands in the nave.
(DNB online; Hicks, 62-9)

HUNGERFORD, Sir Walter, 1st Baron

Founder of St John's Hospital, Heytesbury

Sir Walter Hungerford was born in 1378, the son of Sir Thomas Hungerford and his wife, Joan, and early on showed prowess in the tournament; he is known to have defeated a French knight in 1406 during negotiations at Leulingham. He rose to be a first-class statesman and, among other things, Speaker of the House of Commons. A steward in the household of Henry V, he fought at Agincourt in 1415 and it was he to whom was attributed the wish that he might have 'ten thousand of the best archers in England who would have been only too glad to be there'; to which the king replied that God would overcome the French with 'these His humble few'. He was made a Knight of the Garter in 1421 and was raised to the Peerage in 1426. During Henry's reign and the minority of Henry

*Tomb of Walter and Catherine Hungerford, Salisbury Cathedral   SMT
(By kind permission of the Dean and Chapter, Salisbury Cathedral)*

VI, Hungerford was a prominent ambassador. He was named in Henry V's will as a trustee and an executor. In 1428, he became Treasurer of England.

With his wealth, he founded and endowed a chantry chapel in Salisbury Cathedral, with two chantry houses in the Close, where the chantry priests could live. He died in 1449 and was buried with his first wife, Catherine Peverell, in Salisbury Cathedral, within his iron chantry, but later, their tomb was moved to the south aisle. As well as the Hospital of St John and St Katherine at Heytesbury, Walter founded a total of four chantries and two obits, and was admitted to the confraternity of the Cathedral in 1413. However, he failed to obtain the required licence for endowing his foundation at Heytesbury and it remained to his daughter in law, Margaret, (vide supra) to finally achieve this.
(Martin, 5-7; Curry, 77, 167; Hicks, 62-9; RCHM 1993, 213)

Alderman William Hussey
(by kind permission of Salisbury Guildhall)

HUSSEY, William
Founder of Hussey's Almshouses, Salisbury

William Hussey came from a wealthy, west country family. His father, John, married as his second wife, Margery, the widow of Richard Rumsey of Salisbury. Their son, William, was baptised in Salisbury in 1725, and in 1737 John became Mayor of the City of Salisbury. William eventually inherited considerable wealth from his father and set up as a Salisbury clothier. He entered fully into the life of the City and became a Councillor, an Alderman and eventually Mayor in 1758. From 1774 until his death, he represented Salisbury in Parliament. He married firstly, in 1752, Mary, the daughter of John Eyre of Landford Lodge. In 1758, he married Jane, the daughter of Robert Marsh, a London merchant and sometime Governor of the Bank of England, and they had one son and one daughter. William built a fine house with a large bay window in New Street and today it bears a City Blue Plaque. He died in 1813 and is buried in St George's, West Harnham.
(www.historyofparliamentonline.org)

JENNER, Robert

Founder of Jenner's Almshouses, Malmesbury

Robert Jenner was born in London about 1584 and became a Citizen and a goldsmith of the City of London. He was made a warden, a freeman and an assistant of the Gold and Silver Wiredrawers Companies at various times and by 1614 was responsible for the purchase of silver bullion from the Cumbrian silver mines. The purchase of gold and silver for the wiredrawing trade was held responsible for the economic crisis of the 1620s and its use was banned; in a short time, Jenner was arrested, as it was suspected that he had contravened the ban. However, it seemed to have little effect on his

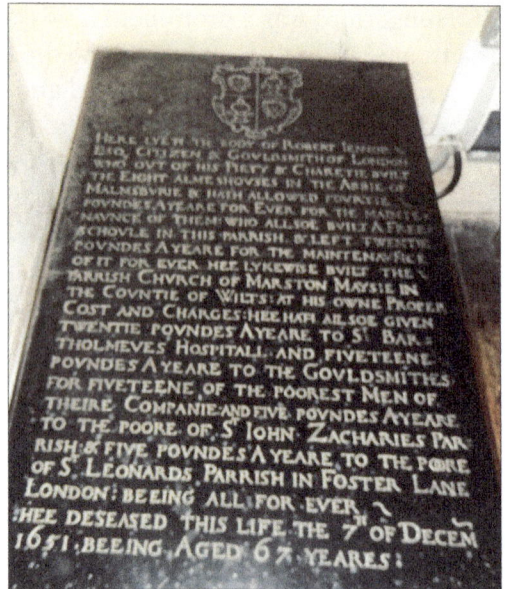

Tomb of Robert Jenner in St Sampsons Church, Cricklade SMT

career. By 1627, he had acquired the manor of Widhill, Cricklade, Wiltshire, and on the basis of this, was elected to represent Cricklade in Parliament the following year. He was twice elected in 1640 and continued to be active in the House of Commons during the 1640s, though his house was plundered by Royalist forces during this time; he was in the Short Parliament, but was secluded by Prides Purge of 1648. He married Elizabeth, the daughter of Thomas Longston, a Citizen and grocer of London, though they do not appear to have

The grave of Dr John Kent in St Nicholas' Church, Boscombe SMT

had any surviving children. At his death in 1651, Robert left money for eight almshouses in Malmesbury and a Free School in Cricklade. He was buried in St Sampson's Church, Cricklade, where there is a large, black, tomb inscribed to his memory in the north aisle.

(will TNA, PROB 11/219; Thomson, 1961: 55, 79, 146,147; www. historyofparliamentonline.org)

KENT, John

Founder of Kent's Almshouses, Boscombe

John Kent was the eldest of eight children born to Robert and Dorothie

Kent. The children were all baptised in Winterbourne Dauntsey church, so it is assumed they were born in the village. John was baptised in 1626, his parents probably marrying around 1624 or 25. It is not known what the family's status was, but the manor of East Boscombe was sold to one William Kent in 1628 by Simon Clifford, whose family had held it for over one hundred years. It passed to William's son, William, a royalist in the Civil War, and then to his son, another William, who in about 1675 sold it to his cousin, John Kent, who held it until his death in 1710. John probably lived in the large mansion house called Boscombe House, which was sited on the east of the village. This house was described as having a large saloon and hall in 1768, with four parlours, eighteen bedrooms, gardens and a bowling green. It was demolished in about 1770, but the outlines of some of the remains could still be seen in the early 1990s. John Kent never married and left no children; so in his will, drawn up in 1707, he left all his real and personal estate to his nephews, nieces, cousins and servants, with the manor of Boscombe going to his brother's son, John, and his farm (called in his will 'Snellsdayes and Haylestones livings') to John's brother, Robert. John senior must have been a fairly wealthy man, having lent money to various relatives at different times in his life; these debts he cancelled in his will, making the loans into gifts, some of which were to be distributed to the children of his debtors. He asked to be buried, if possible, in Boscombe church, and his grave remains today in the floor of the north chancel, where a memorial to him reads:

H.S.E.

Johannis Kent, Armigeri,

Obiit xi die Aprilis

Anno{ Dom.}1710

{Aetat.} 84

Arms: A lion statant guardant, a chief ermine.

(will TNA, PROB 11/515; www.ancestry.co.uk; Stevenson, 57)

LAVERTON, Abraham

Founder of the Laverton Almshouses, Westbury

William Laverton and his wife, Penelope Davis, had ten children, the last but one of whom was Abraham. He was born in Trowbridge in 1819, where his father, who had been born in Shepton Mallet, Somerset, was a master weaver. Abraham must have learned the craft from his father, for, after an education in one of the Trowbridge schools, he went to work in the cloth mills of that town. Eventually, he leased Angel Mill in Westbury and built up his business from there. He never married and his spinster sister, Charlotte, kept house for him for most of his life. He lived first in Westbury House, in the centre of the town, and later in Farleigh Castle, where he died, having spent almost forty years in Westbury. For that town, he became an MP and a JP, a local figure and benefactor, providing furnishings for the church, building a public baths (still in use today) and a

Abraham Laverton SMT
(By kind permission of The Laverton
Centre, Westbury)

boys' school (now a pottery). As well as the almshouses, he built a community hall, The Laverton Hall, still in use by the Town Council of Westbury. His considerable wealth was built up through the cloth industry. He died in 1886 and his funeral at Westbury was a local event. A notice in the Wiltshire Times called him ' A remarkable instance of a self-made man' and went on to extol his virtues of tenacity and perseverance. He was buried in Westbury Cemetery.
(Laverton, 2011)

LOUVAIN, Adeliza of, wife of Henry I

Founder of St Giles Hospital, Wilton

Adeliza was the daughter of Geoffrey I, Count of Louvain, and Ida of Namur. She was born about 1103 and married, firstly, Henry I of England, as his second wife, his first wife, Matilda of Scotland, having died in 1118. Adeliza was known to chroniclers as the 'Fair Maid of Brabant'. She was too young to assist in ruling, but was present at several councils and played no small part in royal administration. She was the first example of an English queen receiving 'Queen's Gold', a proportion of a tax of an extra 10% on any fine to the Crown. Adeliza received many lands during her time as queen, lands in Waltham and Queenhithe and estates in Essex, Hertfordshire, Bedfordshire, Middlesex, Gloucestershire and Devonshire. She was also given the whole county of Shropshire and the rape of Arundel, which included the Castle. There were no children of her first marriage and Henry died in 1135. Adeliza retired, temporarily, to Wilton Abbey and it was about this time that she founded St Giles Hospital there. She also founded leper hospitals at Arundel and Castle Rising. In 1139, she married William d'Aubigny, one of Henry's chief advisers, and had at least seven children

Adeliza de Louvain
(Internet image)

by him. In September 1139, the Empress Matilda was left in her care at Arundel Castle, while her brother, Robert Earl of Gloucester rode off to Wallingford and Bristol to raise support for his sister's cause. While Robert was away, King Stephen marched on Arundel and frightened Queen Adeliza into surrendering the Empress to him, though he promised that the Empress would have safe conduct to Bristol. Adeliza held the county of Shropshire from the time of her marriage until her death and it was supposedly on account of this that no earl was created for that county. She died in 1151 and was buried in Affligem Abbey, Brabant.
(*DNB online; Davis 37-8, 140; www.livingthehistoryelizabethchadwick.blogspot.co.uk 2014*)

LUCAS, Ann
One of the founders of Mere Almshouses
Little is known of Ann, except that she was the daughter of James Lucas and was baptised in St Michael's Church, Mere, on 20 April 1620 and was buried in the same place, 15 April 1638. There were three other known children, the eldest, Thomas, being the only one to survive to adulthood. Their mother, Elizabeth, died at the beginning of 1629 and their father in 1635. Ann must have had some independent means, since she was able to leave £5 for the poor of Mere, of which £4 went towards the building of the almshouses and the remaining £1 was distributed among the poor at her funeral.
(*Mere Parish Book; Mere parish registers*)

LYTE, Isaac
Founder of Lyte's Almshouses, Kington St Michael
By his own admission, Isaac Lyte was born about 1620 in Kington St Michael, though the baptismal register gives the date of his baptism as 26 December 1612, the son of 'Nycolas, gent., Alderman of London, born at Easton Piercy, founder of the almshouses'. There was another brother, Benjamin, baptised on the same day, though whether he was a twin of Isaac is not known; and there were at least two sisters. Isaac was educated at the Merchant Taylors School, but his progress into London business is not known. He was a skinner by trade and eventually became a citizen of the City of London and in 1666 an Alderman, while the following year saw him made a Master of his craft. In 1647 he married Elizabeth Hadley, the daughter of George Hadley and Elizabeth White, at St Laurence Jewry, in the City, and they seem to have lived most of their married life in St Mary Aldermanbury. There were at least seven children of the marriage, three of whom are known to have died in infancy. Isaac made his will in 1672 and died later that year, or early in 1673. At the time, he was living in Mortlake, Surrey, but in his will he remembered the place where he was born and left £600 for the founding of the almshouses there. He also owned a great deal of

property in Brickinghall, Lincolnshire, most of which he left to his two unmarried daughters Elizabeth and Ann. The Lyte family is a confusing one, because there were a number of Isaacs during the 17th century, including the antiquarian John Aubrey's grandfather, who died about four years before this Isaac and who was buried in the nave of Kington St Michael church. Another Isaac Lyte, gent., was buried in Kington church in February 1659/60. Isaac, the founder of the almshouses, mentions in his will a cousin Lyte at Lytes Cary in Somerset, which is where the family originated, but the connection with Aubrey's Grandfather Lyte is not at present known.
(will TNA, PROB 11/342; Boyd's, 9840; Kington St Michael parish registers)

MOMPESSON, Susan
Founder of the Almshouse, Deptford
The Mompesson family appear to have lived in the Wylye Valley since at least the mid-15th century, when John Mompesson, a Lancastrian sympathiser, twice represented Wilton in Parliament. Susan was his great granddaughter, the sister of Anne, Mary, Elizabeth and Edmund Mompesson; their parents were John (the son of Drewe) and Alice Mompesson. Edmund, who remained on the county justice system from the age of twenty-one until his death in 1553, was born about 1511 and inherited the Great Bathampton estate from his father, who died about the same time. Susan remained a spinster and eventually inherited Little Bathampton Manor, now known as Ballington Manor, in 1556, which, in her will she devised to her cousin once removed, Thomas Mompesson. His son and heir was the notorious politician and extortioner, Giles Mompesson. Ballington Manor house was largely rebuilt in the early 18th century, but has a reset stone bearing the inscription 'SM 1580' and there are beams inside the house considerably earlier than the 18th century. Susan Mompesson founded her almshouse at Deptford sometime before her death in 1583.
(will TNA, PROB 11/66; Crowley, 1995: 193, 195-6, 305; Thornton, 42, 43)

NEELD, Joseph
Founder of Neeld's Almshouses, Leigh Delamere
Joseph Neeld was born in 1789, one of five sons of Joseph Neeld, a London solicitor, and Mary Bond, his wife. They lived in Hendon on the north-west outskirts of the City. Joseph junior became a barrister at the Inner Temple and in 1828 inherited substantial wealth from his great uncle, a silversmith. Young Joseph had looked after his uncle for thirteen years and his reward was well-deserved. He bought Grittleton Manor in Wiltshire and married Lady Caroline Ashley Cooper, daughter of the 6th Earl of Shaftesbury in 1831. However, Joseph already had an illegitimate daughter by a Frenchwoman and it is thought that he wanted to bring her into his new household. But his new bride objected and the

Joseph Neeld, ca. 1825, by Sir Francis Leggatt Chantrey
(© National Portrait Gallery, London)

fate of the marriage was sealed, almost before it had begun, and the couple were legally separated. Joseph had no legitimate heirs. He rebuilt Grittleton Manor in Victorian Gothic style and filled it with antiques and paintings. But he was a great philanthropist; he built the Town Hall at Chippenham, houses for his tenants in Grittleton, a church at Leigh Delamere and, of course, the almshouses in the latter parish. He was MP for Gatton in Surrey in 1830, and for Chippenham from 1832 until 1856, when he died. He left his property to his brother John, who became a baronet and was High Sheriff of Wiltshire in 1872.
(www.historyofparliament.ac.uk)

PALMER, Brig.G.L.
Founder of Palmer's Almshouses, Trowbridge
George Llewellyn Palmer was born on 12 March 1857, probably in Bradford on Avon, the only son of Michael Palmer and Mary Ann Bates, his wife. Michael was a cloth manufacturer and George was to follow him into the business. By the time George was born, Michael and his family were living in Berryfield House, Bradford on Avon. George was educated at Harrow and his military attachment came through the Wiltshire Yeomanry, where he rose to the rank

Brigadier George Llewellyn Palmer (Courtesy of T.Pratt, Wiltshire College, Lackham) from Dorling, 1906

of Brigadier-General, though it is unlikely that he was ever deployed. On 21 September 1881, George married Louie Madeleine Gouldsmith, daughter of William, at St James's in Trowbridge and they had at least four children, William, Allen, Michael and Madeleine, all carrying the middle name of Llewellyn. George's father was born in Pembroke, so one assumes the Welsh name came from that side of the family. In 1895, George became the Master of the Avon Vale Hunt, for which he provided the pack and had kennels built at Semington at his own expense. He continued as Master for four years, until the Duke of Beaufort, after an acrimonious dispute over land which remained unhunted in the Vale of Pewsey, became the Master, despite strong protests from the hunting fraternity; Palmer resigned. He and a colleague purchased and levelled some ground at Trowbridge and gave it to the Trustees of the Wiltshire County Cricket Club, who built a pavilion at their own expense. In 1900, George bought Lackham House, Lacock, where he had a number of repairs and alterations made before moving in. He and his family had been living at Springfields, Trowbridge, and from at least 1911 onwards, he was a JP for Wiltshire, as his father had been. In Lacock, George and Madeleine (as she was generally known) erected kennels and new stables and the Michael Palmer Institute to the memory of George's father. It contained reading and billiard rooms and other rooms suitable to a village club. In Trowbridge the almshouses at Islington were founded in Michael's memory. At some point, George was made a Companion of the Order of the Bath and his wife was awarded the OBE in 1920 for her war work. Tragedy struck the family twice; in 1908, their son Michael died from gas fumes in rented accommodation and Allen was killed on the Somme in November 1916; he had served originally as a Captain in the 14th Hussars in the South African Campaign, but was a Major in the Royal Wiltshire Yeomanry when he died. He was buried in the St Pierre Cemetery at Amiens. George sold Lackham in 1919 and temporarily moved out of the county, though he and his wife were eventually to return to Berryfield House, where Madeleine died in 1925; she was buried at Lacock. George moved away to Bexley and died there on 31 March 1932.
(*UK census returns; Kelly's, 1915; Pratt*)

PEMBROKE, Catherine, Countess of
Rebuilder of Mary Magdalene Hospital, Wilton
Born Ekaterina Semyonovna Vorontsova in 1784, she was the daughter of Count

Semyon Romanovich Verontsov, the Russian Ambassador to Britain, and his wife, Ekaterina Alekseevna Senyavina. She had one brother, Field Marshall Mikhail Semyonovich Vorontsov, who was raised to the dignity of Prince after a certain military encounter in the forests of Chechnya. In 1808, Catherine became the second wife of George Herbert, 11th Earl of Pembroke and the couple had six children. As well as rebuilding the Magdalene Hospital, the Countess also rebuilt St Nicholas's church in Wilton, (now known as the Italianate Church), during the years 1841-45. The original had long been in a ruinous state and the new church was built along Byzantine lines, influenced by the Countess's homeland and designed by Thomas Henry Wyatt and David Brandon, with elaborate decorations and furnishings, for which Catherine later left £1,000 in trust. Wyatt also designed a transformation of Wilton House, but was dismissed in 1810. The Countess took personal control of the refurbishments, keeping the clerk of the works and the sculptor to put her ideas into practice. Catherine died in 1856 and was buried in her new church at Wilton, in a magnificent tomb, alongside that of her husband, near the high altar, loved and admired by all.

(Robinson, 11; Lever, 203)

Catherine, Countess of Pembroke   SMT
(from her tomb at St Nicholas' Church, Wilton)

PIERCE, Dr Thomas
Founder of Dr Pierce's Almshouses, North Tidworth
Thomas Pierce (Peirce or Peirse) was a native of Wiltshire, the third son of John
Pierce of Devizes, baptised on 4 August 1621. He was educated at Magdalen
College, Oxford, which he entered as a chorister in 1633, matriculating in 1638
and later progressing to be a scholar, a Fellow and in due course, President of
the College. In 1648, he was ejected from the Fellowship by the Committee for
the Reformation of the University of Oxford, his views being staunchly royalist.
He was known as a poet and a wit, but he ridiculed the reforms, being of the
anti-entertainments lobby, and by all accounts was a difficult and tetchy man. He
became the Rector of Brington, Northamptonshire from 1656-76 and was much
admired by his parish. At the Restoration of the Monarchy, he was created a DD
and was made chaplain in ordinary to Charles II. He also became a Prebendary
in the Cathedrals of Canterbury and Lincoln and in 1675 was made Dean of
Salisbury, where, according to John Evelyn the diarist, he was known as a 'learned
minister' and an 'excellent musician'. However, correspondence between the two
men shows that feelings against the Roman Catholic Church were highly critical
at that time, in fact, almost derogatory and Evelyn also criticised one of Pierce's
sermons at Whitehall as being 'a little over-sharp, and not at all proper for the
auditory there'. He seems to have been a generally difficult man, for he quarrelled
with his Chapter at Salisbury and even involved the Bishop, Seth Ward, [vide
infra] in a lengthy dispute about a prebendal stall for his son, Robert. Thomas
purchased an estate in North Tidworth, where he spent his final days, dying in
1691. He was buried in the churchyard of North Tidworth, beneath an ornate
tomb and in 1696, his wife, Susanna, was buried next to him.
*(Aubrey, 36; Todd, 277-282; Bray, 360-1, 601-2; Foster, 1131-54; Devizes St John parish
registers)*

POORE, Edward
Founder of Poore's Almshouses, Figheldean
Edward Poore was descended from the same family that produced Bishop Poore,
the founder of Salisbury Cathedral. His parents were George Webb Poore of
Devizes and Jane Philips, who were married about 1740. George was a son of
Smart Poore and Elizabeth Webb of Figheldean and he was commonly known as
'Counsellor [sic] Poore', though it is not known what profession, if any, the family
followed. George and Jane had at least seven children, the last of whom died in
infancy, the day after her mother. Edward was the eldest surviving child and, as
an adult, became a barrister, though nothing is known of his career. His will
indicates that he was much travelled, particularly to Italy, where he took a native
of Rome, one Carlo Trebbi, under his wing and educated him, and where he
collected works of art. He was also the patron of a young English artist, William
Beare. Edward's namesake and uncle left him the bulk of his wealth in 1787

Edward Poore's grave in the Protestant Cemetery, Rome

and this may have been the trigger for his travelling. In his will, made in July 1802, he admits that he may die abroad; so his travelling days had not ceased at that time. He died in a convent hospital on the outskirts of Rome in 1803 and was buried in the Protestant Cemetery in Rome, where a stone over his grave was erected by Carlo Trebbi; his will was proved in London in February 1804. He left nothing to anyone in his immediate family, though he made generous bequests to the local poor and to his almshouses in Figheldean. The bulk of his estate was left to a second cousin, once removed, living in Hertfordshire – another Edward Poore. It is interesting to note that Gilbert White, the naturalist, had a brother, Henry White, who for a time was curate at North Tidworth and both Henry and Gilbert visited George Poore's house frequently; Edward would have met the great naturalist as a child and young man. The inscription on his gravestone translates as follows:

To the memory of/ Cavaliere Edward Poore/ of Tidworth/ in the county of Wilts/ in England/ a man in both art and science/ profound and learned/ amongst the scholars of his time/ very esteemed/ died in the Convento del Palazzuolo/ on the 17 August 1803/ of years 60/ this humble tribute/ was erected/ out of affection and the education/ given in early years to his/ always loved and faithful friend/ Carlo Trebbi Roman.

(An expanded version of this article may be found in The Recorder, the newsletter of the Wiltshire Record Society, no.13, February 2014).

(Will TNA, PROB 11/1405; Clutterbuck, 79-80; FamilySearch.com)

POORE, Bishop Richard

Co-founder of St Nicholas's Hospital, East Harnham

Richard Poore was the brother of Herbert Poore and they are thought to have been the sons of Richard of Ilchester, one time Bishop of Winchester. Richard was a pupil of Stephen Langton and became a canon lawyer. He was, by all accounts, a learned, erudite and holy man. He became a dean of the Cathedral (then at Old Sarum), Bishop of Winchester and when his brother died, in 1217, he was elected to take his place. Having obtained the necessary Papal blessing in 1218,

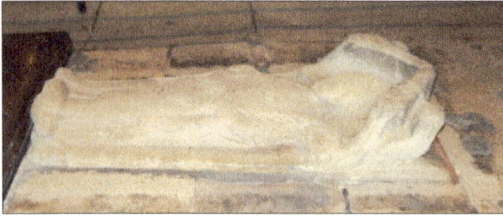

Supposed burial of Bishop Poore's heart, Salisbury Cathedral SMT (By kind permission of the Dean & Chapter, Salisbury Cathedral)

he continued his brother's work of moving the site of the Cathedral from the heights of Old Sarum down into the valley, where it now stands. He was also instrumental in implementing the Lateran Decree of 1215, which created vicarages and in 1219 he was a Papal delegate for this, checking unregulated appropriation of parish revenues. As a result, he created a series of statutes, governing the clergy, which was published among the clergy by the Deans of the Cathedral. His immediate successors followed his example. *(Templeman, 13; Chandler 1983, 12 et seq.)*

POYNDER, William Henry
Founder of the Poynder Almshouses, Hilmarton
William Henry Poynder was born on 5 February 1821 and was baptised on April 10 that year in St George's Church, Bloomsbury, by a clerical relative, Henry Poynder. His parents are recorded as Thomas and Sarah and they were living at Montague Place, Bloomsbury, at the time. His father, Thomas Poynder, acquired the Hilmarton estate in 1813, when it was sold by the then owner, Benjamin Ansley. Thomas had two sons, Thomas Henry Allen and William Henry. The family built many of the houses in Hilmarton village and they all reflect the same style and date of building. Thomas Henry inherited the estate from his father and William succeeded on the death of his brother in 1873. In 1874 he added a sixth bell to the church peal and five years later he completely restored the church at his own expense. His seat was at Hartham Park, Corsham. He died in London on 3 August 1880 and was brought back to Hilmarton, where he was buried on the 10 August.
(Crittall, 1970: 63; www.wiltshire.gov.uk/community; Hilmarton Parish Registers)

SALTER, Samuel
Founder of Salter's Almshouses, Trowbridge
The Salters were a Non-conformist family, possibly from Kington St Michael, where there were a great many Salters in the 17th and 18th centuries. Samuel was born about 1778, the son of Ephraim Salter, who, by the 1790s, had built up a profitable business in woollen manufacture with his partner, Joseph Dunn. Certainly by 1800 the firm of E.Salter & Son was established at Home Mills in the centre of Trowbridge, making fancy trousering (mole- and doe-skin) and silk mixtures. In the early 1790s Ephraim bought a large house in Fore Street and in 1810, his son was to buy the fine house opposite. Ephraim died in 1822 and

Samuel Salter
(By kind permission of Trowbridge Museum)

Samuel continued to build up the business, with 150 people employed in his mill during 1816-33, and 450 outside workers. He never altered the good habits of a lifetime and remained living close to his workplace, now part of The Shires shopping complex in the centre of Trowbridge. Samuel married Mary Davies of Lewes, whose brother William was a rector in Canterbury. Samuel appears to have had one sister, Margaret, who, in 1802, married another of Trowbridge's wealthy clothiers, William Stancomb. Thus, the two firms were closely connected over the course of the 19th century. At his death in 1850, at the age of 72, Samuel was said to be worth a staggering £350,000. He and Mary, had no children, but his money was used for many charitable purposes about the town and he provided well for his nieces and nephews, both those of his and his wife's families.
(Ponting 1973, 178-9; Rogers 1994, 65)

SEYMOUR, Sarah, Duchess of Somerset
Founder of the Duchess of Somerset's Hospital, Froxfield
Sarah was the second daughter of Sir Edward Alston, a London physician and a leading Presbyterian, and his wife Susanna Hudson. She was born in 1631 and baptised the same year at the church of St Martin Orgar in London. She married three times, but failed to produce any living issue. Her first husband was George Grimston, whom she married in 1652 and by whom she had two sons, who died in infancy. After George died, in 1655, she married Lord John Seymour, Duke of Somerset, in 1671. Their marriage was doomed from the start, mainly because of the Duke's debts, and they separated the following year. He died in 1675, but Sarah's title was confirmed to her permanently by Royal Warrant. In 1682 Sarah married her third husband, Henry Hare, 2nd Lord Coleraine, whose father had purchased the Manor of Tottenham in Middlesex, which the couple eventually inherited; but the marriage was not a happy one and they lived apart. Sarah died on 25 October 1692, aged 61, and was buried in Westminster Abbey.
(faithforduty.co.uk; Crowley, 2013, 1-2)

Sarah, Duchess of Somerset (by kind permission of the Principal & Fellows of Brasenose College, Oxford)

SMITHE, Cleophas (see also BARRETT, William)
Co-founder of Devizes Old Almshouses
Cleophas Smithe, the son of Thomas and Margery Smithe, was born in Devizes and baptised on 27 March 1568 in St John's. According to his will, he had at least

two brothers, John and Robert, and the parish register reveals John baptised in 1569/70 and Robert baptised 1570/1. There was also an older brother, Thomas, baptised in 1566, probably dead by the time Cleophas made his will. Presumably when a young man, Cleophas took up an apprenticeship and made his way to London, for in 1595 he married Sarah Wilcocks in the church of St Margaret Lothbury, London. He became a citizen of London and a Freeman of the Drapers' Company. In his will, made in October 1616, he left money to the poor of Devizes and also to those of Edmonton in north London. He also left money to be loaned out for up to three years to any poor householder or young tradesman in the parish of St Antholin, Budge Row, in the City. His will was made on the 29 October 1616 and proved on the 30th. This seems extraordinary and one wonders if there is a mistake in the dating within the register copy.
(will TNA, PROB 11/128; Boyd, 8648; Devizes St John parish registers)

STUMPE, John
Early benefactor of St John's Hospital, Malmesbury
John Stumpe was born about 1525, the second son of William Stumpe (the well-known 'cloth baron') and his first wife, Joyce Berkeley of Gloucestershire. The Stumpe family originated in Gloucestershire and moved to Malmesbury about the time John was born. His older brother, James, entered the ranks of knighthood, but John followed his father into the cloth business. William had purchased the Abbey Church of Malmesbury at the Dissolution and installed twenty looms in it; he had planned to convert the building to housing for his weavers, but this came to nothing. In 1544, he finally gave or sold the church to the parish of Malmesbury. John's first marriage to a daughter of Matthew King appears to have been very much a business affair, since Matthew succeeded John's father as the leading Malmesbury clothier, when William died in 1552. From this marriage there were three sons, but John's wife died young. His second wife, whom he married about 1566, was Christian, daughter of William Chaffin of Bulford and widow of Thomas Dowse of Collingbourne Ducis. There were no children from this second marriage. In the 1550s, the family, through Sir James Stumpe, were held for a time under suspicion of conspiracy, following the acquisition of monastic property by laymen after the Dissolution; and John himself was mentioned in court, when his brother's servant was summoned to the Council and a suspect was examined. When William Stumpe died, he left John the leases on three houses, ten broad looms and £500 in cash. In time, John became a burgess of the town and was a public-spirited man, firstly surrendering his patent as bailiff and holding the office voluntarily, so that the fee might be used to public good. Then, in about 1570, he acquired the former hospital of St John the Baptist and conveyed this to the Corporation for 40 marks. On the strength of his relationship with his niece's husband, Sir Henry Knyvet, Stumpe was returned to Parliament for Malmesbury in 1584. His second wife died in

1595 and John followed her on the 3 May 1600. He does not appear to have made a will, but the IPM taken on his estate in 1601 showed him to be the owner of numerous properties in the Malmesbury area. His son and heir, James, died in 1602, making his third son, Basil, his only descendant to reach old age. John was buried in the Abbey Church of Malmesbury.
(www.historyofparliament.ac.uk; Ramsay, 36-39; Freeman, 143)

SUTTON, Robert
Founder of Sutton's Almshouses, Salisbury

Robert Sutton was the third of four known children of Thomas and Anne Sutton and was baptised in St Martin's, Salisbury, on 24 September 1643. It is not known where the family lived at that time, nor what his father's occupation was, but Robert became a successful and fairly wealthy clothier in Salisbury. In 1670, he married Elizabeth Garland in Mere, in the south-west of the county. They had no children, but Robert left much of his wealth to numerous cousins of his and to kinsfolk of his wife. At the time of his death, around December 1699, Robert and Elizabeth were living in Brown Street, Salisbury, but he also owned property in Tanner Street (now St Anne's Street), Castle Street and Scots Lane, and a malthouse in Tanner Street. These all border on or are close to Marsh Chequer, which may have been named for a relative of his; there are Marshes mentioned in his will and Richard Marsh was one of his executors. Although he left £100 for the rebuilding of Trinity Hospital and set up a charity for St Martin's parish, whereby the poor of that parish were to receive wholesome, twelve-penny loaves of bread in the hardest part of winter each year, he also seems to have had connections with the Non-conformists. He left a similar bequest of loaves to the poor of the Presbyterian Congregation of Salisbury and his cousin, Robert Shergold, may well have been the Dissenter whose Salisbury house was certified as a Quaker Meeting House in 1703.
(Will TNA, PROB 11/459; Chandler, 1985: 12; Familysearch.com)

TAYLOR, Alderman Thomas
Founder of Taylor's Almshouses, Salisbury

Little is known of Thomas Taylor; he does not appear to have married, though his extended family stretched to some thirty-six kinsmen and women, according to his will, made in 1695. He classed himself as 'gentleman' and lived in Salisbury at the time of his death, where he employed one of his kinswomen and her daughter as his servants. His kinsfolk included members of the Bright, Bushel, Hurle, Eckett, Jeofferies, Mitchell, Crooke, Adlam, Copeland, Oram, Bryant, Batt and Powell families, and he had godsons in the Cousens and Hayward families. He also had Taylor kinsmen in Draycott, Wiltshire, though which Draycott is not made clear. From his will it appears he owned a garden above Castle Gate, an inn by the name of The Sign of the Three Tuns and a messuage in Castle Street,

all in Salisbury. He owned an estate in Bramshaw, on the borders of Wiltshire and Hampshire, and made it clear in his will that if timber were needed for the building of his almshouses, then ten good oaks could be brought from that estate. He was a benefactor of all three parishes in Salisbury, but it is not known where he was finally laid to rest, though he probably died in 1697.
(Will TNA, PROB 11/435)

TERUMBER, James
Founder of Terumber's Almshouses, Trowbridge

James Terumber is believed to have been born in Bristol, where he had humble origins as a fuller. He was also known as James Tucker, the latter being an alternative name for a fuller. In the mid 15th century, he flourished as a major figure in the Wiltshire cloth industry. Almost certainly he contributed to the rebuilding of St James's Church in Trowbridge in 1450 and was long remembered as a wealthy and principal benefactor of Bristol, Bradford and Trowbridge. In 1458, he contemplated founding a chantry in Bradford on Avon and by 1461 he held the advowson of an Oxfordshire parish. In 1463, when he was living at Bradford, he was in trouble over twenty-nine woollen cloths sold at Bridport to a Venetian merchant. They were seized from the merchant in London as not properly alnaged, but this had been done already in Wiltshire. James was released on bail after examination in the Exchequer. Three Venetian merchants and a fellow Bradford clothier stood surety for him. By 1469 he had moved to Trowbridge. In 1476 he held fairs and markets from the Crown and invested in lands and property in and around Trowbridge and Studley, Broughton Gifford, Bradford and Beckington. All this land and property he transferred to a body of trustees in 1484, to support him and his wife – they had no children – and after their demise, to appoint a chantry priest to pray for the couple. The chantry rules were very carefully laid out, involving a timetable of prayer throughout the day. He built a fine house for himself on the site of 52-3 Fore Street, a timber-framed house along the same lines as his almshouse in St James's churchyard. Towards the end of his life, he gave up this house and returned to Bristol, where he made his will in 1488. In it, he bequeathed money (though very modest sums) for the repair and upkeep of both conduits in Redcliff, to the vicar of Redcliff and for the upkeep of St Mary Redcliff itself. He also left money to the almspeople and the children of St John's House, Bristol, to the almspeople of Bradford and of Trowbridge, and to the poor in Weavers' Hall and Tuckers' Hall, Bristol. These people would have been living in the undercroft of both Halls. He willed that his body should rest in the chapel of Our Lady 'within the hospital and house of Saint John the Baptist at Redcliff Pitt'. The House of St John has long gone and with it, no doubt, James' final resting place.
(Pugh, 1953a: 134-144 ; Rogers 1984: 29-30, 35; 1994: 20-21, 22; 2014; will TNA, PROB 11/2)

Sir James Thynne, by Jacob Huysmans (1633?-1696)
(© Reproduced by permission of the Marquess of Bath, Longleat House,
Warminster, Wiltshire)

THYNNE, Sir James

Founder of the Thynne Almshouses, Longbridge Deverill

Sir James was the eldest son of Sir Thomas Thynne and his first wife, Maria Audley. He was born in 1605 and married Isabella Rich, the daughter of the Earl of Holland. James and Isabella became estranged and the marriage was childless, Isabella running up huge debts, for which her husband published a disclaimer, denying all responsibility. Isabella was also notorious for her scandalous behaviour. Among other things, she is purported to have danced naked on (Old) London Bridge. Eventually, King Charles I banished her from Court. Having inherited Longleat in 1640, James maintained neutrality during the Civil War, although Longleat suffered a raid in 1643 and it was James who employed Sir Christopher Wren to work on the house. He died in 1670 and Longleat passed to his nephew, ' Tom o' Ten Thousand', who was murdered in 1682. Sir James was buried in the family vault at Longbridge Deverill, the village where he founded his almshouses and where he preferred to live when visiting Wiltshire.

(Longleat Enterprises,4; www.historyofparliament.ac.uk)

TOPP, John

Founder of Topp's Almshouses, Stockton

The Topp family had been tenants of Stockton manor under the Bishop of Winchester. At the end of the 16th century, John Topp inherited the manor and built a fine manor house of stone and flint. He died in 1642 and was buried in the parish church, but he left instructions in his will for the foundation of his almshouses, which were finally

John Topp and his wife, Stockton Church   SMT

erected in 1657. It is said that he founded them in fulfilment of two vows, made when he was under duress, the first vow not having been fulfilled. In order to compensate for his laxity, he established the almshouses for eight people, seven to represent each of the seven years between his two vows.

(Crowley, 1980: 214, 221-2; Tenant, 79-80; Hutton, 155-6)

TOUNSON, Dr John

Founder of Dr Tounson's Almshouses, Calne

John was a son of Robert Tounson, of Cambridge. Robert was born in 1576 and was made a Royal Chaplain and installed as Dean of Westminster in 1617. He attended Sir Walter Raleigh in prison and on the scaffold. In 1620, he was made Bishop of Salisbury and died in 1621. He was the son of Renold Toulnesonn and in 1604 married Margaret, daughter of John Davenant, a London merchant and sister to John Davenant, who succeeded him to the see of Salisbury. Robert and Margaret had a large family, of whom two sons were Robert and John. One daughter, Gertrude, married James Harris of Salisbury Close, the father of the 1st Earl of Malmesbury (vide Hayter supra). John was born in April 1610 and went on to gain his degrees from Magdalen College, Oxford, and Christ Church and was made a Canon of Sarum in 1633 and Vicar of Bremhill in 1639. He was also made a Prebend of Highworth in 1633, succeeding his brother, Robert. He held this post until his death on 24 July 1687 and is buried in the chancel of Bremhill church. His will, made in 1685 and proved the following year, shows how closely interconnected his family was with the higher clergy of the Church and the important families of The Close, Salisbury, and other parts of Wiltshire. He married, though his wife's name is not known, but there were no children of the marriage.

(will TNA, PROB 11/389; Sherlock, 13; en.wikipedia.org)

UTTERSON, Mrs Elizabeth
Founder of Mrs Utterson's Almshouses, Chippenham

Elizabeth Utterson was born Elizabeth Blake and baptised in Peterborough on 7 January 1821, the daughter of James and Ann Blake. By 1841, James had died and Elizabeth was living in Peakirk with her widowed mother, some 6 miles north of Peterborough. It is not known how she came to the West Country, but on 26 November 1854, she married William Lewis, a man some ten years younger than herself, at Bedminster in Somerset. William, like the rest of his family, was a Welshman, born in St David's, Pembrokeshire. By 1841, he had come to Chippenham, with his father Thomas, a journeyman, to learn the shoemaking business from his uncle, Henry Evans. In 1851, he was a partner in his uncle's business in the Market Place, Chippenham. In the same household, in 1851, was Elizabeth Lewis, aged fifteen, a house servant, born in St.David's, almost certainly William's younger sister. In the 1861 census, William is found as a Master Shoemaker, possibly having taken over his uncle's business. He is still in Chippenham Market Place and employs nine men and three boys. His wife, Elizabeth, is there as a 'shoemaker's wife', together with their five year old son, William H., who was born in Chippenham. William senior died in January 1866, aged 36. In 1871, Elizabeth was living as a widow in Cleveland, Somerset, with a servant, but it is not known where else she may have lived. Then, on census night, 1881, she was a visitor to the house of James Utterson, a widower, in Chippenham. James had been born in Eyemouth, Berwickshire, and was the Municipal Registrar of Births and Deaths in Chippenham. He had just lost his thirty-year old son, who had lived with him since his first wife's death, and in the autumn of 1881, James and Elizabeth were married. But their marriage was to be short-lived. James, who was seventy-five when they married, died in early

July of 1884 and Elizabeth on the 23 January 1890. She had purchased the land for her almshouses in the spring of 1884, and dedicated their foundation to the memory of her husband, presumably James, though her money may well have come from her first husband, since she was recorded as an annuitant after his death. His effects were given as £3,000, James's as £2,000 and Elizabeth's a mere £224; clearly, most of the money she had inherited had been invested in her almshouses.

(www.findmypast.co.uk; www. freebmd.org.uk; UK Census Returns; Nat.Prob. Calendar. for 1866, 1884, 1890)

WARD, Bishop Seth

Founder of the College of Matrons, Salisbury

Seth Ward was born in 1617 at Aspenden in Hertfordshire, the son of John Ward, an attorney. He was educated first by his mother and then at the local grammar school. He matriculated at Sidney Sussex College, Cambridge in 1632 and concentrated his studies on mathematics, which he largely taught himself. When Civil War broke out in 1642, he was a Fellow of his College and had entered the Church. He was imprisoned for a short period, for refusing to take the oath of loyalty to Parliament, now in control of Cambridge. He was eventually released and allowed to teach in the University, but soon abandoned this in favour of teaching in friends' houses, until 1649, when he was invited to become Professor of Geometry at Oxford. Here he devoted himself to mathematics, law and experimental sciences. At the Restoration, Ward lost his position and so concentrated on the Church, where he accrued his wealth as Precentor of Exeter Cathedral. In 1662, he was made Bishop of Exeter, at 45, the youngest bishop at the time. Much of his work involved making good the damage done by years of Puritan influence. In 1667 he became Bishop of Salisbury, which, being such a large Diocese, entailed careful administration. He was an accomplished horseman and took regular exercise on Salisbury Plain. But he also suffered with his health and some disastrous quarrels with his Dean, Thomas Pierce (vide supra), left him ill and prematurely aged. His major foundations of the College of Matrons, Salisbury, and the Hospital for Poor Men, Buntingford, had already been established, but he was munificent in many other ways; those who benefited from his generosity were Salisbury Guildhall and Gaol and the poor in The Close and the City. He also gave towards the canalisation of the river from Salisbury to Christchurch, completely restored the Bishop's Palace after the ravages of the Interregnum and bequeathed many 16th and 17th century scientific books to the Cathedral Library. In Hertfordshire he gave to the poor apprentices of Buntingford and both Christ's College, Cambridge, and Wadham College in Oxford benefited from his charity. In London, he was a benefactor of Chelsea College. By 1668 he had left the Diocese to the administration of his Chancellor and had retired as an invalid. He died in Knightsbridge in January

1689 and was buried in his cathedral in the southeast transept.
(Latham; Dale, 74, 75, 78; Ransome,1962: 12; Crittall,1962: 169)

Bishop Seth Ward by John Greenhill
(By kind permission of Salisbury Guildhall)

WARREN, Louisa
Founder of the Warren Almshouses, Warminster

Louisa Warren was the eldest of four daughters of Francis and Mary Bennett and she was baptised in Warminster the 25 July 1793. Her mother, Mary Halliday, came from Sutton Veny and married Francis Bennett in that parish in 1792. Both

the Bennetts and Hallidays were long-established families in the area. On 19 July 1821 Louisa married John Warren in the parish church of Warminster. He was then a maltster by trade and was born into a family of ten children in 1791, the youngest son of William Warren and his wife, Ann Eastmond. Although there were Warrens in Warminster going back to at least the 18th century, involved in both the cloth and malting industries, John was born in Bishop's Nympton, near South Molton in Devonshire. The last of his siblings was baptised in Burrington, some ten miles away, and John variously gave his birthplace on Census returns as Bishop's Nympton or Burrington. John and Louisa had no children of their own and seem to have spent their entire married lives in Warminster. In the Commercial Directories of the time, John is recorded as a maltster in Silver Street from 1830-42; then from at least 1851 onwards he and Louisa were living in George Street, in both of which streets there were malthouses. In 1851 John employed seven men and two boys, but by 1861 he seems to have retired. He died in 1870 and Louisa lived on with a house servant at the same address until her death in 1880, aged eighty-six, having founded her almshouses in 1873 in memory of her husband.
(Rogers, 1992: 97, 145; UK Census Returns)

WICKS (or WEEKS), Michael,
Benefactor of St John's Hospital, Malmesbury
Michael Wicks was baptised in Malmesbury on 21 July 1633, the son of George; and twenty-three years earlier, his father's baptism is recorded: 22 April 1610, George, son of Giles Weekes. It is not known how Michael's early life was spent, but in 1663 he became the receiver of plantation customs, a post in which he appears to have remained until his death in 1694, and regarded himself as a 'gentleman'. In 1663, he made his first marriage, by licence, to Mary Midwell of Welham in Leicestershire, by whom he had one son, who probably died young. It appears that he may have married a second time, to Elizabeth Griffin, the widow of Thomas Griffin, an apothecary from St Martin in the Fields, London. Elizabeth was a Holford before she married and came from Steeple Ashton in Wiltshire. She and Thomas had at least a daughter, also called Elizabeth, who became Michael's ward. She may have married someone with the surname Burgh, whose brother was John Burgh, whom she referred to as 'brother in law' and who was named as Michael's 'nephew' and executor in his will. Elizabeth also referred to Michael as her 'father in law'; this was a common term at that time for a step-parent. Although Wicks lived in London, he kept his connections with Wiltshire, buying a farm at Great Somerford in 1693. At some point, he fell into serious debt to the Crown, to the tune of £185,000. Some of this he managed to clear, but he took various measures to delay the legal proceedings against him, one of which was to stand as MP for Malmesbury. This would give him immunity from such proceedings; but in order to do this, one of the ways in

which he prepared his way into Parliament, was to endow St John's Hospital and
School in Malmesbury. This he did in 1695. He made one stand in Parliament,
but it was not to last. Eventually he obtained a private act (1705) which allowed the
Treasury to compound with him. However, the act lapsed and it was left to John
Burgh to arrive at a settlement with the Treasury. In his will (proved 1708) Wicks
left everything to John Burgh and no further mention is made of any charitable
donations. He died the same year.
(Will TNA, PROB 11/502; FamilySearch.com; www.historyofparliamentonline.org)

YERBURY, Dr.Henry
Founder of the Yerbury Almshouses, Trowbridge
The Almshouses of Trowbridge which bore this name, were founded, according
to some accounts, by three Yerbury brothers, William, John and Richard. Henry
was their brother and by his will of 1686, he left £100 to each of them. But
according to the Benefactors' board in St James's Church, Trowbridge, Henry,
Edward and William were the three family members who erected the almshouse
and endowed it with £22 per annum in perpetuity. This Edward may have been
the eldest of the brothers, or the father himself. Edward Yerbury, gentleman, and
Ann, his wife, had five sons and a daughter, between 1617 and 1634. Henry was
baptised at Trowbridge in 1627/8. Both Henry and his father were educated at
Magdalen College, Oxford, where Henry became a Fellow and doctor of physic. He
displayed a great interest in natural sciences, becoming a pupil of Peter Sthael, (a
noted chemist from Strasbourg, who taught at Oxford). He was a staunch royalist
and was expelled by the notorious Thomas Pierce (*vide supra*). He travelled to
Italy and obtained a degree from the University of Padua and on his return to
England, became a tutor to the family of the Howard Dukes of Norfolk. At the
Restoration, he recovered his fellowship and died at Oxford in 1686, where he
was buried in the Chapel of Magdalen College. In his will, Henry left £22 to
the Bishop of Oxford and his Chancellor (Henry's brother in law and executor),
to be used for charitable purposes, as the Bishop and Chancellor saw fit; and
eventually they decided on an endowment for the almshouses. In St James's
Church, Trowbridge, where his parents are buried and commemorated, there is
a memorial to Henry and to his brother, William, gentleman, born in about 1619
and who spent most of his life in Bath; he died in 1698, aged 79.
*(will TNA, PROB 11/383; Alumni Oxoniensis; Sherlock, 146, 147; Trowbridge parish
registers)*

Bibliography

Aubrey, J., (ed. Jackson.J.) 1862 *The Topographical Collections: Wiltshire: 1659-70*. Devizes: WANHS.

Badeni, J., n/d. *Wiltshire Forefathers*. Wiltshire: privately published

Bailey, B., 1988 *Almshouses*. London: Hale

Baker, T., 'The Trinity Hospital, Salisbury' in *WAM*. Devizes: WANHS, vol 36.

Battersby, R., 1990 *The Heraldry of Wiltshire*. privately published.

Boyd, P., 1939 *Inhabitants of London 1209-1948* www.findmypast.co.uk/ search/ boyds-inhabitants (2014) [*Original MS at Society of Genealogists*].

Bray, W., ed. n/d *Diary and Correspondence of John Evelyn, FRS*. London: G.Routledge & Sons, Ltd.

Burke, 1976 *Irish Family Records*. London

Caffrey, H., 2006 *Almshouses in the West Riding of Yorkshire 1600-1900*. Kings Lynn: Heritage Marketing & Publications Ltd.

Capes, A., & Dew, E., 2006 *Westbury Parish Church through the Ages*

Chandler, J., 1983 *Endless Street*, East Knoyle: Hobnob Press.

Chandler, J., ed. 1985 *Wiltshire Dissenters' Meeting House Certificates 1689-1852*. Devizes: Wiltshire Record Society, vol.40.

Cheetham, J., & Piper, J., 1968 *A Shell Guide: Wiltshire*. London: Faber & Faber, Ltd.

Chettle, H., & Crittall, E., 1956 'The Hospital of St John, Malmesbury' in *VCH Wiltshire*. London: IHR & OUP, vol. iii.

Clutterbuck, R., 1896 'Gilbert White's Wiltshire Friends' in *Wiltshire Notes & Queries*, Devizes: Gazette Office, vol.1 1893-5

Clay, R., 1909/1966 *The English Medieval Hospital*. London: Frank Cass & Co.Ltd..

Crittall, E., ed. 1952 *Andrews' and Dury's map of Wiltshire, 1773: a reduced facsimile*. Devizes: Wiltshire Record Society, vol.8.

Crittall, E., 1956 'Abbey of Wilton' in *VCH Wiltshire*. London: IHR & OUP, vol.iii.

Crittall, E., 1962 'Charities for the Poor' in *VCH Wiltshire*. London: IHR & OUP, vol. vi.

Crittall, E., 1965 'Westbury' in *VCH Wiltshire*. London: IHR & OUP, vol. viii.

Crittall, E., 1970 'Hilmarton' in *VCH Wiltshire*. London: IHR & OUP, vol.ix.

Croman, D., 1991 *A History of Tidworth and Tedworth House*. Chichester:

Phillimore.

Crowley, D., 1980 'Stockton' in *VCH Wiltshire*. London: IHR & OUP, vol. xi.

Crowley, D., 1991 'Stanton St Quintin' in *VCH Wiltshire*. London: IHR & OUP, vol. xiv.

Crowley, D., 1995 'Amesbury' in *VCH Wiltshire*. London: IHR & OUP, vol.xv.

Crowley, D., 1995a 'Bathampton' in *VCH Wiltshire*. London: IHR & OUP, vol.xv.

Crowley, D., 1999 'Pewsey' in *VCH Wiltshire*. London: IHR & OUP, vol.xvi.

Crowley, D., ed. 2009 *The Court Records of Brinkworth and Charlton*. Chippenham: Wiltshire Record Society, vol. 61.

Crowley, D., 2013 *The Minute Boooks of Froxfirld Almshouse, 1714-1866*. Chippenham: Wiltshire Record Society, vol. 66.

Cunnington, B., 1925 *Some Annals of the Borough of Devizes*. Devizes: George Simpson & Co. Ltd., 2 vols.

Curry, A., 2010 *Agincourt*, Stroud: The History Press.

Dale, M., 1962 'The Liberty of the Close' in *VCH Wiltshire*. London: IHR & OUP, vol. vi.

Daniell, J., 1879 *The History of Warminster*. London: Simpkin, Marshall & Co.

Davis, R., 1990 *King Stephen*. London: Longman, third edition.

Dorling, E., 1906 *Wiltshire and Dorset at the Opening of the 20th Century*. Brighton: W.T.Pike & Co.

Edwards, K., 1956 'Hospital of St Nicholas, Salisbury' in *VCH Wiltshire*. London: IHR & OUP, vol. iii.

Fassnidge, H., 1988 *Bradford on Avon, Past and Present*. Bradford on Avon: Ex Libris Press.

Foster, J., ed. 1891 *Alumni Oxoniensis*. London: Parker & Co.

Freeman, J., 1991 ' Malmesbury' in *VCH Wiltshire*. London: IHR & OUP, vol. xiv.

Freeman, J., 1991a 'Garsdon' in *VCH Wiltshire*. London: IHR & OUP, vol. xiv.

Freeman, J., 1991b 'Dauntsey' in *VCH Wiltshire*. London: IHR & OUP, vol. xiv.

Freeman, J., 1995 'Maddington' in *VCH Wiltshire*. London: IHR & OUP, vol. xv.

Freeman, J., 1995a 'Orcheston St Mary' in *VCH Wiltshire*. London: IHR & OUP, vol. xv.

Freeman, J., 1995b 'Tilshead' in *VCH Wiltshire*. London: IHR & OUP, vol. xv.

Freeman, J., 1995c 'Shrewton' in *VCH Wiltshire*. London: IHR & OUP, vol. xv.

Freeman, J., 1995d 'Winterbourne Stoke' in *VCH Wiltshire*. London: IHR & OUP, vol. xv.

Ginever, E., 1974 (revised Murray, D.1995) *The Ancient Wiltshire Village of Heytesbury*. Bridport: Creeds, for Heytesbury Parochial Synod.

Grubb, P., 1974 (revised 2000 Bull, G.) *The Hospital of St John Heytesbury*. Privately published.

Harte, N., & Ponting, K., eds. 1973 *Textile History & Economy: Essays in honour of Miss Julia de Lacy Mann*, Manchester: University Press.

Hasted, E., 1797 *The History & Topographical Survey of Kent, 1793*. Canterbury:

W.Bristow, vol. viii.

Hatcher, M., 1998 Lecture *Leper Colonies in Wiltshire*, given at Devizes, by Nuffield Foundation researcher. Wiltshire Local History Forum Study Day.

Hicks, M., 1984 'St Katherine's Hospital, Heytesbury: Prehistory, Foundation and Re-foundation 1408-1472' in *WAM*. Devizes: WANHS, vol 78.

Hird, E., 1997 *Corsham Almshouse and Free School*. Bradford on Avon: privately published.

Hoare, R.Colt, 1831 *History of Modern Wiltshire*. London: J.B.Nichols & Son. vol iv.

Hobbs, S., ed. 2003 *Wiltshire Glebe Terriers 1588-1827*. Trowbridge: Wiltshire Record Society, vol. 56.

Horn, J., ed. 1982 *The Register of Robert Hallum, Bishop of Salisbury, 1407-17*. Torquay: The Devonshire Press, for The Canterbury & York Society, vol. 72.

House of Commons, 1908 *Endowed Charities Reports: Wiltshire*. London: HMSO, vol.i North, vol ii South.

Howson, B., 1993 *Houses of Noble Poverty*. Sunbury on Thames: Bellevue.

Howson, B., 2008 *Almshouses: a social & architectural history*. Stroud: Tempus.

Hughes, C., n/d *Marlborough: The Story of a Small and Ancient Borough*. Marlborough: Privately Published.

Humphrey, B., 1991 *A Pictorial History of Ludgershall*. Ludgershall: privately published.

Hutton, E., 1917 *Highways and Byways in Wiltshire*, London: MacMillan & Co.Ltd.

Jackson, R., *et al* 1980 *Looking around Tisbury*. Tisbury: Tisbury Local History Society.

Jessup, M., 1975 *A History of Oxfordshire* London & Chichester: Phillimore

Johnson, N., *et al*, eds., 1958 *The Story of Mere*. Gillingham: The Blackmore Press.

Jones, J., 1859 'A History and Description of Bradford on Avon' in *WAM*. Devizes: WANHS, vol. v.

Kelly 1915 *Directory for Wiltshire*.

Kightly, C., 2006 *Farleigh Hungerford Castle*, London: English Heritage.

Kirby, J., 1956 'The Preceptory of Ansty' in *VCH Wiltshire*. London: IHR & OUP, *vol. iii*.

Kite, E., 1855 'The Churches of Devizes' in *WAM*. Devizes: WANHS, vol. ii.

Larking, L., ed. 1857. *The Knights Hospitallers in England*. London: The Camden Society.

Latham, R., 1982 *Seth Ward, Bishop of Salisbury, 1667-89*. Salisbury: The Dean & Chapter.

Laverton, A., 2011 *Abraham Laverton, JP MP, 1819-1886*

Lever, T., 1967 *The Herberts of Wilton*. london: John Murray

Longleat Enterprises Ltd., 2003 *Longleat*. Longleat: Longleat Enterprises Ltd.

Longbourne, D., 2004 *The Book of Mere*. Tiverton: Halsgrove.

Luce, R.H., 1949 'The St. John's Almshouse, Malmesbury' in *WAM*. Devizes: WANHS, vol. 53.

Martin, D., 2002 *The Hungerford Family.* Privately printed.

McBain, A., & Nelson, L., 2003 *The Bounding Spring.* Teffont: Black Horse Books.

Mee, A., ed. 1949 *The King's England: Oxfordshire* London: Hodder & Stoughton

Mee, A., ed. 1964 *The King's England: Wiltshire* London: Hodder & Stoughton

Moffatt, J., 1805 *The History of the Town of Malmesbury.* Tetbury: J.Goodwyn.

Niblett, B., 1981 *Memories of Bradford on Avon.* Trowbridge: Wiltshire Libraries & Museum Service.

Parsons, M., 1956 'Hospital of the Holy Trinity, Salisbury' in *VCH Wiltshire.* London: IHR & OUP, vol.iii.

Pelly, R., ca.1968 *Seven Centuries of Service.* Privately published.

Pevsner, N., 1963 *The Buildings of England: Wiltshire.* Harmondsworth: Penguin Books.

Phillips, A., 1989 *The Warminster Trail.* Warminster: privately published.

Powell, A., 2006 'A possible site for the Hospital of St John the Baptist and St Anthony at Old Sarum, Salisbury' in *WAM.* Devizes: WANHS, vol. 99.

Pratt, T., 2011, rev.2013 *The Manor of Lackham, vols.iii & iv. Online at* www.lackham.co.uk/history/documents.asp (2014).

Prescott, E., 1992 *The English Medieval Hospital 1050-1640.* London: Seaby.

Pugh, R., ed. 1947 *Calendar of Antrobus Deeds before 1625.* Devizes: Wiltshire Record Society, vol.3.

Pugh, R., 1953 'Bradford on Avon' in *VCH Wiltshire.* Kent: Wm.Dawson for IHR & OUP, vol.vii

Pugh, R., 1953a 'Trowbridge' in *VCH Wiltshire.* Kent: Wm.Dawson for IHR & OUP, vol.vii

Pugh, R., & Crittall, E., eds. *VCH Wiltshire.* London: IHR, vol.iii.

Pugh, R., 1962 'Fisherton Anger' in *VCH Wiltshire.* London: IHR, vol.vi.

Pugh, R., 1975 'Devizes' in *VCH Wiltshire.* London: IHR, vol.x.

Pugh, R., ed. 2001 *A History of the Devizes (from VCH vols.iii & x)* Trowbridge: Wiltshire County Council & Kennett County Council.

Ramsay, G., 1965 *The Wiltshire Woollen Industry in the Sixteenth and Seventeenth Centuries.* London: Frank Cass & Co.Ltd.

Ransome, M., 1962 ' The City of New Salisbury: Economic history before 1612' in *VCH Wiltshire.* London: IHR & OUP, vol.iv.

Ransome, M., ed. 1972 *Wiltshire Returns to the Bishop's Visitation Queries 1783.* Devizes: Wiltshire Record Society, vol. 27.

RCHM, 1980 *Ancient & Historical Monuments in the City of Salisbury.* London: HMSO, vol.i.

RCHM, 1993 *Salisbury: The Houses in the Close,* London: HMSO.

Richardson, J., 1993 *The Local Historian's Encyclopedia.* New Barnet: Historical Publications

Rix, A., 1986 *A Short History to mark the Tercentenary of the Will endowing the Duchess of Somerset's Hospital.* Privately Published. Printed in Marlborough.

Robinson, J., n/d (21C) *Wilton House,* Wilton: Wilton House.

Roffey, S., 2009 *Chantry Chapels and Medieval Strategies for the Afterlife.* Stroud: Tempus.

Rogers, K., 1965 'Warminster' in *VCH Wiltshire.* London: IHR & OUP, vol. viii..

Rogers, K., 1984 *The Book of Trowbridge,* Buckingham: Barracuda Books, Ltd.

Rogers, K., 1986 *Warp and Weft,* Buckingham: Bararacuda Books Ltd.

Rogers, K., 1994 *Trowbridge,* Stroud: Alan Sutton Publishing Ltd.

Rogers, K., 2014 *The Domestic Woollen Industry at Bradford-on-Avon.* Bradford-on-Avon Museum.

Rogers, K., & Chandler, J., eds. 1992 *Early Trade Directories of Wiltshire.* Trowbridge: Wiltshire Record Society, vol. 47.

Rogers, K., & Marshman, M., 1994 *Trowbridge History vol.2,* Bradford on Avon: Silverthorne Press.

Rogers, K., ed. 1992 *Early Trade Directories of Wiltshire,* Trowbridge: Wiltshire Record Society, vol.47.

Rutter, J., (1821-1899) Notes for a history of Mere Temperance Society and the associated Band of Hope. (Microfilm at WSHC).

de Salis. R., 1934 *De Salis Family: English Branch.* Henley-on-Thames

de Salis. R., 2003 *Quadrennial di Fano Saliceorum,* vol. i. London

SLHG (Salisbury Local History Group), 1987 *Caring: A Short History of Salisbury City Almshouses & Other Charities from 14th to 20th Centuries.* Salisbury: Salisbury City Almshouse & Welfare Charities.

Sheppard, F., ed. 1960 *Survey of London: vols.29 & 30: St James, Westminster, part 1.*

Sherlock, P., ed. 2000 *Monumental Inscriptions of Wiltshire,* Trowbridge: Wiltshire Record Society, vol.53.

Skinner, T., 1880 *The Directory of Directors.* London

Slack, P., ed. 1975 *Poverty in Early Stuart Salisbury.* Devizes: Wiltshire Record Society, vol.31.

Slocombe, I., 2012 *Wiltshire Village Reading Rooms.* East Knoyle: Hobnob Press for The Wiltshire Buildings Record.

Slocombe, P.M., 2012 *The Hall, Bradford-on-Avon.* Bradford on Avon: Ex Libris Press.

Smith, L.Toulmin, ed., 1906-10 *The Itinerary of John Leland in or about the years 1535-1543.* London: Bell, 5 vols. (reprinted 1964: Centaur Press of Fontwell & S.Illinois University Press of Carbondale, USA.).

Stacey, N.E., 2006 *Charters and Custumals of Shaftesbury Abbey 1089-1216.* OUP.

Stedman, A., 1944 'A History of Marlborough Grammar School' in *WAM.* Devizes: WANHS, vol. 51.

Stevenson, J., 1983 'Marlborough and Preshute' in *VCH Wiltshire.* London: IHR & OUP, vol. xii.

Stevenson, J., 1987 'Teffont Evias' in *VCH Wiltshire.* London: IHR & OUP, vol. xiii.

Stevenson, J., 1995 'Boscombe' in *VCH Wiltshire*. London: IHR & OUP, vol. xv.

Stevenson, J., 1995a 'Figheldean' in *VCH Wiltshire*. London: IHR & OUP, vol. xv.

Stratton, C., ed. 1909 *Survey of the Lands of William, 1st Earl of Pembroke*. London: Roxburghe Club, 2 vols.

Templeman, G., 1956 'Ecclesiastical History 1087-1547' in *VCH Wiltshire*. London: IHR & OUP, vol.iii.

Tenant, P., 1900 *Village Notes*, London : Heinemann.

Thomson, S., ed. 2011 *The Recorder* Annual Newsletter of the Wiltshire Record Society, No.10.

Thornton, T., 2006 *Prophecy, Politics and the People of Early Modern England*. Woodbridge: Boydell & Brewer.

Todd, H., n/d *Memoirs of the Life & Writings of the Rt.Rev.Brian Walton, Bishop of Chester, vol I, 277-282*.

Waylen, J., 1855 ' Danvers, Earl of Danby' in *WAM*. Devizes: WANHS, vol. ii.

Whitlock, T., 2005 *Crime, Gender & Consumer Culture in 19th Century England*, Aldershot: Ashgate Publishing, Ltd.

Wood, K., 2000 *Westbury and Westbury Leigh*. Westbury: The Westbury Book Group.

Wroughton, J., 1999 *An Unhappy Civil War* Bath: The Lansdown Press

Lightning Source UK Ltd.
Milton Keynes UK
UKOW07f1713080616

275884UK00006B/29/P

9 781906 978358